DELIBERATE TENNIS

Kathleen,

Don't just play tennis,

play deliberate tennis.

Regards,

Bill

DELIBERATE TENNIS

A PLAYER'S GUIDE TO
MAXIMUM EFFECTIVENESS
ON AND OFF THE COURT

Bill Himadi, Ph.D.

ISBN: 0692510087
ISBN 13: 9780692510087

TABLE OF CONTENTS

Dedication

For May, Michele, Elaine, John, and Dad.

INTRODUCTION

If you want to become an effective tennis player, perhaps even a great one, then this book is for you. The central thesis of this book is that every reasonably healthy person, *given the right environmental conditions and belief system*, has the potential to become an expert-level tennis player. By combining the elements found in this book into a program of deliberate tennis, I guarantee that you will become a good or great player. There is one significant catch, however; you will have to commit to a program of tennis excellence and for an extended period of time. Effort, in short, is what makes you talented.

There are some who contend that hard work, although important, is not enough, arguing that performance gains are rigidly determined and limited by our genetic make-up. They would argue that each of us has individual, biologically-based performance thresholds that we cannot transcend. If this were the case, Rod Laver, Ivan Lendl, and Roger Federer, to name a few players, would never have reached the pinnacle of tennis. These players are deliberate-practice advocates, spending thousands of hours on the court to perfect their craft.

If there are any performance threshold limitations, they are most likely to be found in our environment and in our own minds. With the combination of an intensive and innovative training program, competitive environment, and the right psychological "mindset," you can achieve great things. I present five empirically-derived psychological principles or guidelines in this book that I consider critical for skill development and to promote enhanced concentration and focus.

This book is the result of my fifty-five years playing this wonderful game and from my thirty-plus years as a practicing clinical psychologist. I have had a great time and made many friends throughout the years playing tennis. I have only one regret about my tennis background - I wish I had been exposed to the ideas presented in this book when I first started playing the game.

Many of the concepts in this book are illustrated with the exploits of an interesting array of tennis characters, some of whom attained international acclaim and others of more regional notoriety. For select individuals, I have either not mentioned or changed their names to maintain anonymity. Several of the stories in this book are based on my own experiences with tennis and are re-created from memory with, I believe, an acceptable degree of accuracy.

This book constitutes a tennis road map of sorts. Regardless of your age or specific circumstances, this book will help you define your tennis values and maximize your time on the court to reach your potential as a tennis player. When you are ready, this road map will show you the way.

CHAPTER 1

THE GARDEN AND DREAMS
OF TENNIS GLORY

"His behavior was outrageous, and I loved every minute of it."

FLASH BULB FEVER

It is March 26, 1966, and my dad and I are watching Richard "Pancho" Gonzales battling Ken Rosewall in the semifinals of the $25,000 Invitation Professional Tennis Tournament at Madison Square Garden in New York City. The atmosphere at the Garden is electric; Gonzales is down 2-5 in the first set when he engineers a furious comeback. He breaks Rosewall's serve in the eighth game, saving a set point in the process. He then holds serve easily. Gonzales breaks Rosewall's serve again to even the match at 5-5. Rosewall is momentarily shaken but takes control of the set with his legendary backhand and several well-placed overheads. Rosewall wins the first set 7-5.

Newspaper accounts of the match the following day noted that Gonzales was perturbed by courtside photographers at several points during the match. Allison Danzig, writing for the New York Times and ever the diplomat, stated Gonzales "was annoyed by cameramen who came close to the court. He said afterward that he thought they had been discourteous in refusing his request that they shut off their strobe lights." This didn't sound like the Pancho Gonzales we saw that night. He wasn't quite so polite during the match.

This was what really happened: Gonzales took control of the second set with devastating serving and aggressive net play. He went up 5-3 and was serving for the second set. Rosewall hit several sharply angled service returns to break Gonzales in the ninth game. Rosewall then held serve to even the set at 5-5. At deuce in the eleventh game, Gonzales hit a blistering first serve to Rosewall's forehand that landed just long. As he was about to hit his second serve, there were several camera flashes. He hit the serve in the net. Double fault!

Gonzales strode to the back of the court where my dad and I were sitting in the first row. He glared at us, bellowing, "Goddamn f***ing cameramen!" He then placed the second digit of his index finger of his left hand into his left nostril and blew out a significant chunk of snot from his right nostril onto the back of the court. His behavior was outrageous, and I loved every minute of it. This was not to be Gonzales's day; he lost the second set 7-5.

On-Court Annihilation

As entertaining as the Gonzales-Rosewall match was, I was at Madison Square Garden that evening for one and only one reason: to see Rod Laver. Laver was scheduled to play the Spaniard, Andres Gimeno, in the other semifinal event. Gimeno was the third leading money-winner on the professional tour the previous year and a superb player. What Laver did that day was, as Danzig put it, "almost beyond belief." He destroyed Gimeno in thirty-three minutes, winning 6-0, 6-1. Laver lost only six points in the first set and seven in the second. Laver's topspin groundstrokes had Gimeno completely befuddled. During one point of the match, Gimeno came to net on a deep approach to Laver's backhand. Laver responded with a deftly placed, winning topspin backhand lob - and he executed that shot with a wood racket. The Madison Square Garden crowd was stunned at Laver's devastating display of tennis virtuosity. Sadly, Laver should have saved some of this brilliance for the final; he lost to Rosewall the next day.

Growing up, Laver was my tennis idol. After all, we are both left handers and have George for a middle name. Unfortunately, those are the only two things I share with Laver. I still hold the opinion that Laver was the greatest player to date, although I do acknowledge a generational bias and certainly recognize the majestic game of Roger Federer. But consider Laver's resume: he is the only individual who completed two calendar Grand Slams. That is, he won the Australian, French, Wimbledon, and the United States Championships in both 1962 and 1969. Prior to 1968, these tournaments were only open to amateurs. Although his total Grand Slam victories was eleven, Laver was unable to compete in Grand Slams from 1963 through 1967 due to playing on the professional tour. The Open era of tennis did not commence until 1968. During those five years from 1963-67, Laver was the dominant player on the pro tour. If Open-era tennis had begun in 1963, it is not inconceivable that Laver could have won an additional ten Grand Slams, bringing his total to twenty-one.

Laver was the complete tennis player, possessing few, if any, weaknesses. He could hit winners from anywhere on the court with both his forehand and backhand. He was quick and agile; his volleys were vicious. He had a great serve and overhead. One particularly notable feature of Laver was his "leg-of-lamb" left forearm. The difference between his left and right forearms was pronounced. Laver's left forearm measured twelve inches around and was the same size as that of heavyweight champion Rocky Marciano. I recall reading somewhere that Laver built up his left forearm by squeezing a squash ball while attending school. I attempted the same when I was fourteen years old. In this early attempt at a conditioning regimen, I persisted for about a month. Despite playing tennis spanning a period of over fifty years, there is absolutely no difference between the size of my left and right forearms.

San Antonio

There was another noteworthy tennis development in the early months of 1966 taking place approximately 1800 miles southwest of Madison Square Garden. A Trinity University freshman was tearing his way through the men's intercollegiate tennis scene. This young man had great potential and many believed that he would soon reach the upper echelon of the men's game, perhaps challenging Gonzales, Rosewall, and Laver for tennis supremacy - but more on him later.

THE DEBATE

Jack Kramer promoted the $25,000 tournament at Madison Square Garden and, at the time, it was the most lucrative professional event ever; the *total* prize money was $25,000. Contrast this with the 2016 U.S. Open Championships at Flushing Meadows. The total player compensation for this two-week event in New York will exceed $46,000,000 with the top prize money for the men's and women's champion set at $3,500,000. A first round winner at the U.S. Open will earn $18,300 more than the total prize money designated for the 1966 Madison Square Garden tournament. Yes, tennis has come a long way since the advent of the Open era in 1968. Corporate sponsorship has dramatically increased with extensive media coverage. The level of competition has also risen during the past fifty years at both the junior and professional levels. There is increasing pressure to win and succeed during the early stages of one's tennis career.

Given all these changes, it is surprising that our understanding of how to account for the differences between expert-level tennis players and the rest of us remains rather limited. How do some people become great tennis players whereas others are mired in mediocrity for decades? Traditionally there are two answers to this important question, and this debate is an ancient one. One argument (nature) asserts that select individuals are given a gift from the gods that allows them to excel in some domain of interest. They have inherited a fortuitous combination of genetic material that allows them to perform at a superior level. Since only a few individuals exhibit this level of greatness, it is viewed as a rare event bestowed upon only the select few. John McEnroe is often cited as an example, an apparent "natural" when he first picked up a racket.

The other approach (nurture) contends that people become great at what they do because they work at it, devoting substantial amounts of sustained practice to perfect their skills. Rod Laver would fall into the nurture camp; he put countless hours on the practice court and is considered one of the greatest players ever to play our sport.

Contemporary thinking does not conceptualize this nature/nurture issue as dichotomous, but one involving complex interactions of the two.

Individuals enter this world with different genetic dispositions, but the role of the environment is crucial in shaping and developing elite performers.

Psychological research during the past several decades has illuminated this issue of how to promote the development of the elite performer. One established finding from the work of K. Anders Ericsson, Ph.D. and his colleagues is that the amount of *deliberate practice* is crucial to account for expert-level performance. Elite tennis players are exceptional because they practice in a more effective, innovative way than others.

Carol Dweck, Ph.D., and her students present data from their research that addresses how the *beliefs* we hold about whether behavior is innate or acquired can have dramatic effects upon how we are motivated to achieve. Their research on fixed and growth mindsets is crucial to consider when designing a tennis development program at either the individual or group level.

This book is about tennis, its psychological aspects, and my fifty-plus year journey with this great game. I've played tennis since age ten, and I continue to play on a regular basis. I obtained a Ph.D. in clinical psychology in 1982, and my clinical practice involved two primary areas: anxiety disorders and the more severe mental illnesses. Throughout the years, I often speculated how one could apply psychological principles to improve tennis performance.

In general, this book could be described as the psychology of expert-level performance with a focus on tennis. Anyone who has ever played tennis or those who may be interested in how to improve performance regardless of their area of interest may find this book helpful. I present some information on psychological theory, research, and practice but have tried to make it as readable, and entertaining, as possible. You, the reader, will be the judge as to whether I have been successful.

One theme that runs throughout the book involves innate vs. acquired characteristics of greatness. Is someone born with the capacity for superior performance or is it the result of an intensive, focused, and innovative training regimen? Does the right psychological "mindset" in combination with a rigorous, deliberate training program make any initial innate advantage irrelevant? Can almost anyone become an expert-level performer? I believe the answers found in this book will be interesting and informative.

FATHER AND SON

Leaving Madison Square Garden that evening, I was still harboring the fantasy of becoming a professional tennis player. And a fantasy it was. Looking back, it seems as though I frittered away a great deal of my adolescence hanging out with my friends, watching *The Man from U.N.C.L.E.* and the *Soupy Sales Show*, and eating tons of potato chips. This was not the recommended training regimen for a future professional athlete. As a consequence, my early tennis career was not exactly stellar, although I did manage to attain some local notoriety in northern New Jersey as a pusher. I would camp out on the baseline and keep the ball in play until my opponent became frustrated and missed. Despite my rather slothful adolescence existence, I did spend hours on the court and played in an occasional local or United States Lawn Tennis Association (USLTA) sanctioned junior tournament. I made it to the semifinals of several of these events but never on a sustained enough basis to warrant a top-ten Eastern Section ranking.

My dad introduced me to the game when I was ten years old. Family legend has it that my dad was playing tennis while my mother was in labor with me. He absolutely loved the game. He was fiercely competitive but gracious in both victory and defeat. Dad had this uncanny ability to make a vanquished opponent, despite having just lost 6-0, 6-0, feel good about the way he performed on court.

My dad's "tennis style," forged during the mid-1930s, would probably be characterized as a retriever and counter-puncher. He was very steady with a deadly slice backhand. His forehand had some technical flaws, and he did not like hitting overheads. He enjoyed grinding it out from the baseline. He emulated his game after Frankie Parker, the tennis great of the 1930s and 1940s.

As with many tennis players, my dad was a bit of a fanatic when it came to playing the game. During the winter months in New Jersey, prior to the advent of indoor courts in our area, he kept a tennis net in the trunk of his car. One day in January 1960, he woke me up at 7:00 a.m. and said, "Come on, let's get some breakfast and then go hit some." It was probably twenty degrees outside. After eating some oat meal with brown sugar and raisins, off we went to one of the public hard courts with our winter coats, ski caps, gloves, and tennis rackets. We also brought along an ice and snow shovel. We spent about thirty minutes chopping the ice on the court and then shoveling it past the doubles sideline. We then hit for about forty-five minutes. I recall trying not to fall and injure myself. By the time we left the court, I was freezing and thought, "What a way to start the day." My dad seemed perfectly happy, having had his January "tennis fix."

GET A GRIP

"Who cares about girls' tennis?"

My early tennis years had some other, interesting moments. Sometime in July 1961, I broke a string in my racket for the first time. I was quite proud of this, particularly since the strings had worn out in the center of the racket. I was actually making contact with the ball in the "sweet spot." One of the few people in our area who strung rackets was Frank X. Brennan. My dad and I drove to Mr. Brennan's house in Fairlawn, New Jersey. We then proceeded to his basement, where he kept his stringing equipment and supplies. Mr. Brennan was stringing a racket and changing a grip when we arrived. There was this young woman, about seventeen or eighteen years old, who was sitting on a stool and talking to Mr. Brennan. It was Billie Jean Moffitt (the future Billie Jean King). She had just returned from her first Wimbledon excursion, where she won the Ladies doubles title with Karen Hantze. Billie Jean lost in the second round in singles that year to the Mexican Yola Ramirez Ochoa, 11-9, 1-6, 6-2. We were introduced to Billie Jean and had a pleasant conversation for a few minutes. Mr. Brennan was beaming. He seemed very proud of her. As we were about to depart, Mr. Brennan asked me if I wanted to have him put Billie Jean's grip that she used at Wimbledon on my racket. I politely declined, thinking, "Who cares about girls' tennis?" So, at age eleven, I summarily dismissed this to-be transformative figure in the history of tennis - *and* with a sexist thought no less.

Frank Brennan later billed himself as the "Coach of World Champion Billie Jean King." His son, Frank X. Brennan, Jr. would have a remarkable career as the coach of the Stanford University women's tennis team. His record was 510 wins with only 50 losses. I remember Frank Jr. playing in some local New Jersey tournaments in the early 1960s. He could hit some big shots, but he was somewhat erratic. I believe someone in my peer group nicknamed him "Fuzz," for either his rather large sideburns or his facial peach fuzz.

MAC THE KNIFE

In December 1962, our family went to Miami for a vacation, because grandparents on both sides of the family resided there. Sometime in November of that year, my dad suggested that I submit an entry form for the Orange Bowl Junior Tennis Championships held every December. I thought he was nuts. After all, the Orange Bowl championship was one of the pre-eminent international junior tournaments. Since I had a limited tennis "track record," I figured that my entry would not be accepted for the boys' 14-and-under division. I was wrong. I got in. These were still the early days of tennis, and the Orange Bowl tournament officials probably needed all the participants they could get. So in I was.

I was scheduled to play Mac Claflin of Coral Gables in the first round. I completed several practice sessions at the Silver Thatch Inn, a well-known tennis resort in Pompano Beach prior to the match with Claflin. The head tennis pro at the Inn was a guy named Wayne Sabin, who played tennis during the 1930s and 1940s. Following one of these practice sessions, I asked Mr. Sabin if he knew Claflin and the level of his game. Sabin said, "Well, look at it this way kid: It's like a guy with a knife going up against a guy with a machine gun. And *you* got the knife." It definitely was not Mac the knife. He mowed me down with machine gun-like efficiency, beating me 6-0, 6-1. Claflin was about five inches taller than I, had a huge kick serve, volleyed well, and had solid groundstrokes. He wiped me out. Claflin was a highly ranked national player, and he lost in the next round, demonstrating the depth of talent in the tournament. Tony Roche, the future Australian tennis great and coach of Ivan Lendl, won the 18-and-under division that year. Claflin did, however, win the Orange Bowl tournament several years later and had a stellar junior tennis career.

WHITE CASTLE BLUES

Another tennis experience worth noting occurred in February 1968. My family had just moved to Fort Lauderdale from New Jersey, and I finished up my senior year at Ft. Lauderdale High School. The high school tennis team had been practicing for about a month when I arrived, and the formal season was to start in two weeks. I approached the coach and asked him if I could try out as a "walk on." The boys' team had depth; I wasn't sure if the coach would go for this. But he agreed to give me a try. When I arrived at the courts the following day, all the guys had been paired up. I thought, "This doesn't look promising." Well, the coach suggested that I play the number one girl from the high school girls' team. I agreed, figuring this would be a piece of cake. It wasn't. This girl, Carol Groefer, was a good player and beat me in three sets. I was despondent. "There goes my high school tennis career," I said to myself. As I was packing up to leave the court, one of the guys from the team approached me and asked how I did against Carol. Somewhat reluctantly, I said, "Lost in three." He replied, "That's not too bad; she consistently beats about half the guys on the team." We talked for several minutes, and then he suggested that we go to the White Castle restaurant across the street to get some burgers and fries. From what I recall, you could buy seven or eight burgers for a dollar. I figured I could drown my tennis sorrows with several burgers, fries, and a milkshake. As we were heading to the White Castle, he said, "See that little kid hitting on court three?" There was this petite but intense-looking girl about thirteen years old trading groundstrokes with some guy, who appeared to be in his early twenties. I replied, "Yeah." He then said, "She can beat Carol 6-0, 6-0." It was Chris Evert! I thought, "Man, am I out of my league." From that moment on, I started to notice girls' tennis. It was Billie Jean's revenge; I should have taken that grip.

SENIOR TENNIS MOMENTS

"That's the greatest forehand I've ever seen."

Probably the most fun I had with tennis involved hanging out with my dad and his tennis buddies. These guys were hilarious. They all looked forward to reaching that magic age of forty-five. While most of their friends and colleagues were commiserating about their advancing years, these aging tennis players relished it. After all, at forty-five one could play in the "seniors." That's one of the great things about tennis: advancing years for the competitive tennis player has its advantages. There is selective attrition among tennis players over time. This could result from the many responsibilities of middle age, getting out of shape, loss of interest, injuries, and disease, among other factors. Another perk is that you avoid playing someone significantly younger as you advance to the next age division. At the present time, adult tournaments based on age are divided into five-year increments from ages twenty to ninety-five. During my dad's era, for the majority of tournaments, there was a ten-year interval from ages thirty-five to forty-five. There was a clear advantage to playing in the forty-five-and-over division. At age forty-four, one could be playing someone nearly ten years younger.

In 1965 and 1966, my dad and his friends competed in several senior events, including the national clay- and grass-court championships. I would tag along with my dad for most of these events. I brought my racket along in the hope of finding a game.

GOLIATH

These tournaments proved amusing on occasion. There was one small tournament in Nyack, New York, in which my dad was scheduled to play Archie Oldham in the first round. Archie was a former basketball player for St. John's University and was the basketball coach for Columbia University in the mid-1960s. He was probably six feet ten, a definite oddity for a tennis player of that era. Archie created quite a stir when he walked onto the court. There was this rather exciting atmosphere with Archie's matches. He had an enormous serve and came to the net on every conceivable opportunity. And with his huge wingspan, it was challenging to get anything by him once he camped out at the net. As my dad, who was five feet eight, went out to do battle with this racket-armed Goliath, I quipped, "I don't think I'd recommend lobbing this guy." Well, my dad lost in three sets. Archie was serving and volleying. My dad countered by hitting soft returns at Archie's feet. Fortunately, my dad did not take my line against lobbing seriously because he executed several well-placed lobs when Archie crowded the net. It was a good match and one involving contrasting styles.

WASTE OF TIME

At another senior event in North Jersey, a little blond-headed kid approached me and asked if I wanted to hit a few balls. He looked to be about ten or eleven years old. I reluctantly agreed since there were no other available prospects. I distinctly remember thinking, "Oh, great. I'll probably have to stand at the net and feed balls to the kid until he gets bored. This is going to be a waste of time." As we were heading out to one of the outside courts, I asked him his name, and he said, "Peter." His last name was Fleming. Yes, the future doubles partner of John McEnroe. Together they won 50 professional doubles titles, including four Wimbledon and three U.S. Open Championships. Peter's record as a singles player was also impressive. He reached the finals of the 1976 NCAA tournament, losing to Bill Scanlon. As a professional, he was ranked number eight in the world in 1980. He had a great singles year in 1979, winning ATP events in Cincinnati and Los Angeles. He was runner-up that year in San Jose, San Francisco, and Maui.

Let's return to 1965. I was five years older than Peter and believed that he wouldn't provide me with much competition. When we started warming up, I realized that the kid had some game. His forehand was tough - good velocity and penetration. His backhand was erratic; his serve was surprisingly good. It was a tougher match than I expected. During the second game of the match, Peter hit a deep ball crosscourt to my backhand and approached the net. I responded by slicing a backhand down the line. He quickly moved over and put away the volley. I couldn't believe it, thinking, "What is this *little* kid doing at the net?" Well, following his winning backhand volley, I stood there for a moment and gave him this look that communicated, "Alright kid, you've had it." I turned up the juice and won the match. But it wasn't easy. He was one tough competitor.

Approximately six years later, Peter began training at the Port Washington Tennis Academy in Port Washington, New York. Harry Hopman, the legendary Australian Davis Cup captain, was the tennis director at the Port Washington facility. Peter was sixteen years old in 1971 and approaching his full height of six feet five. One of the academy teaching pros thought it would be entertaining to arrange a challenge match between Peter and this new academy trainee, twelve-year-old John McEnroe. Peter towered over the young Mac and probably figured the match would be too one-sided. So, he offered McEnroe a handicap. At the beginning of each set, McEnroe started at 4-0, 30-love. To Peter's shock and dismay, John won five consecutive sets. If I had thought about a handicap in my 1965 match with Peter, I may have offered him some similar deal. I'm glad I didn't.

In 1966, my dad and I played Peter Fleming and his dad in a father-son event in New Jersey. Strangely, I can still visualize the court we played on but cannot remember the name of the club. Peter's dad was an accomplished player and probably the best player of the foursome. But Peter was still the weak link, and my dad and I were favored to win the match. The tournament was scheduled in June, at the height of the New Jersey pollen season. I have always been allergic to grasses and trees and was having a particularly bad reaction for several days preceding our match with the Flemings. I was prescribed chlortrimeton, an antihistamine, to control my allergy symptoms. It came in this little yellow pill, but I wasn't a proficient pill swallower back then, so I would chew it. It tasted horrible, very bitter. Anyway, several hours before the match, I chewed up two of them. Big mistake. I was feeling drowsy and my coordination was off. I played terribly, but we managed to squeak out a three-set win. Our opponents in the next round were the fourth-seeded team. They finished their match early and were doing some scouting of our match with the Flemings. At one point, I looked over at them and thought, "I'm sure their strategy will be to play me tomorrow if we happen to survive this match."

And that's exactly what they did. During the first set, they played to me at almost every opportunity. My eyes were itching and my nose was running, but I refused to take the allergy medication. That doubles match was probably the best I played all year. We scored the upset, 6-4, 6-2. My dad and I progressed to the semifinals, losing to the second seeded team, Karl Hedrick and his dad.

So, my record against Peter Fleming is 2-0. Timing is everything.

The 45-and-over national clay-court event in 1965 was held at the Mount Lebanon Tennis Center in Pittsburgh. My dad was not having a particularly successful rookie senior season. He was becoming discouraged. To make matters worse, he was scheduled to play Ed DiLeone in the second round. Ed was an accomplished player. He was the 45-and-over National Public Parks Champion in 1959 and 1960. He was ranked third nationally in 1964 in singles in the 45-and-over division. Ed looked like the character, Santiago, from Hemingway's *Old Man and the Sea*: weather beaten with leathery skin. My dad played one of the best matches of his tennis career. Ed won the first set 6-1; my dad, the second at 6-1. The third set was hard fought. At 4-4, my dad held serve to go up 5-4. Ed was looking concerned when he went out to serve in the tenth game. He quickly went down 15-40. I vividly recall my dad turning to me and mouthing, "One more point." The next point seemed interminable. They probably traded thirty groundstrokes. Finally, one of Ed's shots hit the top of the net and dribbled over for a winner. There were probably twenty people watching the match by then, and you could hear the collective groans when the ball dropped over the net. The crowd was pulling for the underdog. On the next match point, Ed served and came to net. He served to my dad's backhand, which was not a wise thing to do. My dad hit a sharply angled cross-court return that appeared to be a winner. Ed dove for the ball and managed to pull off a drop volley. Ed won that game and the set 9-7, escaping a major upset. There was a nice article in the local newspaper the next day detailing the match.

The following day, my dad and I were watching a match when I noticed a rather diminutive senior player casually walking by. My dad called out,

"Hey Bitsy, could you come over here for a minute?" He replied, "Hi George, sure."

Bryan Morel "Bitsy" Grant was an Atlanta native and tennis legend. He was born on Christmas 1909 and died on June 5, 1986. He was nicknamed Bitsy because of his small stature. He was also known as the "Mighty Atom." Bitsy stood 5 feet 4 and weighed 120 pounds. He was a giant on the court, however, and defeated all of the tennis greats of the 1930s including Don Budge and Ellsworth Vines. He defeated Vines in the championship match at Forest Hills when Vines was ranked number one in the world. The scores were 6-3, 6-3, 6-3. Vines allegedly cut the gut out of his racket after the loss, stating, "I'm through."

Grant won the Southern Championship title eleven times, the first when he was sixteen years old. He secured his eleventh title in 1952 at age forty-three. He won the National Clay Court title in 1930, 1934, and 1935. He was ranked in the top ten in the United States on nine occasions from 1930-41. He was ranked number three in the U.S. in 1935 and 1936. He attained a career-high ranking of six in the world in 1937. Later, Grant was actively involved in competitive senior tennis, winning nineteen U.S. titles.

My dad explained to Bitsy, somewhat to my chagrin at the time, that I was concerned about my own small stature (I was about the same size as Bitsy) and was wondering if he could offer me some words of encouragement. He said, "Sure," and then ripped off a section from one of those yellow Wilson cardboard containers that held four cans of tennis balls. He took out a pen and wrote, "Dear Bill, remember the best things in life come in small packages." During the next year, I grew seven inches.

I met Bitsy again in 1981. I was completing a year-long clinical internship at The University of Mississippi Medical Center in Jackson, as part of the requirements for a Ph.D. in clinical psychology. There was an article in the sports section of the Clarion-Ledger highlighting Grant, who was scheduled to compete in the annual Southern Senior Men's Clay Court Championships in May. I managed to break away from the internship for a few hours to watch Grant's quarterfinal match. He was playing in the 70-and-over division. His opponent was an effective player with solid groundstrokes. I was amazed at Bitsy's footwork. Even at age seventy-one, he was fast and a great retriever. I got a sense of how he must have been in his prime. During one point of the match, Grant's opponent hit a monster, winning forehand. Bitsy was picking up the ball at the end of the court near to where I was standing and muttered, "That's the greatest forehand I've ever seen." I had to laugh. Bitsy faced some of the greatest forehands in the history of the game, including those of Fred Perry, Ellsworth Vines, and Jack Kramer.

Following the match which, by the way, Bitsy won, I introduced myself and told him about the time he had written the small packages line to me. He looked up at my six-foot frame, and we both started to laugh. We talked for a few minutes and as he departed toward the clubhouse, he turned around and said, "Say hi to your daddy." I thought about catching up to him to tell him my dad died in 1979 but decided against it and returned home.

THE WEST SIDE TENNIS CLUB

The most exciting event for seniors was the 45-and-over National Grass-Court Championships held at the West Side Tennis Club in Forest Hills, New York. This wonderful facility is rich with tennis history. The West Side Tennis Club was initially organized in 1892 and included three clay courts located at Central Park in Manhattan. The club moved to its current location in Forest Hills in 1914. By 1915, the West Side Tennis Club was home to the USLTA National Championships and remained so for the next sixty years. The historic stadium and the Tudor-style clubhouse are defining features of the club and provide a cloistered tennis experience only twenty minutes from the hustle and bustle of Manhattan.

Despite being referred to as a national-level event, most of the participants in the grass- court championships were from the New York metropolitan area. There were several players from other areas of the country. There was one entrant, however, who generated a great deal of excitement during the 1966 tournament. Jaroslav Drobny entered the field, and the other participants were thrilled at the possibility of matching their skills with this international star.

Drobny was one of the giants of the game. He won the French Championships (now the French Open) in 1951 and 1952 and was runner-up on three other occasions (1946, 1948, and 1950). Drobny won Wimbledon in

1954, defeating a young Ken Rosewall in the finals 13-11, 4-6, 6-2, 9-7. He was runner-up at Wimbledon in 1949 losing to Ted Schroeder. He lost the Wimbledon final in 1952 to Frank Sedgman. Drobny was ranked number one in the world in 1954.

Even when he was a younger player, Drobny had a small paunch, but his athleticism more than made up for his less than optimal physical conditioning. During the intervening years since defeating Rosewall at Wimbledon, Drobny had definitely neglected his physical status. His small paunch had grown into a rather large gut. With his left-handed, serve-volley game and great court anticipation, however, Drobny dominated the early rounds of the tournament. He defeated Morris Adelsberg 6-3, 6-3 in the first round and then won the next three rounds with the loss of only four games. In the semifinals, he defeated Emory Neale 6-4, 6-4. He then played the hard-serving Californian, Robert V. Sherman in the finals, prevailing 9-11, 6-4, 6-2. He had too much experience and game for the best of the United States' senior players. My dad lost in the first round that year, defeated by Robert Kamrath 6-2, 7-5.

PHYSICAL CONDITIONING

"The secret to playing tennis at this age is…mobility."

My dad's best tennis buddy was one Andrew Jackson Herschel, better known as "Bob." This guy was unique, a wonderful eccentric. According to his daughter, Janet, Bob announced to his family in 1962 that he was quitting his job as a mechanical engineer for the Curtiss-Wright Corporation to pursue a career in tennis. The family's reaction was, "Are you nuts?" After all, he was forty-five years old. But pursue he did.

Bob was an imposing figure on the court, standing six feet three. He had an athletic build and moved around the court like a gazelle. He sported a shaved head long before Michael Jordan popularized the style. Bob graduated from the University of Chicago with a degree in mechanical engineering. One of his classmates at college was Charles (Chuck) Percy, future United States Senator from Illinois.

With some notable exceptions, physical conditioning was never a priority for tennis players in the 1960s. Most players of that era stayed in shape by playing tennis.

Now, here's a contrast in conditioning styles. Herschel was scheduled to play in the semifinals of a 45-and-over senior event in upstate New York in 1965. During the warm-up, Bob was smoking a cigarette, a Chesterfield unfiltered. So there he was, hitting groundstrokes, overheads, and serves smoking a Chesterfield. During a match, he even smoked during the changeover, leaving a lit cigarette on the bench when he resumed play.

Steve Ogilvy, an accomplished player from New England, had just won the other semifinal match and was "scouting" Herschel's upcoming match. Ogilvy was known for his dedication to the game, healthy lifestyle, and conditioning regimen. As he was watching the warm-up, Ogilvy was eating some strange-looking concoction in a clear plastic cup. Someone asked him what he was eating, and he replied, "Oh, this is yogurt, granola, and honey." Now remember, this was 1965. Few had even heard of yogurt or granola. The recommended diet for tennis players of that era was steak, eggs, and salt tablets. Ogilvy was dismissed by his tennis peers as a bit of a "health nut."

So, Ogilvy was munching on this stuff and commenting, "Look at Herschel. He's smoking during the warm-up! And he will probably down several scotches after the match...His serve and forehand are great...He's going to win this match and will probably kill me tomorrow." Ogilvy was partially correct. Herschel did win his semifinal match and then had a competitive match against Ogilvy in the final, prevailing 6-4, 7-5.

Both Herschel and Ogilvy had remarkable senior tennis careers. Herschel was routinely ranked in the top ten in the Eastern Section before moving to Sarasota, Florida in 1980. Ogilvy was ranked number one in the Eastern Section at the 45 and 55 age divisions. He also held the number-one ranking in the New England Section in all the age divisions from 55 to 85. He was inducted into the United States Tennis Association (USTA) New England Hall of Fame in 1995. He died from injuries sustained in an automobile accident at age eighty-eight. He was returning home from a tennis tournament in Killington, Vermont, when he veered into oncoming traffic several times before colliding with a tractor-trailer truck.

Herschel continued to play tennis in Florida and was a top-ranked player for many years. He finally retired from the game in 2007 at age ninety. He died in May 2010.

Several days prior to attending a professional workshop in Sarasota in 1993, I contacted Herschel. I had not seen or talked to him since 1967. He was surprised, but delighted, to hear from me. We agreed to meet for dinner. During dinner, he was cracking me up with stories about playing tennis with Enrico Fermi (the physicist) while attending the University of Chicago. One of his comments about Fermi was "the little man couldn't play tennis."

Herschel was seventy-six years old in 1993, and he was ranked number three in Florida and number nine nationally in the 75 age division. We agreed to "hit some" the next day. Following my return to the hotel, I received a call from Herschel at about 10 p.m. He said, "I just wanted to call to say get some sleep tonight. You're going to need it." This seventy-six-year-old was trying to psych me out!

In 1993, I was playing tennis on a regular basis as a member of a NTRP 4.5 team. Our team had just won the regional championships in Pensacola and was scheduled to play in the state championships in a few weeks. Even with this, Herschel's telephone gamesmanship was having an effect on me. I remember thinking, "Could I actually lose to this seventy-six-year-old guy tomorrow?"

For the uninitiated, NTRP stands for the National Tennis Rating Program. It is a classificatory schema to rate tennis players by skill level. Many tennis leagues and tournaments, and now ladders, are presently organized according to the skill level of the players. Ratings range from 1.5 to 7.0 in .5 level increments. For example, a NTRP rating of 1.5 indicates a player who just started the game, a beginner. A rating of 7.0 indicates a world-class player who competes on an international level. Most club players have ratings in the 3.0 to 5.0 range. A player at the 4.5 level, for example, is one who "has begun to vary the use of pace and spins, has good movement, can control distance and depth of shots, and is beginning to develop game plans according to strengths and weaknesses. This player can hit the first serve with power and accuracy and can place the second serve. This player tends to over hit on difficult shots. Aggressive net play is common in doubles."

Bob and I played the next day and had a great time. There were several changes in Herschel's game. First, he only used a cigarette holder during the warm-up. He explained that, in 1973, a physician tennis friend said, "Bob, if you continue to smoke, you'll probably be dead by age sixty." Herschel quit cold turkey. The thought of no longer playing tennis rather than death probably scared Herschel into quitting cigarettes. Second, his powerful and penetrating serve had declined. His forehand still had some punch, and he moved effortlessly around the court. Amazingly, he could serve and volley.

We had a good match. Some of the games were long and hard-fought. Well, youth, relatively speaking, prevailed in the match. Had Herschel been ten years younger, the outcome may have been different. After the match, we proceeded to the club house for a soda (no scotch). At one point during our conversation, he talked about playing tennis at age seventy-six. He then leaned over to me, partially violated my personal space, and said, "The secret to playing tennis at this age is (pausing for effect) mobility."

CONDITIONING REGIMEN

Herschel is correct about mobility, although this holds for any age. I am only going to offer two rules in this book and here they are:

Rule Number 1: Footwork is the single most important part of the game.

Rule Number 2: Never forget rule number 1.

In order to hit the ball well, you need to be balanced and in position. There is a differential advantage for those players, senior or not, who are quick on their feet and have the physical conditioning to play three hard sets of tennis. I am aware of some excellent players who "lose their legs" in the third set. As the legs go, so goes the match.

I am not going to pretend to be an expert in exercise physiology because I'm not. The following conditioning regimen is based upon my personal experience in tennis, which spans a fifty-five year period. I've experienced a variety of minor and not-so-minor ailments that plague the competitive tennis player: shoulder problems, tendonitis in the wrist, elbow, and knees, and back, groin, and ankle sprains. All of these injuries have led me to a specific stretching and conditioning regimen that has been helpful to me. Perhaps it will be helpful to you as well.

STRETCHING

I never stretched in my younger years and managed to avoid most injuries. And if I did suffer the occasional muscle strain, it resolved quickly. When I turned forty, my physical status changed. I was more susceptible to injuries, and the recovery time was longer. One day in 1992, I was discussing the topic of sports and injuries with a clinical psychology graduate student whom I was supervising at Florida State Hospital. He asked me if I stretched on a regular basis. I replied, "No." He said, "Start," and introduced me to Bob Anderson's book, *Stretching*.

Anderson's book is excellent and I heartily recommend it to all tennis players. The first half of the book delineates specific stretches for various muscle groups. Anderson makes a distinction between the "easy" and "developmental" stretch. The "easy" stretch is where one experiences a mild tension while holding the stretch for 10-15 seconds. After the tension from the easy stretch subsides, Anderson recommends moving to the "developmental" stretch, where one stretches further until mild tension is again experienced. Hold this stretch for an additional 10-15 seconds. On pages 188-189 of his book, Anderson presents sixteen stretches for the tennis player. I do these stretches before a match; a sequence of sixteen stretches takes approximately ten minutes.

RUNNING

If you want to improve your cardiovascular efficiency and endurance, start running. Remember the two rules about footwork? Start running. Running has a central place in my conditioning regimen. I run ten miles per week over three sessions. Fortunately, I've always enjoyed running and have been doing it for over five decades. Just prior to turning fifty years old, I marked the occasion by running five miles, one mile for every decade that I had lived.

My thought was to turn the table on the aging process. Many people become more sedentary as they age with all the attendant health consequences.

I devised a plan to become progressively more active as I aged. It was my hope that I could at least slow down the rate of physical decline. Following my five miles at fifty run, I planned a 5.1 mile run when I turned fifty-one, a 5.2 mile run at fifty-two, and so on. I do these age-adjusted "symbolic" runs about four times a year. In between these times, I do my usual ten-miles-per-week routine.

I used to carry around this bulky, hand-held portable compact disc player to listen to music while I ran. One day at the track, perhaps in 2002 or 2003, I noticed a young woman wearing this sleek-looking electronic device on her arm. It appeared to be a musical device of some kind, given the attached ear buds. I asked her what it was, and she replied "an iPod." She then explained that it had been introduced by Steve Jobs of Apple Computer in 2001 and briefly described what it could do. As she was talking, I felt like a dinosaur holding this ridiculous portable CD player. The next day, I purchased my first iPod. It added a new and enjoyable dimension to my jogging regimen.

FARTLEKS ANYONE?

What in the world is a fartlek?? I'll explain shortly. Running at a regular pace for several miles is good for conditioning, but it does not meet the realities of the tennis experience. A competitive tennis match involves multiple short sprints. The movement patterns are ever-changing; there are short bursts of speed followed by brief periods of rest. Fartlek training is ideally suited for tennis conditioning.

Fartlek is a Swedish word meaning "speed play." Fartlek training is most often associated with running, but it can be adapted to most forms of exercise. It essentially involves changing your pace while exercising. Fartleks tend to be unstructured, alternating moderate to intense efforts with easy ones. In essence, you are incorporating occasional sprints into your workout.

Tennis players can take advantage of fartlek training by gearing their off-court training to the demands of a tennis match. My own approach to fartlek training involves running and completing the first mile at a steady pace. During the second mile, I will run hard for about 50 yards, jog for about a tenth of a mile, and then do an all-out sprint for 40 yards, followed by a jog for a quarter mile. I repeat this sequence until I have finished my three or four mile run. Sometimes, I will include a walk for about 30 seconds. There are multiple variations to use. Find one that works for you.

THE M-DRILL

The M-Drill is an on-court drill that I use during practice sessions and just prior to a match. This drill is helpful for enhanced mobility and footwork. Arthur Ashe described the M-Drill in his book, *On Tennis: Strokes, Strategy, Traditions, Players, Psychology, and Wisdom*. Ashe stated, "Start at the right-hand corner of the court, where the baseline meets the doubles sideline. Sprint forward and touch the net, then shuffle sideways to the singles sideline. From there, backpedal to the service line, shuffle sideways to the center service line, then sprint forward to touch the net at the strap. Backpedal straight back to the service line, shuffle sideways to the other singles sideline, sprint forward to touch the net, shuffle sideways to the doubles sideline, backpedal all the way to the baseline, then turn and sprint to the corner where you started."

Tennis players will immediately recognize that this drill incorporates many of the movements used during a match - forwards, backwards, and sideways all with short, quick steps. One piece of advice when doing the M-Drill: remove all tennis balls from the court. You don't want to be backpedaling and step on a ball.

STRENGTH TRAINING

This is a critical part of a tennis player's training regimen. Strength training results in improved strength, energy capacity, bone density, balance, and co-ordination. And it will reduce the frequency of on-court injuries. I do weight training two times per week. I initially consulted with a trainer to design a weight-training program appropriate to the demands of tennis; this program focused on strengthening the areas of my body most susceptible to injuries - shoulders, elbows, back, groin, knees, and calf muscles.

BALLET

Here's a radical suggestion for you - take a ballet class. Want to improve your footwork? Ballet. Want to improve your balance? Ballet again. Want to improve your coordination? You guessed it, ballet. Lynn Swann, the great Pittsburgh Steeler wide receiver, studied ballet and reported that it helped him with his timing, balance, and body control. The Australian Davis Cup teams during the Hopman era also studied ballet. When I was thirty-eight, I took a ballet class and continued with it for five years. I've been thinking about taking classes again. So, buy a pair of ballet shoes and give it a try. You might enjoy it.

PRACTICE WITH A PURPOSE

You know that old joke about "How do you get to Carnegie Hall? Practice, practice." The same holds true for tennis. I know several club players who detest practicing. They love to play matches and may do so five times per week. If you want to improve your game, however, you need to schedule some practice sessions. Take a lesson from a teaching pro. Use the ball machine. Hit against a wall. Purchase a ball hopper and hit some serves.

As a kid, I spent hours hitting tennis balls against the wall of a local elementary school. Now, I prefer the ball machine. I will work on groundstrokes, hitting hundreds of balls during one practice session. I work on keeping the ball deep, getting my racket back early with good, ballet-like footwork. Since my backhand is my weaker stroke, I will hit the majority of groundstrokes on my backhand side.

I never hit a topspin backhand until recently. I learned the game during the era of wood rackets and underspin backhands. As a result of focused practice sessions, I can now hit an effective topspin backhand, particularly when an opponent has taken the net by approaching my backhand side. Although I will hit the majority of backhands during a rally with slice, I now have the capacity to drive the backhand with topspin on occasion. This has added a new dimension to my game and has only occurred because of - practice.

Another shot that I routinely practice is the serve. Since I am a lefty, I work on the slice serve on both the deuce and ad sides of the court. I'm attempting to develop a heavy slice, or as some would refer to as the "can-opener," to the ad court. Another focus of service practice is to develop a reliable, deep second serve.

Finally, take a lesson from a teaching professional. A good teaching pro can offer helpful suggestions for your game.

Now, I have to admit I always felt somewhat self-righteous when I completed two practice sessions per week. This self-righteousness evaporated when I reviewed research from the expert-performance literature, addressed in Chapter 3, indicating that this level of practice, although important, is woefully inadequate if one is interested in becoming an elite performer.

THE THREE TIERS

"It was sort of a depressing wake-up call that few of us thought we could answer."

When I was playing junior tennis in New Jersey, I classified my competitors into three tiers. The first tier included the guys who won most of the tournaments. They were routinely ranked in the top ten of the Eastern Section. There was a subset of this first tier whom I would classify as the "elites." Dick Stockton was the best player of this elite group. Several of my tennis friends referred to Stockton as the "god of junior tennis." Additional elites, to name a few from other areas of the country, included Mac Claflin, Brian Gottfried, Harold Solomon, and Erik Van Dillen. The majority of these players went on to play on the professional tour, with some having solid careers. The rest of the players in the non-elite, first tier were solid players and later played for some of the top college tennis teams in the country.

The second tier consisted of good players who would occasionally challenge some of the guys in the first tier. At times, they scored a major upset over one of the elites but this rarely occurred.

The third tier players were the guys who loved to play the game but who typically lost in the first or second round of the sanctioned junior tournaments. They were the "cannon fodder" for the rest of the field, playing the role of the Washington Generals to the Harlem Globe Trotters.

When I was playing my best junior tennis, I resided at the middle to the bottom of the second tier. There were times, albeit rarely, when I defeated one of the better second-tier players.

I was fascinated by the differences among these various tier players. What made the elites so good? Did they possess some innate advantage or ability that the rest of us lacked? And there always seemed to be this predictable consistency with respect to the ranking of these various players. How could this be?

I recall one match that brought home this issue with particular force. The best junior player in northern New Jersey during the mid to late 1960s was a guy named Steve Siegel from Teaneck. He had this great forehand, was fast, and seemed destined for tennis greatness. I never played Steve, but if I had, I would have been lucky to win one or two games.

The one tournament that we looked forward to every summer was the Eastern Junior Championships held at the West Side Tennis Club. Steve Siegel was the top seed in the 18-and-under division in 1966. One entrant to the tournament received most of the attention because of his age. Fourteen-year-old Brian Gottfried from Florida entered the tournament in the 18-and-under division. We couldn't believe the temerity of this kid, playing up two divisions. We were all interested in how he would do. I saw him play one of his early round matches. He was wearing this Australian style "floppy hat" and played mostly from the backcourt. He was very steady. Well, to the surprise of us all, Brian knocked off a couple of seeds and made it to the finals against Siegel. There was no way we believed this kid could defeat Siegel, but he did in three sets. The rest of us were stunned. It was sort of a depressing wake-up call that few of us thought we could answer.

Did Gottfried possess some innate talent that the rest of us didn't have? Is there a way to adequately account for how accomplished this kid was at such a young age?

CHAPTER 2

SIR FRANCIS GALTON AND THE INNATE TALENT HYPOTHESIS

"You've either got it or you don't."

You've heard it all before. When describing the accomplishments of a Bobby Fischer, Tiger Woods, Mozart, or Roger Federer, people use the typical metaphors – "He's from another planet"; "That performance was out of this world"; "He's inherited a special gift"; "His skills are encoded into his DNA." At its most basic level, the innate talent hypothesis states that select individuals are born with the ability or capacity for superior performance in some domain of interest. You've either got it or you don't.

SIR FRANCIS

Where did the innate talent hypothesis come from and does it provide an explanatory account of expert-level performance? To answer these questions, we need to turn to the work of Sir Francis Galton, the nineteenth century British aristocrat. Galton was born in 1822 near Birmingham, England. He was the youngest of nine children. He came from a prominent British family. His mother, Francis Anne Violetta Darwin, was the daughter of Erasmus Darwin, Charles Darwin's grandfather. Galton's father, Samuel Tertius Galton, was a prominent banker. Francis was considered a child prodigy, excelling at reading and mathematics by the age of five. His I.Q. was estimated to be 200. As a young man, he studied medicine and mathematics. He was an explorer and adventurer. He traveled to the Sudan in 1845 and to Southwest Africa in 1850. His published accounts of his travels earned him a medal from the Royal Geographic Society.

Galton's intellectual pursuits were widespread including anthropology, geography, psychometrics, and statistics. He introduced the statistical concept of correlation, provided an account of regression toward the mean, and quantified a measure of normal variation, the standard deviation. He coined the phrase nature vs. nurture. He gave scientific credibility to the analysis of finger prints in criminal forensic work, delineating several specific types of finger print patterns. Galton was knighted in 1909.

The publication of Charles Darwin's *The Origin of Species* in 1859 had a profound impact on Galton's life. He was particularly influenced by Darwin's first chapter, "Variation Under Domestication," which involved the selective breeding of domesticated animals. In that chapter, which was a prelude to his revolutionary idea of natural selection, Darwin detailed the process of differentially selecting certain physical characteristics of animals for breeding purposes. Galton extended the notion of the evolution of physical characteristics to human talents or abilities. He began investigating the possibility that genius may be a function of hereditary factors when he noticed that the achievements of his contemporaries "seemed to go by descent."

In his book, *Hereditary Genius: An Inquiry into Its Laws and Consequences*, Galton proposed to show "that a man's natural abilities are derived by inheritance, under exactly the same limitations as are the form and physical features of the whole organic world." Thus, Galton believed that the hereditary mechanisms responsible for physical features such as height and body size could also account for humans' mental capacities. He categorically rejected the idea that humans were born with equal abilities, stating, "It is in the most unqualified manner that I object to pretensions of natural equality." Galton contended that persons of eminence had a particular nature that would result in exceptional performances regardless of environmental circumstances. These individuals were "urged by an inherent stimulus" to excel. For Galton it didn't matter whether or not someone was born to unfortunate circumstances; if they possessed natural talent, they would rise above the masses to perform great things.

Galton founded the discipline of eugenics and believed that humans could be improved via deliberate selection. He argued that intelligence tests could be used to identify the most gifted men and women for selective breeding. Those receiving the highest scores could be introduced to one another and offered financial incentives to marry and for producing a large number of children. Ironically, Galton never fathered any children.

To support his eugenic ideas, Galton became immersed in measurement and statistics. He applied statistics to problems of heredity and classified successful men into certain categories according to the frequency with which their level of success occurred in the British population.

Galton reasoned if human abilities were hereditary in nature, then persons of eminence should be found more frequently among close relatives of eminent individuals than for distant relatives. He contended that an individual's reputation, based on a track record of accomplishments, was a reasonable measure of natural ability. He obtained copious amounts of biographical data from eminent individuals and reported that the number of eminent relatives declined as one progressed from first degree to second degree relatives and from second degree to third. He presented these biographical data as support for his hypothesis of the inheritance of abilities rather than to environmental factors such as educational opportunities and other advantages accorded to individuals from families of considerable wealth and influence.

GALTON'S THREE TRAITS

Galton proposed that three separate traits were necessary to achieve eminence: *intellect, zeal, and power of work*. He also made a distinction between eminent and illustrious individuals. He noted that eminence involved persons having assumed a societal position attained by only 250 persons in each million. He reserved the term "illustrious" for persons attaining a position in society of only one in a million.

Galton acknowledged the need for training to improve oneself but noted that these gains were only rapid during the initial stages of training and that "maximum performance becomes a rigidly determinate quantity." Thus, hereditary factors set limits for attainable performance in both the mental and physical domains.

Galton discussed this maximal performance limitation with a story of a rather undistinguished university student who graduates and then enters the competitive employment arena. Galton reported, "The same kind of experience awaits him here that he has already gone through. Opportunities occur – they occur to every man – and he finds himself incapable of grasping them. He tries and is tried in many things. In a few years more, unless he is incurably blinded by self-conceit, he learns precisely of what performances he is capable, and what other enterprises lie beyond his compass. When he reaches mature life, he is confident only within certain limits, and knows, or ought to know, himself just as he is probably judged of by the world, with all his unmistakeable weakness and all his undeniable strength. He is no longer tormented into hopeless efforts by the fallacious promptings of overweening vanity, but he limits his undertakings to matters below the level of his reach, and finds true moral repose in an honest conviction that he is engaged in as much good work as his nature has rendered him capable of performing." Spoken like a true British aristocrat. As Geoff Colvin, author of *Talent Is Overrated*, wryly noted, at least Galton made mediocrity sound noble.

THE RAGE TO MASTER

A contemporary, albeit more balanced, version of Galton's innate talent hypothesis was presented by Ellen Winner, Professor of Psychology at Boston University. One of her primary research areas involves gifted children. She noted that there are two "diametrically opposed" myths with respect to giftedness. One myth, she argued, is that giftedness is entirely inborn. She cites Mozart, Picasso, and Einstein as examples of born geniuses according to this myth. The other myth, she asserted, is offered by some psychologists who state that giftedness is exclusively the product of the environment. With optimal training conditions, these psychologists would argue that one could produce the highest levels of giftedness.

According to Winner, gifted children present with three defining characteristics:

1. They are *precocious* - they strive toward mastery of some area or domain of interest at an early age.
2. They insist on marching to their own drummer. Gifted children learn faster and in a *qualitatively* different way than do the typical or bright child. Gifted children require minimal support from adults to master their particular domain.
3. They present with a *rage to master*. These children are "intrinsically motivated" to master a domain. They manifest an obsessive and intense interest in their chosen domain. This rage to master idea sounds quite similar to Galton's concept of eminent individuals being "urged by an inherent stimulus" to excel.

Prodigies, according to Winner, are more extreme versions of gifted children. They are so accomplished that they perform at an adult level.

Winner noted that giftedness is only found in areas that are highly structured and rule-governed. These include areas such as language, mathematics, visual arts, music, chess, and sporting events including gymnastics, skating, swimming, and tennis. Gifted children are not found in areas such as law, medicine, or the sciences that require vast accumulations of knowledge. So, for a child to excel in some area, it needs to be one where the underlying principles are structured and can be readily grasped by these highly motivated children.

Although Winner suggested that giftedness is neither entirely inborn or exclusively a result of a highly focused environment, she argued, "for a strong inborn, brain-based component of giftedness." She noted there are neurological and genetic differences between the gifted and ordinary child, but this appears to be more an article of faith than a reality. She related that the field of genetics is evolving in a way that *one day* may be able to relate specific traits or abilities to specific genes or clusters of genes.

Winner raised an interesting issue: Although noting that no one disputes the biological basis of mental retardation (now referred to as intellectual disability) or would suggest that the adaptive skill deficits found among these individuals are exclusively a result of insufficient training, she asked, quite appropriately in my judgment, "if biological retardation exists, why not biological acceleration?"

What is the evidence for the genetic transmission of specific human talents? Did the mapping of the human genome isolate genetic determinants for expert-level performance? Not yet, but there are some interesting leads. For instance, an individual's visual acuity involving the capacity to discern the detail and depth of moving objects appears, at least to a significant degree, genetically predetermined. Superior visual acuity may allow the individual, with sufficient training, to quickly discern the anticipatory cues involved, for example, in an opponent's tennis serve. Thus, it may be possible that some tennis players may have the capacity for superior cue identification that may contribute to an effective return of serve.

Another area having a genetic component involves aerobic capacity, which is a measure of the amount of oxygen an individual uses while exercising. With respect to endurance, the more oxygen one can use the better. Recent research indicates that twenty-one gene variants, a genetic signature of sorts, differentiated high and low responders with respect to their aerobic improvement.

And, of course, a simple trait such as height is largely determined by heredity and that in several sports (e.g., basketball, gymnastics) elite performers are either taller or shorter than the general population. Even with this apparent "simple" trait, research suggests that nearly 300,000 single nucleotide polymorphisms (SNPs), bits of DNA, are only able to account for forty-five percent of the variance in height among individuals. Given the complexity of the human genome, it is not surprising that a single gene or even several thousand can account for elite athletic performance.

Although it is generally accepted that both the environment and genes determine an individual's athletic skills, the relative contribution of these factors to the development of elite athleticism is presently unknown. And, most likely, this relative contribution will differ depending on the particular sport in question.

A ridiculous assertion came from Billy Mitchell, the great arcade video gamer, who suggested that his video game skills were a direct manifestation of his DNA. Yes, it is true that he is one of the greatest video gamers of all time. Genetic changes occur over extremely long expanses of time and arcade video games have only been around for approximately forty-five years. It is absurd to consider that his video game skills have somehow been differentially selected as part of some evolutionary process. But in other skilled areas such as golf, music, and chess these apparent explanations are routinely accepted.

Are all reasonably healthy children created equal? Of course not. Children present with different physical and emotional characteristics and in their capacity to pursue various interests. The more interesting question is whether this "giftedness" or "rage to master" makes any significant difference with respect to the development of an expert-level performer. There are many eminent adults who were considered ordinary as children – Darwin, Tolstoy, and Michael Jordan to provide a few examples. Their accomplishments were not hindered by any inborn limitations.

A review of the backgrounds of individuals widely considered to be gifted or prodigies –Mozart, Bobby Fischer, or Tiger Woods – reveals that they were the recipients of early and highly enriched learning environments. Gifted or eminent individuals may or may not have exceptional genes. We do know they are the products of exceptional environments.

How does one account for the continued dominance of the innate talent hypothesis? Part of the reason is that these apparent explanations give solace (or moral repose) to the vast majority of us with mediocre skills. We can be content with the belief that we just didn't receive the special talent as a gift from the gods. After all, it's not our fault. We were just not one of the lucky few. And for those with extraordinary skills, they probably won't object to be seen by others as possessing some special endowment.

A more important reason for the continuation of these types of apparent explanations is the lack of an alternative, data-based conceptualization for the performance of highly skilled individuals. Is it possible that "the huddled masses" have the potential to become expert-level performers?

CHAPTER 3

CAN ORDINARY PEOPLE DO EXTRAORDINARY THINGS?

"[T]his study contained the seed of a *potentially revolutionary idea*."

THANKS FOR THE MEMORIES

In a paper titled "Acquisition of a Memory Skill," K. Anders Ericsson, a postdoctoral fellow, under the direction of the eminent cognitive psychologist, William G. Chase of Carnegie-Mellon University, addressed this question of whether ordinary people could perform at extraordinary levels. The authors investigated the oft-noted limited capacity of short-term memory captured by the formula seven plus or minus two. This means that the number of objects humans can readily hold in short-term memory ranges from five to nine. It is no coincidence that telephone numbers, excluding the area code, have seven digits. This standard limit to short-term memory stands in marked contrast to the amazing feats of memory experts, who can recall copious amounts of information. Could it be that these extraordinary feats of memory are only reserved for a select few with some innate gift for memory recall? Or can memory skills be developed through extended practice? These were the questions of interest for Ericsson and Chase.

The authors recruited an undergraduate volunteer, known in the literature as S.F., for this project. Along with rats, undergraduate students are the most popular subjects for psychological research. Prior to the initiation of training, S.F. was assessed for his level of cognitive abilities. There was nothing extraordinary about either his intellectual or memory functioning, both falling within average levels "for a college student." The authors trained S.F. on what is known as a digit span test. One of the researchers read a list of random digits to S.F. at the rate of one digit per second. The starting sequence of digits was seven. An example of a random seven digit sequence would be 8-3-4-0-6-1-9. The task for S.F. was to recall the sequence of numbers. If he was successful on a particular trial, the following sequence was increased by one. If not, the next sequence was decreased by one. The investigators were interested in the strategies that S.F. used to recall the digits and asked him to provide verbal reports of his recall approach following half of the digit trials.

The results of this investigation were intriguing. Following twenty months of testing involving more than 230 hours of practice, S.F. was able to improve from recalling a list of seven randomly presented digits to almost eighty. Think about this for a minute. Each trial involved a new sequence of digits, and S.F., in a relatively brief period of time, was performing at the level of noted memory experts. How was he able to do this?

The analysis of S.F.'s verbal reports provided the answer. The critical part of his strategy involved the use of a specific mnemonic device. A mnemonic device involves associating something novel, like a randomly presented list of digits, with something known. The "known" element for S.F. involved running times. S.F. was an accomplished long-distance runner, and he fashioned a mnemonic device based on running times. For example, he would chunk 3- and 4-digit sequences as a race result. Thus, the digit sequence 4-2-0-3 would be classified by S.F. as "4 minutes, 20 point 3 seconds." He supplemented this mnemonic strategy with ages and dates for the digit sequences that could not be classified as running times. He never generated a mnemonic unit greater than 5 digits. The vast majority involved 3- and 4-digit sequences.

Interestingly, following three months of practice, the investigators presented S.F. with a random sequence of letters from the alphabet. He manifested no transfer of training effects. He could only recall six randomly presented letters. Thus, his memory training was limited to recalling digits (not a particularly employable skill). The authors concluded, "With an appropriate mnemonic system and retrieval structure, there is seemingly no limit to improvement in memory skill with practice."

This study was important for several reasons. First, it demonstrated that an individual, who possessed average levels of intellectual and memory functioning, could perform extraordinary feats of memory solely as a function of extended practice. Second, this study contained the seed of a *potentially revolutionary idea*: does extended, deliberate practice provide an adequate account for individuals of eminence, for those high achievers in fields such as the arts, sciences, and sports?

Ericsson has devoted his academic life to articulating the principles for the development of highly skilled performances. These principles have been bandied about in the academic psychology literature for the past two decades and have received increasing attention in the popular press during the past several years.

THE GREAT VIOLIN STUDY (1993)

We turn now to another stringed instrument, the violin, to help us discern the principles of how to develop the great tennis player. K. Anders Ericsson and his colleagues, Ralf Th. Krampe, and Clemens Tesch-Romer, proposed that the development of highly skilled performers is directly related to the amount of deliberate practice. The authors chose music as the domain of interest because violin performances can be readily identified and measured and where skilled mentors guide and shape the development of their students.

This study took place at the Music Academy of West Berlin (Hochschule der Kuenste), which has a long history of producing accomplished musicians, some of whom go on to perform at the international level, either as soloists or with major symphony orchestras. There were four comparison groups in this study. The researchers asked the music professors at the Academy to nominate violin students who had the potential for careers as international soloists. This elite group was known as **"the best violinists."** The Academy professors also nominated a second group of violinists who were likely to have careers with major symphony orchestras. This group of highly skilled violinists was called **"the good violinists."** A third group of students, having a primary background with the violin, was selected from the music education department affiliated with the Academy. This group was labeled **"the music teacher"** group. Each of these three groups consisted of seven women and three men. The mean age of these violinists was 23.1 years. The researchers also included a group of ten male, middle-aged violinists who were performing either with the Berlin Philharmonic Orchestra or the Radio Symphony Orchestra.

Each violinist in the first three groups was interviewed during three sessions. In the **first session**, biographical data were obtained including the age at which each started violin practice, history of music instruction, and involvement in music competitions. The participants were also asked to estimate how much time they spent in *solo-violin practice* since taking up the violin.

Study participants were then given a list of ten daily non-music activities (e.g., household chores, sleep, and leisure time) and twelve music-related activities (e.g., practice alone, taking lessons, and solo performance). Participants were asked to rate how much time they spent on each of the activities during the most recent week.

Participants were also asked to rate each of the twenty-two activities on three dimensions on a 0-10 point scale. The dimensions included: (1) how relevant each activity was to improving their violin performance, (2) the effort involved in performing the activity, and (3) how enjoyable the activity was.

In the **second session**, participants answered questions about practice and concentration. They also recalled all of the possible twenty-two activities they had engaged in during the previous day. This recall was aided by the use of a self-monitoring tool, more commonly known as a diary, that was organized by dividing the day into ninety-six, 15-minute segments. Participants were then instructed to complete this diary of activities for an entire week. The participants sent the daily diary sheet to the investigators at the end of each day.

The **third session** involved some additional data-coding activities. Then the investigators asked the participants about their life goals and gave them a general debriefing.

The results of this study were quite interesting and have major implications for the design and implementation of tennis training programs. Biographic data collected by the investigators revealed that the participants from the four groups were similar in many ways. Participants initiated formal lessons and systematic practice at approximately age eight and committed to becoming musicians by age fifteen. All participants had similar musical backgrounds and, by age twenty-three, they had amassed at least ten years of violin practice.

The vast majority of the young violinists (27/30) assigned *solitary practice* the highest rating for improving violin performance. Although almost all of the participants acknowledged that solitary practice was the critical vehicle for improving violin performance, they all didn't spend the same amount of time doing it. At the time of the study, the "best" and "good" groups spent approximately an average of twenty-four hours per week in solitary practice. The third group, the "music teachers," practiced alone for about nine hours per week. The two top groups practiced alone for 3.5 hours per day, whereas the music teacher group performed this activity for 1.3 hours per day. The two best groups preferred practicing in the morning when they were awake and refreshed. No particular pattern was found for when the music teachers practiced. The average practice session duration for all groups was about eighty minutes.

Of the ten rated non-music daily activities, only *sleep* was rated as important for improving violin performance. The two top groups actually slept more, with an average duration of 8.6 hours of sleep per night. The music teacher group slept, on average, for 7.6 hours per night. The two top groups also took more afternoon naps with the average nap duration per week of 2.8 hours vs. 0.9 hour for the music teacher group. *So, it appears that sleep is important to recover from the rigors of intensive, solitary practice.*

Recall that all the violinists reported that solitary practice was the single most important task that they could do to improve their violin playing. The investigators analyzed the data obtained from retrospective accounts of the participants with respect to the amount of time that they engaged in solitary practice from the inception of formal practice to age eighteen. The results were striking. The best violinist group amassed an average of 7,410 hours of practice; the good group accumulated an average of 5,301 hours of practice; the music teacher group logged in 3,420 hours of practice by age eighteen. The investigators asked the middle-aged violinist group to estimate how much practice time they accumulated by age eighteen, and the results indicated an average of 7,336 hours.

So, despite the fact that the best and good violinist groups were practicing about twenty-four hours per week at the time of the study, the differences in their performance levels were found to be in their *history* with the violin. The violinists who amassed a greater amount of solitary practice during their youth were performing at a superior level. Thus, the advantage of practice was cumulative in nature.

THE TEN-YEAR OR 10,000 HOUR RULE

There has been some discussion in the expert-performance literature as to what extent these rules – the ten-year or 10,000 hour rule – accurately reflect how much effort one needs to put forth to become an elite performer. Where did these rules come from and what do they mean? The ten-year rule is the proposition that one can achieve expert-level performance in some domain of interest with at least ten years of focused, intensive preparation. Note that the elite violin performers in the above study began studying the violin at approximately age eight and were accomplished musicians by young adulthood.

The earliest reference to this ten-year issue can be found in a paper dated 1899 addressing the development of telegraphic skills. Telegraphy involves the sending and receiving of Morse code, an important skill in 1899. The authors, William Lowe Bryan and Noble Harter, reported, "Our evidence is that it requires ten years to make a thoroughly seasoned telegrapher." Simon and Chase (1973), in a landmark study with chess players, noted that no one reached the elite of the chess-playing world without approximately a decade or so of intensive preparation. In Ericsson's 1993 violin study, he referenced this as the "10-year rule" and noted that this rule is not limited to telegraphers and chess players but applies to a wide array of skilled areas including mathematics, music, and sports.

This ten-year rule is not a hard and fast one. As with most things in life, there is some variability. The great Bobby Fischer required nine years of intensive preparation with chess before attaining grandmaster status. And basketball players around seven feet tall can perform at the highest professional level with only six years of focused training.

A modern equivalent of the ten-year rule is the 10,000 hour rule, which posits that expert-level performance can be reached with 10,000 hours of deliberate training. This rule was articulated by Malcolm Gladwell in his magnificent book, *Outliers*. Following his review of Ericsson's 1993 violin study, Gladwell stated the "idea that excellence at performing a complex task requires a critical minimum level of practice surfaces again and again in studies of expertise. In fact, researchers have settled on what they believe is the magic number for true expertise: ten thousand hours." Is this really the magic number and can someone *only* become an expert performer with 10,000 or more hours of training?

A review of the research data suggests otherwise. Even in Ericsson's violin study, the elite group of violinists *averaged* 10,000 hours of solitary practice by age twenty. This means there was some variability among the ten elite participants, with some logging in more than 10,000 hours and some fewer. Unfortunately, Ericsson and colleagues did not present any measures of variability to determine how much spread there was in the data. An interesting question would be what accounts for the differences among the elite performers? Apparently some of the participants reached an elite level of violin performance with fewer than 10,000 hours of training. Could it be that some innate factor explains why some of these elites reached a high level of violin performance in less time? I would suggest that one needs to rule out all environmental influences, such as the quality of practice time, prior to speculating about hereditary or innate factors.

There is no critical number of hours to attain expert levels of performance and 10,000 hours is not magical. Ericsson does not use the term "10,000 hour rule" in his scholarly papers and cautions against others interpreting this in a literal way. What appears critical for the development of the elite performer is extended involvement in deliberate-practice activities typically, but not always, involving ten or more years.

PRACTICE MAY NOT MAKE PERFECT, BUT A CERTAIN TYPE OF PRACTICE DOES

I'm sure that readers of this book recognize that there are many people, including tennis players, who spend a great amount of time with their area of interest but who never become great at what they do. I am a prime example of this. I have been playing tennis for the good part of fifty-five years and yet my skill level never advanced beyond a NTRP rating of 5.0. I am now playing at about a 4.0 level. I occasionally joke that my tennis career is characterized by years of mediocrity punctuated by a few brief moments of near adequacy. I know I have lots of company; there are many tennis players who have played for decades at about the same skill level. How can this be?

For the vast majority of us, skill development follows a similar path. When someone is initially introduced to some area of interest such as tennis, one can attain a level of proficiency within a relatively short period of time, usually around fifty hours. During this initial phase, the aspiring tennis player is learning the basics of the game and concentrating hard on keeping the ball in play. The primary goal at this stage is to reduce major mistakes and to be able to rally with one's opponent. As the aspiring tennis player acquires additional experience, mistakes become less frequent and his[1] game becomes increasingly nuanced. His tennis skills reach a level of automaticity, and he finds he does not need to concentrate as intensely as during the initial phase of skill development. But this is where problems arise. Many tennis players will become arrested at this automatic level despite years, and even decades of additional experience.

Are we to be content with Francis Galton's contention that we are born with certain innate limitations that we cannot transcend? Is greatness reserved for the select few? I don't think so. Ericsson has proposed a different and data-based conceptualization with respect to skill development.

---

1   This author uses "his," "he," and "him" as gender-neutral personal pronouns in select areas of the text.

GUIDELINE 1: DELIBERATE PRACTICE

Ericsson's central thesis is this: skill level is directly related to the amount of deliberate practice. The more deliberate practice you do, the more skillful you will become. And if you do lots of it, you can become very good. Ericsson defined deliberate practice as "the engagement with full concentration in a training activity designed to improve a particular aspect of performance with immediate feedback, opportunities for gradual refinement by repetition and problem solving."

There are several important, interrelated components to deliberate practice:

1. **Deliberate-practice activities need to account for the current skill level of the individual.** In the jargon of behavioral psychology, one needs to assess the individual's baseline level. What can he do? Since this book is about tennis, one needs to have information about the individual's current level of groundstrokes, service returns, approach shots, drop shots, volleys, and overheads. How steady is the individual? How hard can he hit the ball? How is his footwork? Once this baseline assessment has been completed, deliberate-practice activities can be designed to improve his skill level.

2. **Deliberate practice requires a teacher or coach.** No one attains expert-level status alone. Elite performance emerges gradually and performance improvements require the design of tasks that can be mastered in a step-wise manner. A parent typically introduces the aspiring tennis player to the game. If the parent is an accomplished player, he designs the initial practice tasks and will spend many hours with his child on the court. As the player becomes more proficient, there will come a time when a certified instructor or coach will be enlisted to assist the player in further skill development. Feedback is continuously available to the player in the form of verbal praise for task persistence and improvement. Practice activities continue to change based on the emerging skill level of the student.

3. **Practice activities need to be repeatable**. High volume repetition is the key to skill development. The tennis player needs to put in the practice hours on specific tasks designed by a coach or teacher to effect improvement. As noted in the great violin study, there was a positive relationship between the amount of deliberate practice and skill level. The more deliberate practice you do, the better you will become. For the tennis player, much of this practice time can be done alone. Service practice only requires a tennis court and a ball hopper. The ball machine is an ideal practice tool. For more sophisticated drills, a practice partner will be necessary. Regardless, to show improvement on specific tennis skills, one needs to repeat these tasks many times.

4. **Deliberate practice requires intense focus and concentration**. Elite performers note that the one factor that limits their deliberate-practice activities is the ability to sustain a high level of concentration. Recall that the best violinists in Ericsson's 1993 study practiced for about 3.5 hours per day with each practice session lasting about eighty minutes. Elite performers from multiple areas including the arts, chess, and sports practice about the same amount per day. The amount of daily practice rarely exceeds five hours. There may be an upper limit to the amount of deliberate practice that one can do on a sustained basis without producing fatigue or burnout.

5. **Deliberate practice is not particularly enjoyable:** Ericsson argued that deliberate-practice activities are "not inherently enjoyable" because they are designed to stretch the individual's skill level. That is, practice activities are designed by a teacher or coach to be just out of the comfort zone of the student. The student is unable to perform these particular skills on a reliable basis and, thus, this type of practice requires a significant amount of effort and focus. What is enjoyable or reinforcing about deliberate practice is its impact on improved performance. Deliberate practice requires a considerable amount of effort and not many people will engage in this type of activity. For those willing to put in the time and effort, the rewards will be considerable.

6. **The effects of deliberate practice are cumulative**. It should be apparent by now that protracted involvement in some domain of interest is necessary to produce expert-level performance. Whether or not you call it the "ten-year rule" or the "10,000 hour rule," lots of deliberate practice is required to produce an elite performer. All individuals improve gradually. There are no data indicating that someone can exhibit expert-level performance without a significant amount of practice and experience. The process of skill development, however, is invisible to most individuals. When one watches Roger Federer or Novak Djokovic on the tennis court, one can only be amazed at their skill level. After all, they are executing shots that the vast majority of tennis players can only do in their dreams. Since the tennis fan does not have access to all the grueling hours of practice involved in producing this level of expertise, it is easy to assume that their performance reflects some extraordinary innate ability. Elite athletes are great because they train longer and *more effectively* than the rest of us. As a corollary to this, Ericsson noted the infrequency of greatness results from the lack of optimal training environments and the requisite years of practice necessary to produce expert-level performance.

The knowledgeable tennis fan might, at this point, ask: "How is it that only a handful of tennis players reach the elite level?" Not only do they reach this elite level, but they tend to dominate the competition. After all, most of the Grand Slams are won by just a handful of players. And they win these events over some extremely skilled individuals. The elite must have inherited some special gift or are genetically different from the rest of the pack. This appears to be unlikely. The search for specific genes that can account for the elite performer has not been particularly productive. Another problem with the "innate talent hypothesis" is that many elite performers from a wide range of fields showed no evidence of talent but only reached a level of greatness after decades of hard work.

Allen Fox, the celebrated tennis strategist, coach, and regular contributor to *Tennis* magazine, articulated the key factor that discriminates elite tennis players from the other professionals. He noted, "A major reason the very *best* pros rise above the pack is because they are better at identifying and shoring up their weaknesses. The others practice and stay in shape, but their games remain essentially unchanged." And this is the essence of deliberate practice. It is not just the number of hours that one practices but the *quality* of practice time.

Ericsson and his colleagues are skeptical of the hypothesis that individual differences in innate talent have a determinative impact on expert-level performance. They do acknowledge the potential for differences with respect to activity levels and emotionality that may facilitate individuals' engagement in deliberate practice for extended time periods. Ericsson appears to be saying that some individuals come into this world with two of Galton's three traits that purportedly lead to eminence – zeal and the power of work – but that the importance of these traits is to facilitate involvement in deliberate practice. Whether or not one has some innate capacity for protracted effort or this amount of effort is developed over time by those of us without any special "gifts," it is the amount and quality of deliberate practice that are the critical elements in producing elite performers.

DO THE MATH

Several caveats are in order at this point. For someone to attain expert-level status in tennis or some other domain of interest, he has to put in the necessary amount of work and do so within an environment that will support optimal training conditions. How often does this occur? Rarely. This may be the reason for the paucity of elite performers rather than some genetic anomaly. And the window of opportunity for these conditions appears rather limited. International-level performers begin their training activities from ages three to eight. This gives them the time to log in an extended amount of deliberate practice. For example, if someone begins playing tennis at age six, they could theoretically amass approximately 10,000 hours of focused practice by age sixteen. But, and here is the important point, this individual would have to engage in deliberate-practice activities for approximately three hours a day, seven days a week, for ten years. Not only that, but they would have to do this within an optimal training environment. Sounds daunting, doesn't it?

Childhood would appear to be the ideal time to do this. But these children would sacrifice other significant parts of their lives for this quest to become an elite performer.

Now, let's take another situation. Someone who begins a deliberate-practice regimen at, say, age sixteen will need to do this for a ten-year period. He might be able to pull this off, but it would require a supportive environment with few distractions. And distractions abound at this age. Once he begins college or start working, the odds of becoming an expert-level performer decreases significantly. And can you imagine someone starting the process at age twenty. With a deliberate-practice regimen and regular tennis competition, he will improve and may even reach a high level of skill. Will he achieve international-level tennis stardom? To put it bluntly, it probably ain't going to happen.

The innate talent hypothesis, however, continues to reign supreme. Advocates of this position state that it is just a matter of time before a genetic basis can be found to account for elite performance. I contend that the genesis of elite performance most likely is complex, but one cannot deny the critical role of environmental factors in the development of the expert-level performer.

Ericsson has provided a data-based framework that can account for many characteristics of expert-level performance. His is also an "optimistic" approach. After all, if you don't subscribe to the belief that you-either-have-it-or-you-don't, you are more likely to do the work necessary to attain a high level of performance. Beliefs, in the words of the phenomenologists, reshape experience. With the right beliefs and years of requisite deliberate practice, one can accomplish remarkable things. Geoff Colvin concluded, although somewhat overstated, "great performance is not reserved for a preordained few. It is available to you and to everyone."

CHAPTER 4

GAME, MINDSET, MATCH

"No one ever accused Ivan Lendl of being a natural."

O ne area that has profound implications for the development of expert-level performers is the belief system that individuals hold regarding achievement and expertise. Carol S. Dweck, Professor of Psychology at Stanford University, has devoted her academic career to understanding how individuals' beliefs impact their motivation to achieve.

Dweck noted that successful individuals share several common characteristics. They enjoy learning, embrace challenges, work hard, are optimistic, and persist when presented with obstacles. These individuals, according to Dweck, manifest a *"mastery-oriented"* behavioral pattern. Others will avoid challenges and show performance decrements when confronted with obstacles. This is known as the *"helpless"* behavioral pattern and can affect some of the most skilled and intelligent individuals. Is there a way to build this durable, mastery-oriented pattern for the aspiring tennis player? Dweck's research strongly suggests that the answer is yes.

GUIDELINE 2: MINDSETS

Belief systems or *"mindsets"* give meaning to our experiences and help structure our world. Dweck posits two major types of mindsets. Individuals with a **fixed mindset** believe that one's talents, intelligence, or abilities are fixed entities that cannot be appreciably changed by experience. I suppose this could be called the Galton mindset because, for one with a fixed mindset, you *do* either have it or you don't. Having to expend a lot of effort or deliberate practice to improve in some performance domain suggests that you do not have talent. And if talent is some type of fixed entity, with some having more than others, why bother doing all that training? If you had talent you wouldn't have to work so hard to be great. As a result, in performance situations, those holding a fixed mindset find themselves having to prove themselves, to demonstrate that their talent is intact. When they prevail in some competitive situation, they can bask in the glory of their own special, inherited superiority. When they fail, this may imply that they may not be so talented or they have to generate excuses for why they failed: "The weather conditions were not right"; "The tournament officials were biased against me"; "I didn't get enough sleep last night," and so on. And, God forbid, should those with a fixed mindset actually begin to train hard and continue to fail, this is irrevocable proof that they are "losers." At this point, the fixed mindset individual has few options. Since talent is conceptualized as a fixed entity, effort is not going to be particularly helpful so they either find "true moral repose" in their own mediocrity or they quit.

The **growth mindset** is one in which skills or abilities are conceptualized as malleable and can be developed through focused training and experience. Effort, as Dweck noted, is what makes you talented. During a competitive or performance situation, those holding a growth mindset view this as an opportunity to increase their skills or level of competence. If one succeeds in some competitive arena, this is validation for one's effort and hard work. When someone with a growth mindset fails, this is viewed as a valuable learning opportunity for further improvement. Perhaps the individual did not expend a sufficient amount of preparatory effort or perhaps the training methods were not optimal. Failing provides an opportunity to learn and develop.

Dweck, through years of deliberate, thoughtful, and programmatic research, has developed a theoretical model having several inter-connected elements. One's particular belief system or mindset (fixed or growth) leads to the adoption of either a *performance* or *learning* goal. Those adopting a performance goal are primarily concerned with securing favorable judgments of their expertise, by having to prove themselves over and over again. For those adopting a learning goal, the object is to increase their skill level. These two goals, in turn, can result in either the helpless or mastery-oriented behavioral pattern noted above.

Allow me to illustrate Dweck's model with a selection of her research studies. One study (Diener & Dweck, 1978) examined the differences between children holding either a mastery or helpless orientation following a failure situation and how this impacted their emotions, behavior, and thinking. Study participants were late elementary-school children classified into two groups as likely holding either a helpless or mastery-oriented pattern based on their responses to a questionnaire. The investigators had all the children work on a series of problems known as a concept-formation task. All of the children could solve the first eight problems. The next four problems constituted the failure condition because they were too difficult for members of their age group to solve. The investigators were interested in the changes in the children's thinking, emotions, and behavior as they moved from successful problem-solving to failure. The concept-formation task is one that is formulated in such a way that the investigators were able to pin-point the exact strategies the students were using for each problem they attempted to solve. Following the sixth success problem, the investigators had the children talk about what they were thinking and feeling as they worked on the remainder of the problems.

The results of this study revealed that all the children, whether or not initially classified as holding a helpless or mastery-oriented pattern, used effective problem-solving strategies when dealing with the first eight problems. **Two distinct patterns emerged when they started to fail**. Those children classified as helpless started to blame themselves for their failures, citing limited intelligence or problem-solving ability. They manifested negative emotions, made task-irrelevant verbalizations, and showed significant deterioration in their performance across the four failure trials. With some of these students, this deterioration in problem-solving strategies approached a level used by pre-school children – completely irrelevant and ineffective.

The mastery-oriented children manifested a completely different response pattern to the failure items. They worked hard at attempting to solve the problems. They instructed themselves to use more effort and to concentrate more effectively. The mastery-oriented students did not provide excuses for their failure and did not even see themselves as failing. They remained optimistic throughout the task and attempted to improve their problem-solving across the four difficult items.

It is interesting to note that during the initial eight items (the easy items), all of the children were utilizing effective problem-solving strategies and maintained a positive outlook on their performance. Once the children were exposed to the failure items, marked changes occurred in the behavior between the groups. The helpless group lapsed into ineffective problem-solving strategies, blamed themselves for their failures, and became emotionally distraught. The mastery-oriented group continued to work hard, remained optimistic, and exhorted themselves to do better. How does one account for this? Consistent with holding an innate view of talent, the helpless children viewed failing as an indictment of their intelligence or ability with a consequent loss of self-esteem. The mastery-oriented group did not see failing as reflecting on their ability. In fact, these students did not see themselves as having failed. These children approached the difficult items as an opportunity to learn and develop skills.

In the next study, Elliott and Dweck (1988) investigated whether *experimentally inducing* a performance or learning goal would actually produce the helpless or mastery-oriented behavioral pattern. Participants in the study were 101 fifth-graders. The participants were randomly assigned to four experimental conditions. The children were given feedback that their skill level on a concept formation task was either high or low. That is, half of the participants were informed that they had the ability to perform really well on the task, and the rest were told that their current level of ability was rather low. The investigators then gave the children either a performance or learning goal. Those participants given a performance goal were informed that their ability would be evaluated from their performance on the task. Those students given a learning goal were informed that the task would give them the opportunity to learn new things. So, the four groups were:

1. High ability – Performance goal
2. Low ability – Performance goal
3. High ability – Learning goal
4. Low ability – Learning goal

The concept formation task began with a series of successes, and the four groups performed equally well. Then, the participants were presented with some difficult items. The investigators evaluated the students' thoughts, feelings, and behavior as they proceeded from the easy to the difficult items. Those students from the first group (high ability – performance goal), who believed that their ability to do well on the concept formation task was high, continued to persist when presented with the difficult items. The students from the second group (low ability – performance goal) showed the classic helpless response pattern involving negative emotions, poor task persistence, and indicted their limited ability as responsible for their poor performance. The two groups given the learning goal continued to remain optimistic and demonstrated effective problem-solving behavior regardless of whether they had initially been informed that their ability level was high (group 3) or low (group 4).

The results of this study suggested there was something about having a performance goal that makes one susceptible to the helpless behavioral pattern. The participants in this study were not initially identified, as they were in the Diener and Dweck study, as being prone to either a helpless or mastery-oriented pattern. Since the students were randomly assigned to the four groups, one can assume that those prone to the helpless or mastery-oriented pattern were equally distributed across the four groups. It was merely being told that their ability would be evaluated created the helpless behavioral pattern for many of the performance-goal participants. Those participants with the learning goal continued to persist and maintained a positive outlook when confronted with the difficult test items whether or not they believed they had sufficient ability for the task.

Dweck argued that the goals pursued by individuals create an interpretive framework for ongoing events. Thus, the same event may have an entirely different meaning if it occurs within the context of a performance or learning goal. Individuals holding a performance goal are primarily concerned with measuring their ability. The outcome of some task or competitive event will be the primary source of information regarding the adequacy or inadequacy of their ability. Failing at some event, like losing an important tennis match, may lead those with a performance goal to believe that their ability is inadequate. For those individuals holding a learning goal, the same outcome only means that their strategic plan was insufficient or that they need additional skill development.

The effort one expends is influenced by the two goal orientations. Those holding performance goals believe that high effort implies low ability. When you have the talent, you don't need to work hard to be great. Conversely, if you have to work really hard at something, you must not have much talent or ability.

Individuals pursuing learning goals view effort in an entirely different way. They see it as a way to achieve mastery. High effort is the path to expert-level performance.

The different goals can also, as indicated in the above studies, impact one's emotions. For those individuals pursuing a performance goal, a challenging or failure situation can produce negative emotions such as anxiety, depression, or anger. This makes sense because failure for performance-goal individuals implicates their self-worth. Failure suggests that they don't have talent. Those holding a learning-goal orientation maintain a positive emotional orientation during challenging tasks or failure situations. Learning-goal individuals view failure as an opportunity to learn and develop.

The ideal situation for those holding performance goals is one that maximizes positive self-judgments about their ability level and produces accolades from others. Performance-goal individuals with limited confidence in their ability view challenging tasks with trepidation because of the potential for failure and loss of self-esteem.

Performance-oriented individuals who have high confidence in their ability level would be more challenge seeking but would be wary of situations where the risk of failure was significant. And if they experienced repeated failures, their talent, or lack thereof, would be painfully exposed. They would not be likely to engage in a regimen of protracted effort because of the belief that greater effort would only confirm their talent deficit.

The situation couldn't be more different for learning-goal individuals. Success does not imply some innate talent but is the result of a program of sustained effort. And failure situations do not imply a lack of ability but energizes the individual to expend more effort. Effort, for learning-goal individuals, is the means for task mastery.

Now, consider this hypothetical situation: Two tennis players enter a tournament and are assigned to different halves of the draw. One player disdains practice but enjoys performing. His game is fluid, nuanced, and highly effective. He is considered by others to be a "natural." He breezes through the draw, losing only one set on his way to the finals.

The other player is the classic grinder. He is committed to practicing and will spend three to four hours a day on the practice court. His strokes are mechanical, almost robotic. His matches tend to be long and grueling, but because of his work ethic, he wins the majority of his matches in straight sets. He loses only one set on his way to the final round. Of these two players, who is the more talented?

A TALE OF TWO MINDSETS

John McEnroe

John Hall and I had just reached the semifinals of a 45-and-over senior tennis event in Dover, Delaware in February of 1996. We went out to dinner that evening and were, of course, "talking tennis." At one point, John asked me who I considered to be the most talented player ever to play the game. My response was, "You mean besides John McEnroe?" The answer was obvious. McEnroe was a Van Gogh or Baryshnikov with a racket. He executed shots with a flair and artistry that was unparalleled in the sport's history. He had great hand-eye coordination and could take the ball early and attack the net. And once at the net, he would angle off volleys or execute those wonderful, deftly placed drop volleys. He had that incredible "can-opener" serve that he sliced out wide to the ad court. His opponent would be pulled so far off the court that, even if they were able to return his serve, John would be at the net to finish off the point. In McEnroe's autobiography, *You Cannot be Serious*, he correctly noted that one of his unnoticed or unappreciated skills was his speed at backing up to hit the overhead. This was an important skill because he frequently crowded the net. If his opponent lobbed him, John quickly backed up and crushed the overhead.

As we continued our discussion that evening, John and I also agreed that Ilie Nastase was close to McEnroe in terms of sheer athleticism. Nastase had this uncanny ability to improvise winning shots from the most bizarre, defensive positions.

Arthur Ashe described McEnroe as the most talented player he had ever seen, as have many others. McEnroe appeared to agree with this assessment, stating that at one point in his career, his head was so big it barely fit through the door. This is understandable. In the fishbowl world of international tennis, McEnroe was constantly receiving accolades from others regarding his tennis skills - and deservedly so.

John McEnroe was born on February 16, 1959, at the Wiesbaden Air Force Base in West Germany. John grew up in a comfortable, middle-class neighborhood, Douglaston in Queens, New York. He attended private schools. He started playing tennis at the Douglaston Club when he was eight years old and received formal tennis instruction from the local pro, Dan Dwyer, who famously predicted after John won a 12-and-under tournament at age eight that "we're going to see John at Forest Hills someday." McEnroe noted that his next tennis instructor was "a nice old guy named George Seewagen."

There was more to Seewagen than being a nice old guy. Seewagen was an outstanding athlete in his youth, starring in baseball, basketball, track, and soccer. He won a national championship in soccer and was named an All-American in college. Seewagen was drafted by the New York Yankees to play baseball. He wasn't interested in playing tennis in his youth, dismissing those who played it as "sissies." Like others who come to the game late, Seewagen was hooked when he started playing the game. Because of his athleticism, he quickly advanced and was ranked in the top ten among men in the Eastern Section. He once played a match against Don Budge. Seewagen was a knowledgeable and skilled tennis player. I'm sure he provided McEnroe with some solid tennis fundamentals. Seewagen noticed young McEnroe's potential, informing others to keep an eye on the kid's development because he had the "goods" to go far in the game. And Seewagen would have known. In addition to being a great athlete himself, he had a son, Butch, who was a dominant junior player in the early to mid-1960s and who later played on the circuit for a few years.

As a developing junior player, McEnroe noted that he was fast on his feet and was able to see the ball early. He stated, "I was fascinated by all the different ways you could hit a tennis ball – flat, topspin, slice." As with many aspiring young tennis players, McEnroe spent hours hitting balls against a backboard.

When he was twelve, McEnroe began training at the Port Washington Tennis Academy. Antonio Palafox, the head pro, was a shrewd and strategic player and a doubles specialist. He was of small stature but quick and knew how to play the angles. He partnered with Rafael Osuna to win the United States Tennis Championships (now the U.S. Open) in 1962 and Wimbledon in 1963. Palafox was a key member of the 1962 Mexican Davis Cup team that lost in the final round to a powerful Australian team that included Rod Laver, Roy Emerson, and Neale Fraser.

Palafox had the young McEnroe look at the court as a mathematical equation. He helped shape McEnroe's approach game, sometimes having McEnroe approach with a deep ball; at other times, McEnroe would slice the ball off the court. And Palafox would have been the ideal person to teach McEnroe about doubles.

In 1971, the great Australian Davis Cup captain, Harry Hopman, became the tennis director at Port Washington. So, the young McEnroe was the recipient of some of the best tennis instruction available in the world. And with other aspiring junior players such as Peter Fleming, Vitas Gerulaitis, Peter Rennart, and Mary Carillo training at the academy, McEnroe was at the "right place and the right time" to develop his game.

Despite the impressions of many, McEnroe was not a tennis prodigy. McEnroe was an accomplished junior player, but he did not dominate the junior ranks. He was ranked number 18 in the 12-and-unders when he was eleven years old and improved to number 7 a year later. He defeated Eliot Teltscher 7-5, 6-1 to win the Orange Bowl 18-and-under Championships in 1976. McEnroe never won the National Boys Championships at Kalamazoo but did reach the finals in the 18-and-under division in 1976, losing to Larry Gottfried 5-7, 6-3, 4-6, 6-2, 6-3.

A year later, at age eighteen, McEnroe's game took off. Gottfried noted, "It was as if one day John woke up, realized he really wanted to be a tennis pro – and took things to an entirely different level." An entirely different level indeed. He won several qualifying rounds at the 1977 French Open and lost to the Australian, Phil Dent, in the second round, 4-6, 6-2, 4-6, 6-3, 6-3. Dent made it to the semifinals that year. McEnroe then had his incredible run at Wimbledon several weeks later. He won three matches in the qualifying tournament held at the Bank of England Club in Roehampton. He defeated Ismail El Shafei in the first round of the main draw 6-0, 7-5, 6-4. He then defeated Colin Dowdeswell, Karl Meiler, Sandy Mayer, and then got a measure of revenge in the quarterfinals, defeating Phil Dent 6-4, 8-9, 4-6, 6-3, 6-4. His Cinderella run ended in a semifinal match against Jimmy Connors losing 6-3, 6-3, 4-6, 6-4. Following the match, Connors said, "The kid is difficult to play. He tees off on everything and hits winners from impossible places."

Wimbledon was the perfect venue for McEnroe's emergence into tennis stardom. His game was ideally suited for grass. His lefty serve, precision volleying, and ability to take the ball on the rise proved a deadly combination. His 1977 Wimbledon run was, in my opinion, one of the more exciting developments in American tennis history.

Over the course of McEnroe's legendary career, he won 77 singles titles and 77 doubles titles. He won seven Grand Slam singles events - three Wimbledon titles and four U.S. Opens. He was a charismatic and controversial individual. His on-court antics were often entertaining and, at times, disturbing.

Despite his impressive record and high level of tennis skill, John McEnroe was, in a strange way, an underachiever. He stated, "I'll confess it: I feel I could have done more. There are nights when I can't get to sleep for thinking about the Australian Opens I passed by when I was at the peak of my game and always felt I'd have another chance; the French Open that I had in the palm of my hand, then choked away."

John McEnroe had the potential to be the game's premier player, possessing a skill set, at least in some aspects of the game that surpassed even that of Rod Laver and Roger Federer. **He also possessed something else: a fixed mindset.**

An individual's mindset appears determined, to some extent, by the reactions of others. In a very real sense, one's mindset may be seen as a social product. McEnroe's environment was conducive for him to develop a fixed mindset. As a child, he was curious, bright, and an excellent athlete. He was an accomplished basketball, football, and soccer player in school. The people around him readily noticed and commented on his considerable athletic talent. Mary Carillo, John's childhood friend and fellow trainee at the Port Washington Academy, frequently played practice matches with John. Following a particularly energetic match, where Carillo gave it her all but succumbed to John's tennis skills, she asserted, "Oh God, John, you're going to be the best player in the world." John was only thirteen years old. That same year, George Lott, a tennis columnist and former Wimbledon doubles champion, proclaimed that John was going to be the next Laver. Pretty heady stuff for a young teenager.

But McEnroe was conflicted about tennis. He stated that he was pushed into something that he didn't really want to do. His parents were the driving force behind John's early tennis career. McEnroe reflected, "My dad...seemed to live for my growing little junior career – he was so excited about having a son with some actual athletic talent." John's dad attended all of his weekend practice sessions at the Port Washington Academy. "He'd just stand there," John noted, "with a huge smile on his face – he never seemed to get bored with watching me play tennis." When John told his dad he wasn't enjoying the game, his dad either attempted to laugh it off or "act hurt." McEnroe senior was obviously thrilled with his son's athletic prowess and communicated to John in many direct and subtle ways of his incredible talent and, despite John's protestations, the need to continue to play the game.

Dweck noted that messages sent to a child or young person from a fixed-mindset perspective can have profound and long-lasting consequences. These messages essentially communicate: *"You have permanent traits and I'm judging them."* So, when others make statements about McEnroe being a future number one in the world, being the next Laver, or having a dad exult in his son's considerable talent, there is an underlying message heard by the young person – "If I don't perform well or become a champion, I'm not talented or worthy."

This may have been the primary dynamic in John's tennis career. Taking a cue from the Elliott and Dweck study noted above, McEnroe would be classified as a high ability – performance goal individual. McEnroe was clear on this issue. He stated that he wanted to perform and that he did not enjoy practicing. He focused his energies on the outcome and not the process of his tennis. His goal was to validate his considerable talent by winning a match, a tournament, or reaching number one in the world.

Recall that with performance-goal individuals, there is a risk, when confronted with failure situations, of a significant deterioration in functioning involving one's emotions, behavior, and thinking. For McEnroe this included tantrums, excuses, and negative thinking. As a junior, McEnroe never thought an opponent was a better player. He was probably thinking, "No one is more talented than I!" He burst into tears whenever he lost a match and offered a variety of excuses for his loss, including the opponent was bigger, luckier, from California or Florida, and so forth.

As a professional, McEnroe noted that he almost always felt inadequate when he lost a match. He had to fight the thought, "I'm a loser; I'm not the same person I was." This is a classic fixed-mindset response. A loss for McEnroe was more than just losing a tennis match – it was a global indictment of his personality or talent. Perhaps he didn't have the goods; perhaps he wasn't worthy.

This same process may be seen in some of McEnroe's classic matches. McEnroe described his loss to Ivan Lendl at the 1984 French Open as the worst of his life and a "total disaster." He stated that match "still keeps me up at nights. It's even tough for me now to do the commentary at the French – I'll often have one or two days when I literally feel sick to my stomach just at being there and thinking about that match." McEnroe won the first two sets and appeared to be cruising to victory. He was up two games to love in the third but lost the set 6-4. He was aware of the enormity of the event and his place in tennis history. A win at the French would have provided him with a credible argument for being the greatest player of all time. After all, he was only twenty-five years old with the potential to win more Grand Slams. But Lendl was beginning to pressure him. McEnroe was losing his concentration, and he was entertaining excuses – he was tired, a call from a former girlfriend the previous night had annoyed him, and then there was the "squawking headset" incident. Apparently an NBC cameraman had taken off his headset and it began to emit a loud, squawking noise. McEnroe stated that his concentration was shot once the squawking noise started. At one point, he walked over to the headset and screamed into the small microphone, *"Shut the f*** up!!"*

McEnroe recalled that the match turned on one key point, and it involved his famous "can-opener" serve to the ad court. McEnroe was leading 4-2 in the fourth set and serving at 40-30. Lendl's coach, the former Australian tennis great, Tony Roche, counseled Lendl to return McEnroe's serve crosscourt with slice. This allowed the ball to stay low, precluding McEnroe from hitting an aggressive volley. McEnroe entertained hitting a drop volley following Lendl's crosscourt return but decided against it because, even for McEnroe, this could be a low percentage shot. Instead, he played it safe and his forehand volley floated long. Following that, McEnroe described the rest of the match as a "blur." McEnroe's performance deteriorated. He lost the match 3-6, 2-6, 6-4, 7-5, 7-5.

Despite having a stellar year in 1984 - winning both the Wimbledon and U.S. Open titles - McEnroe labeled himself as the "Choker-in chief" because of that one match against Lendl. And he only lost three matches that year.

A match against Brad Gilbert in the final round of the 1985 Masters tournament at Madison Square Garden provides another example of classic fixed-mindset thinking. McEnroe compared Gilbert to the Disney character Eeyore, infecting others with his dysphoric (depressive) gloom. Gilbert was an effective, strategic player. There was always the risk that if you entered Gilbert's "cloud of tennis gloom," you would never come out again. Gilbert, for example, defeated Boris Becker in a match at the 1987 U.S. Open, leaving the powerful Becker a quivering mass of tennis goo. The effect of Gilbert's game was like that of a giant syringe, sucking all the strength out of you.

Against McEnroe at the 1985 Masters, Gilbert was at his "Winning Ugly" best. He defeated McEnroe 5-7, 6-4, 6-1. McEnroe's response was, "Someone is telling me something here. Because if I can lose to Brad Gilbert, something is seriously wrong. I've got to take a look at myself. I've got to re-evaluate not only my career but my life." So, again, McEnroe takes the result of one tennis match and transforms it into an indictment of his entire life. When one interprets events from a fixed-mindset perspective, one failure can have global implications.

McEnroe took six months away from the game after his loss to Gilbert. Following his six month hiatus, McEnroe was becoming antsy; he proclaimed that he wanted to regain the number one ranking. He initiated a serious training regimen, eating healthy foods and eliminated the beer and desserts. He practiced yoga in the morning, tennis in the afternoon, and stationary bike and weight-training at night.

As noted above, effort is a bad thing for those holding a fixed mindset. If you have to expend effort, this essentially means you are not talented or special. McEnroe maintained his training regimen for five months but then quit. He never regained the form that vaulted him to the top of the game. He continued to play for several more years and had some impressive wins, but he never won another Grand Slam; he retired from the game in 1992.

Ivan Lendl

No one ever accused Ivan Lendl of being a natural. Upon initial reflection, Lendl reminds one of Ivan Drago, the fictional character from the 1985 film Rocky IV. One could picture Lendl hooked up to electrodes as he sprints on a treadmill while uttering such classic lines as "You will lose" and "I must break you." As a result of sheer determination and will, Lendl dominated the tennis world from 1985 to 1990 and ushered in the modern era of "power tennis." He pushed aside John McEnroe and Jimmy Connors in his quest to become the number one player in the world. He brutalized his opponents with his powerful forehand. Arthur Ashe commented, "Lendl hits the forehand harder than anyone I've ever seen…he deforms the ball when he hits it." His on-court demeanor was dour and intimidating, and his training regimen was austere; second to none. He frequently took thirty mile bike rides, ran sprints, and did on-court drills for hours per day. All aspects of his life were compulsively planned and executed and geared toward achieving tennis supremacy. And that was exactly what he achieved. And Lendl, unlike McEnroe, **possessed a growth mindset.**

Lendl was born in the city of Ostrava in Czechoslovakia on March 7, 1960. His parents were both competitive tennis players. His mother, Olga, attained the number two ranking in Czechoslovakia and was the primary driving force in Ivan's tennis development. Lendl noted that his mother was not a particularly gifted athlete but worked extremely hard on her game. She was relentless on the court. One of her favorite expressions was "I'm going to break you down." (Hmm, watch out, Rocky Balboa.) When Ivan was an infant, his mother always had him courtside in a stroller. He began hitting balls against a backboard at age six. By age eight, he was playing matches against older boys. Ivan's mother was a perfectionist, communicating to Ivan that she wanted him always to improve. He obviously took that lesson to heart.

Lendl defeated his mother for the first time at age fourteen. This was a significant win for Ivan given the skill level of his mom. His mother was not pleased with the outcome of the match, having been relegated to the number two player in the family. During the summer, Ivan competed against all the best juniors in Czechoslovakia involving a concentrated experience of two tournaments a week for eight weeks in both singles and doubles.

At age eighteen, Lendl burst onto the international junior tennis scene by capturing both the French and Wimbledon junior titles. This international experience led to a growing restlessness in Ivan. He found the rigid, authoritarian, socialist Czech system to be stifling. Czechoslovakia in those days was a satellite state of the Soviet Union, and the system was not supportive of individual effort and initiative. There was no payoff for hard work. Ivan was determined to be free of these institutional constraints.

Lendl turned professional in 1978 following his victories in the French and Wimbledon juniors. Sometime in 1979, Ivan began his affiliation with

Wojtek Fibak, a professional tennis player from Poland, who was ranked in the top ten in singles in 1977. In 1980, Fibak reached the quarterfinals at the French Open, Wimbledon, and the U.S. Open. In many ways, Fibak was the polar opposite of Lendl and this included his tennis game and personality. Fibak was not a power player, relying instead upon finesse and guile. He was cultured with a special interest in collecting art.

Fibak became Lendl's friend, mentor, and advisor. Fibak suggested overhauling Lendl's game. Even though Lendl was already a top-ranked player, his game had some significant limitations: his first serve was not particularly effective; he used a defensive, slice backhand; and his volleys were only mediocre. Fibak acknowledged that Lendl's game was neither nuanced nor graceful, and to reach the top of the game, Fibak exhorted Lendl to become a "tennis machine."

Those with a growth mindset are receptive to an honest appraisal of their current skill set and to what steps they must take to remediate their deficits. For Ivan, this involved a multifaceted approach. The first step involved Lendl developing a topspin backhand. This could have been a risky proposition at this stage in his career, but Lendl was up for the challenge. Lendl played two matches against Harold Solomon on hard courts within a four-month time span that serves as a classic illustration of the advantages of a growth mindset. The first match was in April 1980 in Las Vegas when Lendl was just learning to execute the topspin backhand, and Fibak instructed Lendl to hit every backhand against Solomon with topspin. Lendl lost the match 6-1, 6-1. Lendl spent the next four months perfecting the stroke, hitting topspin backhands for several hours a day. During the U.S. Open, Lendl faced Solomon in the round of 16 and destroyed him 6-1, 6-0, 6-0. Lendl was the tenth seed that year. He had transformed his backhand into a dangerous weapon with four months of intensive, deliberate practice.

The next step in Lendl's tennis makeover involved his diet and exercise. Lendl consulted with Robert Haas, a sports nutritionist and author of *Eat to Win*. Haas was well-known in tennis circles, having previously worked with Martina Navratilova in effecting improvements in her physical conditioning. Haas analyzed Lendl's blood chemistry and found that he was in the high risk range for serum cholesterol. Lendl's daily diet prior to working with

Haas consisted of copious amounts of red meat, highly caloric desserts, and four or five Coca Colas. He rarely ate fruit or vegetables. Haas overhauled Lendl's diet to one involving pasta, soup, fruit, vegetables, and little red meat. Haas got Lendl to adopt a draconian physical training regimen that involved, in part, long and arduous bicycle rides. And consistent with the elite violin players from "The Great Violin Study," Haas encouraged Lendl to take a brief, restorative nap each afternoon. Lendl embraced the changes and made significant advances in his conditioning and overall health and well-being. Lendl was on his way to becoming a finely-tuned tennis machine.

By 1981, Lendl was the third-ranked player in the world. He was having a successful career but appeared unable to win the "big matches." He was a finalist in four Grand Slams from 1981 to 1983 but lost all of them. The media labeled him a choker.

Like the mastery-oriented children in the Dweck studies, Lendl knew how to deal with adversity. He planned and strategized how to become the number one player in the world. McEnroe and Connors, both lefties, were standing in his way. In 1984, Lendl hired the great Australian Tony Roche to assist him in reaching the pinnacle of the men's game.

Lendl had his breakthrough match at the 1984 French Open, defeating McEnroe in five sets. As a lefty with a great net game, Roche was ideally suited for designing Lendl's game plan for McEnroe.

His 1984 French Open win validated Lendl's training regimen. But he wasn't resting on his laurels. Unlike McEnroe, Lendl focused his energies on the process of his tennis. He was a proponent of the belief that if you worked hard enough, anything is possible. He stated, "[T]he faraway goal is not the real objective – the methodical day-to-day struggle is."

The next "struggle" for Lendl was the mental aspect of the game. There were too many times in the past when Lendl lost his focus and concentration in important matches. In January 1985, Lendl hired a mental health professional, Alexis Castori, author of *Exercise Your Mind: 36 Mental Workouts for Peak Performance*. Knowing how committed Lendl was to his physical training regimen, Castori conceptualized her work with Lendl as "mental aerobics." Lendl was aware that he needed to focus more effectively on the ball during a match and eliminate outside distractions.

In her work with Lendl, Castori used several exercises to enhance his ability to concentrate more effectively. She had Lendl practice a mental exercise that she termed "Increasing Your Powers of Focus and Concentration" in which he described, in detail, a common household object without judging it in any way. This is how the exercise is done: You only need an object such as a pen or salt shaker and some type of alarm as found on a digital watch, cell phone, or kitchen timer. Practice this exercise in an environment free of distractions. Set the alarm for five minutes and, in a sitting position, place a small household object in front of you. Feel free to hold the object. Then describe out loud everything you can about the object in as much detail as you can. This would include the color of the object, the size, shape, tactile properties, any imperfections such as scratches, and so forth. Examine all aspects of the object by turning it upside down or around but be sure to describe all properties on a particular side of the object before turning it to another area. Continue describing the object until the timer or alarm rings. Castori recommends doing this exercise daily for several weeks. Increase the duration of the exercise by one minute every week until you can concentrate on some given object for eight to ten minutes.

Lendl practiced another exercise, "Overcoming Minor Daily Frustrations," to help him cope with frustrating experiences either on or off the tennis court. Ivan used this exercise whenever he was feeling annoyed and about to "lose it." This exercise is profound but simple. You don't need any special equipment and can use it wherever you happen to be. The focus of this exercise is on the here-and-now. As every tennis player knows, one can experience a variety of emotions during a tight match – excitement, frustration, anger, and for some, rage. These emotional states are invariably accompanied by various dysfunctional thoughts such as "I know I'm going to choke" or "I can't stand playing a pusher." The primary technique in this exercise is known as "witnessing." This is where you just describe what you are doing without judging it in any way. Begin the witnessing procedure whenever you feel yourself becoming frustrated. On the tennis court, between points, this procedure would include descriptions such as "I'm walking over to the ball and picking it up"; "I'm wiping the sweat off of my forehead with my wrist band"; and "Now I'm walking back to the baseline." After engaging this witnessing process, you should begin to notice your frustration lessening and, with continued practice, stopping. This witnessing exercise is to be used between points or during the changeover and is not designed to be used during a point. These exercises are particularly helpful in increasing one's awareness and concentration because one does not become enmeshed in negative thinking or dwelling on emotional states. Lendl learned how to cope with his problematic thinking and emotions by describing his behavior in the moment. In this regard, Lendl had a huge advantage over McEnroe.

Castori also helped Lendl with his on-court movement. She noticed that his movements were rigid and mechanical and had him enroll in aerobic-dance and ballet classes. The goal was to create a "graceful tennis machine."

This combination of a rigorous physical training regimen, extended on-court drills, diet management, and improved mental focus allowed Lendl to become the dominant player of his era. From 1985 to 1987, his match winning percentage was greater than 90%. He won eight Grand Slams. He was victorious at the U.S. Open in 1985, 1986, and 1987. Impressively, Lendl was in eight consecutive U.S. Open finals from 1982 to 1989. He won the French Open in 1984, 1986, and 1987. He won the Australian Open in 1989 and 1990. The only Grand Slam that eluded Lendl was Wimbledon. He did, however, reach the finals on two occasions, losing to Boris Becker in 1986 and to Pat Cash in 1987. He was the number one ranked player for an impressive 270 weeks. By the time he retired from professional tennis in 1994, Ivan had won 94 ATP singles events.

Let's now return to the hypothetical example of the two players, one described as a "natural" and the other a "grinder." Of McEnroe and Lendl, who would you consider to be more talented? The answer appears to be obvious, but we need to digress for a moment. Malcolm Gladwell argued that our culture, in a rather interesting way, values effortless achievement over ability earned through hard work. This may be the genesis of our fascination with movies such as *The Natural*, and McEnroe was closer than any other tennis player to fitting that role. There is no doubt that McEnroe's game was more fluid and nuanced than Lendl's. McEnroe was literally "poetry in motion" on the court. Lendl was clearly not a natural. McEnroe reportedly once joked that Lendl had more talent in his whole body than McEnroe had in his little finger. So how did this alleged innate talent differential impact their careers?

Lendl won eight Grand Slams to McEnroe's seven. Lendl reached the finals of 19 Grand Slams to McEnroe's 11. Lendl was the number one player in the world for a total of 270 weeks versus 156 for McEnroe. Lendl won 94 ATP singles titles to McEnroe's 77. In head-to-head play, Lendl had a 19-14 advantage and won ten of their last eleven meetings with relative ease.

So, who was the more talented? I would argue it was Lendl. The difference was that Lendl *created* his talent through sustained effort and hard work. And he did so to such a remarkable degree that he drove McEnroe into retirement. McEnroe's fixed mindset was not capable of contending with Lendl's growth mindset assault.

Game, mindset, match – Lendl.

Carol Dweck, in her book *Self-Theories: Their Role in Motivation, Personality, and Development*, reported that at a certain landmark age (it was probably the youthful age of 50) she asked herself what she would prefer to be able to say at the end of her life. In true growth-mindset fashion, she noted, "I want to be able to say that I kept my eyes open, faced my issues, and made wholehearted commitments to things I valued. I did not want to be haunted by a litany of regrets or left with a bundle of potentialities that were never realized." When that time comes, how many of us will find peace in this end-of-life review? With respect to his tennis career, I'm sure Ivan Lendl will have few regrets.

DON'T PRAISE TALENT; PRAISE EFFORT

What steps can members of the tennis community take to create that growth mindset for aspiring tennis players? After all, wouldn't we want to inculcate in young tennis players those features that define successful people – sustained effort, optimism, enjoyment in the process of development, and the capacity to endure when faced with challenges? I believe that the answer from coaches, parents, and aspiring tennis players would be a resounding yes.

This is an important issue because there are research data indicating that children as young as three-and-a half-years-old can manifest a helpless response pattern involving a compromised self-concept, lack of task persistence, negative emotions, and feelings of worthlessness. Could it be that some children enter this world with an emotionally helpless disposition whereas others present with a Lendl-like mastery orientation? Although there may be minimal support for the Galton hypothesis of an innate tendency for eminence or expert-level performance, there is acknowledgment that children do come into this world with different emotional dispositions, with some being more active toward the environment whereas others may be more reticent and easily frustrated. Fortunately, these innate differences may not be all that important for the development of the mastery-oriented growth mindset.

Additional research from Dweck and her colleagues clearly indicates that the types of *feedback* children receive from adults can either lead to the development of a mastery-oriented hardiness or a helpless response pattern *regardless of innate differences in emotional dispositions*.

What is the best type of praise to give a child? There are two broad categories of praise. One involves praising the child as a whole when people comment about how smart or talented a particular child may be. The other category involves feedback directed at the child's strategies or effort.

Mueller and Dweck (1996) reported that 85% of parents endorsed the following statement: "It is important to praise children's ability when they perform well on a task to make them feel that they are smart." This would appear to be quite sensible. After all, wouldn't one want to praise children's talents or abilities? This is the standard reinforcing practice of many parents, and the intention of giving this type of praise is to develop children's self-esteem and to develop mastery-oriented behaviors.

Research findings from Dweck and her colleagues on this issue are quite surprising and suggest that this type of global, person-oriented praise can actually prevent the occurrence of the mastery-oriented behavioral pattern that parents and others are attempting to instill. Dweck's primary hypothesis or assumption in this research is that global or person-oriented praise may produce significant vulnerabilities in children. That is, praise directed at children's intelligence, talents, or abilities sends a powerful message to children to measure themselves in a global way based upon their performance on some specific task. If they happen to perform well at some task, this may not be an immediate problem. But when they later fail at some task, and everybody does at some point, there is a risk that these children will make global attributions about their lack of intelligence, talent, or ability. Conversely, praise that is directed toward children's effort or productive strategies should avoid these pitfalls and facilitate mastery-oriented responses.

In one study, Kamins and Dweck (1999) investigated this issue of whether giving global praise to children when they succeed – that is, by telling them that they are talented or smart – will set them up for a helpless response when they later fail at something. Participants in the study were sixty-four kindergarten students. Each participant was assigned to one of several groups. In the first part of the study, each child successfully worked on four tasks for their teacher. The teacher then delivered to the groups a different form of praise. Several groups received **person praise** in which the teacher directed praise to the child as a whole (e.g., "I'm very proud of you," "You're a good girl," or "You're really good at this"). One group received **outcome praise** in which the teacher delivered praise that focused on the outcome of the task (e.g., "That's the right way to do it"). Finally, two groups received **effort or strategy praise** in which the teacher directed praise to the amount of effort or strategy used in solving the problem (e.g., "You must have tried really hard" or "You found a good way to do it, can you think of other ways that may also work?").

The investigators assessed the children on several dimensions after the third success trial. Specifically they looked at how well the children believed they performed on the task, how this reflected on their traits or abilities, and the impact their performance had on their emotions. All of the groups were equally positive about how they had performed at this point in the experiment.

All of the groups then experienced two failure trials. Following these failure experiences, the children were assessed again about their performance, their views on their abilities, and their emotions. The results were clear and convincing. The children who had received the global, person-oriented praise were the ones most vulnerable to the effects of the failure trials. They denigrated their performance on the task, reported their abilities to be low, and reported more negative emotions than did the groups receiving the effort or strategy praise. The investigators also examined how persistent the children were on the tasks. As predicted, those children who received the person praise were less inclined to persist on the task following a failure experience.

Dweck concluded, "[I]f you learn from person praise that success means you're a good or able person, then you also seem to learn that failure means you are a bad or inept person. If you learn from praise that your good performance merits wholesale pride, you also seem to learn that poor performance merits shame." I suppose one could call this "the McEnroe effect." So, the impact of person praise seems to create a condition of "contingent self-worth" in which individuals feel worthy when they succeed but deficient or unworthy when they fail.

Josh Waitzkin, the eight-time United States chess champion and subject of the book and movie *Searching for Bobby Fischer*, noted this process with young chess "prodigies." He stated, "The most gifted kids in chess fall apart. They are told that they are winners, and when they inevitably run into a wall, they get stuck and think they must be losers."

The results of the above Dweck study were obtained with kindergarten children. Would these results hold with older children? Mueller and Dweck (1998) conducted six studies involving over 400 fifth-grade participants. The central question in this research involved the effects of praise for intelligence versus praise for effort. During the initial phase of the research, participants were given an "easy" set of problem-solving tasks and, following completion of the tasks, were informed by one of the experimenters, "Wow, you did very well on these problems. You got [number of problems] right. That's a very good score." Then the experimenters delivered two different types of praise. Those children praised for intelligence were informed, "You must be smart at these problems." In contrast, the children praised for effort were told, "You must have worked hard at these problems."

After the participants received the intelligence or effort praise, their achievement goals were assessed by having the children select an "easy" task that would ensure they would continue to look smart or a "harder" task that they could learn a lot from even if it wouldn't make them look smart. Sixty-seven percent of the children who received intelligence praise chose the easy task. That is, they selected the task that would make them continue to look smart. A whopping ninety-two percent of the children who had received effort praise selected the harder task. So, those children praised for intelligence were no longer interested in learning or taking on new challenges. In contrast, those children praised for effort were eager to take on difficult tasks.

Next, all participants were given a set of difficult problem-solving tasks and were subsequently informed by the experimenters that they had performed poorly on this second set of problems. The participants were then asked about their willingness to persist on the problems, their enjoyment of the problems, and the explanation for their poor performance. Finally, the participants were given a third set of problem-solving tasks, equivalent to the initial easy set of problems, to see how the failure experience impacted their future performance.

The results of this research were stunning. Those participants receiving intelligence praise, after failure, reported the least amount of enjoyment of the task, were least likely to want to persist on the problems, and attributed their failure on the second set of problems to a lack of intelligence. The participants receiving effort praise reported more enjoyment of the task, demonstrated more persistence, and explained their failure on the second set of problems as a result of insufficient effort.

The results for the third set of problem-solving tasks were also interesting. The intelligence-praise group actually showed a decline in performance from the first to the third set of tasks, even though the item difficulty level was the same across these two sets. The effort-praise group showed significant improvement in their scores from set one to three. Thus, the group that received intelligence praise actually manifested a decline in their performance merely as a function of experiencing failure on the second set of items. The effort-praise group continued to improve.

In summary, the results of these research studies, one involving kindergarten students and the other fifth graders, were clear and convincing: The delivery of person-oriented praise resulted in a host of negative outcomes, once individuals encountered failure, including performance decrements, poor task persistence, and a variety of negative emotions. Effort praise, on the other hand, promoted enhanced performance, robust task persistence, and continued optimism.

The Mueller and Dweck (1998) studies also addressed the issue of how the different forms of praise impacted individuals' theories regarding the nature of intelligence. Students who had received intelligence praise endorsed what is known as an "entity theory of intelligence," wherein intelligence is conceptualized as some entity or thing that one possesses. This is the "you-either-got-it-or-you-don't" idea introduced by Sir Francis Galton. Entity intelligence is inferred from the performance of individuals. When you perform well, you are labeled as smart or talented (i.e., you've got it). The problem comes in when you encounter challenges or failure (i.e., you now don't have it). Entity theories do not promote constructive change. For instance, if one doesn't have the requisite talent, intelligence, or ability, why expend effort to make changes?

Those students who received effort praise endorsed the view that intelligence is a malleable or fluid quality that can be changed through effort. When these individuals experienced failure, they engaged in creative problem-solving strategies to improve performance. Deliberate practice is one aspect of this change-through-effort available to those who subscribe to a growth or "incremental" theory of change.

An important thing to notice about Dweck's research is that the significant changes produced in those participants receiving either person-oriented or effort praise were the result of the experimenters uttering a few words such as "You must be smart at these problems" or "You must have worked hard at these problems." These seven or eight words initiated a process in which the person either manifested a maladaptive or adaptive approach to problem solving. Thus, others' reactions can be instrumental in fostering the growth mindset that, in my opinion, is crucial for the establishment of successful individuals. Can you imagine what could be accomplished for the aspiring tennis player if the tennis community would systematically provide messages consistent with that of a growth mindset? *Instead of searching for talent, arrange the conditions to create talent.*

CHAPTER 5

IT'S THE ENVIRONMENT, STUPID

"Properly understood, behavior modification is environmental modification."

The refrain of Bill Clinton's 1992 presidential campaign was, "It's the economy, stupid." James Carville, the brilliant political campaign strategist, coined this phrase to remind Clinton's campaign workers that George Herbert Walker Bush (Bush senior), and incumbent President, was vulnerable on economic issues.

Clinton and his advisors knew that if they were able to keep the focus of the campaign on the economy, they had a good chance of winning the election. As a result of the weak economy and continued budget deficits, Clinton was victorious on election night, winning the election with a 43% to 38% popular vote margin. Ross Perot, the third party candidate, garnered 19% of the vote.

A similar situation holds for the development of the elite tennis player. If you want to be a successful tennis player, your mantra should be: "It's the environment, stupid." No matter what your views are about human behavior, it is difficult to dispute the role of the environment in shaping and guiding our behavior. One can raise issue with the degree of control exerted by environmental factors, but some control is clearly obvious. And don't forget that other people are a significant part of our environment.

BEHAVIORISM

The one approach of psychology that emphasizes the critical role of the environment in developing and maintaining behavior is known as behaviorism. Its founder and most flamboyant spokesperson was John B. Watson. He was born on a farm near Greenville, South Carolina, on January 9, 1878. His mother was a religious fundamentalist, and his father was alcohol dependent, had violent tendencies, and was a womanizer. When Watson was thirteen, his father ran off with another woman and never returned.

One would never have predicted Watson's later academic success from his early school years. Watson's teachers described him as "indolent, argumentative, and not easily controlled." He often got into fights and was arrested twice as a teenager.

At his mother's insistence, Watson enrolled at Furman University to study theology. Despite his rather pronounced rebellious streak, he promised his mother that he would become a minister. He stayed at Furman for several years but, upon his mother's death, enrolled at the University of Chicago to study philosophy under John Dewey. Finding Dewey's work "incomprehensible," Watson changed his major to psychology and received his Ph.D. in 1903. He accepted a teaching position at the University of Chicago, where he remained until 1908. He married a young student of his, Mary Ickes, who was from a wealthy and politically connected Baltimore family.

In 1908, Watson accepted a full professorship at Johns Hopkins University in Baltimore. J. Mark Baldwin, a professor at Hopkins and co-founder of the prominent psychology journal, *Psychological Review*, had recruited Watson. In 1909, Baldwin was forced to resign his position at Hopkins resulting from a sex scandal; he was caught in a police raid on a Baltimore brothel.

Following Baldwin's dismissal, Watson became chairman of the psychology department and editor of the *Psychological Review*. So, at the young age of thirty-one, Watson became a key figure in American psychology. He was also quite prolific during his Hopkins years, writing several classic texts including *Behavior: An Introduction to Comparative Psychology* and *Behaviorism*.

In the former text, published in 1914, Watson declared, "Psychology as the behaviorist views it is a purely objective experimental branch of natural science." Additionally, he asserted that the subject matter of psychology was to be behavior, its methodology entirely objective, and its central focus the prediction and control of behavior. This was a bold pronouncement in 1914 and one that was defiant toward and dismissive of other existing schools of psychology. With respect to the important role of the environment, Watson argued that behavior consisted of responses of an organism to certain antecedent events, more popularly known as stimuli. Thus, Watson argued that behavior was a function of the environment.

Watson's proposal for the subject matter of psychology was a radical one. But it was a statement he made in *Behaviorism* that earned him a considerable amount of notoriety. In marked contrast to the position of Sir Francis Galton, who stressed the predominance of innate factors in accounting for human behavior, Watson asserted: "I should like to go one step further now and say, 'Give me a dozen healthy infants, well-formed, and my own specified world to bring them up in and I'll guarantee to take any one at random and train him to become any type of specialist I might select – doctor, lawyer, artist, merchant-chief and, yes, even beggar-man and thief, regardless of his talents, penchants, tendencies, abilities, vocations, and race of his ancestors.'"

Take that, Sir Francis! Well, Watson was excoriated by some of his contemporaries as an extremist. But he excited several generations of psychologists who shared Watson's vision of developing psychology as a natural science. Even Watson wasn't as extreme as the above pronouncement made him appear. In the next sentence to the above cited passage, Watson noted, "I am going beyond my facts and I admit it, but so have the advocates of the contrary and they have been doing it for many thousands of years."

Watson had a rather colorful but brief career at Johns Hopkins. In 1920, he and his graduate assistant, Rosalie Rayner, carried out the "Little Albert" experiment that earned its place as one of the most controversial (and infamous) in the history of psychology. The idea was to see whether the behavioral conditioning principles of the time could be used to condition a fear response of a child elicited by a loud noise (the clanging of a metal bar) to a white rat. Little Albert was an eleven-month-old infant. The initial stage of this investigation involved presenting a white rat to Albert without the loud noise. Albert's initial response to the rat was one of curiosity and friendliness.

Watson and Rayner then combined the loud noise with the presentation of the white rat on several occasions. After approximately seven pairings, poor Albert showed a strong fear response to the rat. Watson and Rayner reported, *"The instant the rat was shown the baby began to cry. Almost instantly he turned sharply to the left, fell over, raised himself on all fours and began to crawl away so rapidly that he was caught with difficulty before he reached the edge of the table."*

Watson and Rayner also wanted to determine if there was a transfer of this fear response to other objects. Several days later, the investigators presented Albert with several additional objects including a rabbit, a dog, a fur coat, human hair, a piece of cotton, and a Santa Claus mask. Each of these objects produced a fear response in Albert, whereas he had previously played with each of these objects without any type of concern.

Now this was the wild west of applied psychology. One major ethical problem with this investigation is that Watson and Rayner never "unconditioned" Little Albert's fear response. A group of researchers in 2009 attempted to find Little Albert to see how Watson's investigation may have affected his life. What they determined, sadly, was that he died from hydrocephalus at age six. Hydrocephalus is the medical condition in which there is an abnormal accumulation of cerebrospinal fluid in the ventricles of the brain. The resultant intracranial pressure can result in seizures, mental disability, and death.

There is more to this story. Watson's relationship with Rayner, who was from a wealthy Baltimore family, progressed beyond a professional one. Watson fell deeply in love with her. At the time of their affair, Rosalie was living with her parents. A published report from the *Johns Hopkins Gazette Online* noted that the Rayner family invited John Watson and his wife to a dinner party. Mary Watson suspected that her husband and Ms. Rayner were having an affair. She feigned a headache during dinner, found her way to Rosalie's room where she discovered fifteen love letters her husband had written to Ms. Rayner. She took all of the letters and subsequently sued her husband for divorce. The divorce battle was on – the powerful and politically connected Ickes family versus the wealthy Rayner family. A media frenzy ensued, and several excerpts of Watson's love letters to Rosalie were published in the *Baltimore Sun*. One of them read, "Every cell I have is yours, individually and collectively...My total reactions are positive and toward you. So likewise each and every heart reaction. I can't be more yours than I am, even if a surgical operation made us one."

As a result of his affair with Ms. Rayner, Watson was forced to resign his position at Johns Hopkins in October 1920. The Ickes family prevailed in the divorce proceedings and when the divorce settlement was finalized by 1921, Watson was ordered to pay two-thirds of his salary to his former wife in alimony and child support. Watson married Rayner shortly thereafter; he never returned to an academic position.

Watson began a second career in the advertising field. He was recruited by the J. Walter Thompson Company in order to promote the application of behavioral principles to advertising. Upon entering the business world, Watson wrote a former colleague, stating, "It will not be as bad as raising chickens or cabbages." He added, "I shall go into commercial work whole-heartedly and burn all bridges." He initially worked in every department of the agency, did house-to-house surveys, sold coffee, and clerked at Macy's. With his trademark energy and resilience, Watson rose to vice president of the company within three years.

Watson had a major impact on advertising in the United States, arguing that humans were "organic machines" that could be predicted and controlled, as are other machines. He persuaded his advertising colleagues that consumer behavior could be controlled by behavioral techniques of conditioning emotional responses. He pushed for the experimental study of consumer behavior under controlled laboratory conditions.

Watson promoted style over substance in the marketing of products. With respect to automobiles, Watson argued that all models were essentially mechanically similar, so the basis for sales should be on changing design and style to appeal to the consumer. Later, the director of research for General Motors echoed Watson's approach when he stated, "The whole object of research is to keep everyone reasonably dissatisfied with what he has in order to keep the factory busy in making new things."

Watson used his knowledge of behavioral principles to associate various products with consumers' emotional states and needs. He was the first to promote the use of celebrity endorsement of products.

As one might expect, the advertising industry loved John Watson. And, as a plus for Watson, his salary at the advertising company was many times higher than what he was earning at Johns Hopkins.

Behavioral psychology has made significant progress since the pioneering, free-wheeling days of John Watson. Largely due to the work of B.F. Skinner, noted Harvard psychologist, behavioral psychology became an integrated system instead of a loose collection of facts and concepts. Instead of stirring manifestos about the promise of behavioral psychology, Skinner and his colleagues engaged in the painstaking task of experimental research. Experimental data led, inductively, to the emergence of a set of laws or system of behavior. The primary focus of study involved the relationship of the environment to the individual organism. There was a rejection of mind-body dualism, determinism was the operating philosophy, *and hereditary determinants of behavior were relegated a limited role pending a thorough account of environmental factors.*

Skinner made multiple contributions to the field of psychology. His most significant involved the role of operant conditioning. Before presenting a primer of operant conditioning that will be critical to our discussion of tennis, we need to briefly review some historical issues involving voluntary behavior. Watson contended that an analysis of instinctive behavior and the existing conditioning principles of his day involving reflexes and conditioned reflexes would be adequate to account for the entirety of human behavior.

Others disagreed. For many, the most interesting feature of human behavior appears to be its orientation to the future and not behavior that was either instinctive or elicited by some prior stimulus as is the case with reflexes. For example, when preparing for an important match, the tennis player will orient his training for a particular opponent. The player will analyze the opponent's strengths and weaknesses and design a strategic plan. Immediately prior to the match, the player may warm up with a practice partner or hit against a backboard. This whole sequence of behavior is preparatory in nature, seemingly geared toward the future. Future-oriented behavior appears to constitute the bulk of human behavior. How does behavioral psychology account for this within a natural science framework?

To provide an adequate account of future-oriented behavior, we need to turn to Charles Darwin's publication of *The Origin of Species* in 1859. This work, perhaps more than any other, altered the course of intellectual history by emphasizing that species exist on a continuum with the attendant implication that humans may not be unique in their ability to think, reason, and engage in future-oriented behavior. Darwin argued that there was "no fundamental difference between man and the higher mammals in their mental faculties." This was the result of his position that humans were derived from the evolutionary process of change and development. This position constituted a radical break from René Descartes, who argued that animals were "mindless automata," sharing no similarities with humans.

To what extent could animals engage in reasoning and problem-solving behavior? This was a fascinating question because the extent to which other species may exhibit intelligent behavior might provide answers about the development of "mental" evolution. Or would it be possible to account for the reasoning of animals without referring to some hypothetical mental process?

The work of E.L. Thorndike (1898) emerged out of this issue of whether animals could think and reason. Imagine this situation: A hungry young cat, three to six months old, is placed in a box from which it can escape by unlatching a door. The box was 20 x 15 x 12 inches. The front side of the box was constructed of slats or bars an inch apart and functioned as a door that would fall open if the cat could turn a small wooden button from a vertical to a horizontal position. Outside the front of the box, in full view of the cat, was a piece of fish. When first placed in the box, the cat engaged in a variety of behaviors, most of which were not successful at opening the latch. These behaviors included sniffing, clawing, attempting to squeeze through the bars, stretching its paws through the bars, and poking and biting at various features of the box. Eventually the cat engaged in some bit of behavior that actually struck the wooden button, which opened the door and allowed the cat to gain access to the fish. Thorndike found that when this "problem" was repeated on multiple occasions, the cat became more efficient at opening the latch. Thorndike reported that by "repeating the experience again and again, the animal comes to omit all the useless clawings, and the like, and to manifest only the particular impulse (e.g., to claw hard at the top of the button with the paw, or to push against one side of it with the nose) which has resulted successfully. It turns the button around without delay whenever put in the box."

One of the primary measures Thorndike used was the time it took for the cat to escape from the box. Over multiple trials, the cat required less time to leave the box. Was this cat a genius? Did it engage in mental reasoning? Was it born with some innate Galton-like capacity for problem solving? Thorndike did not think so. He did not believe that the cat engaged in any higher-order cognitive processing. Thorndike asserted that a part of the cat's behavior was "stamped in" because it was successful in opening the door.

Thorndike called this stamping in process "The Law of Effect." This has also been called "trial-and-error learning" although Thorndike preferred the term "trial and accidental success." What Thorndike observed was that a given bit of behavior, door opening, took less time to occur over successive experimental trials. He was able to construct "learning curves" by graphing out the time it took the cat to exit from the box on successive trials. The cat's behavior had changed. Opening the door was initially a low probability response. The probability of this response increased as the cat gained access to the fish. The cat appeared to have learned something.

Thorndike made an important discovery, and his work ushered in a flurry of research on this so-called trial-and-error learning. Many types of organisms were examined using a variety of experimental apparatuses including mazes, jumping stands, puzzle boxes, and straight alleys. Each apparatus yielded its own type of learning curve. Unfortunately, the type of behavior examined in these various studies was rather complicated and did not yield a particularly clean measure of behavior acquisition and change.

A productive research program for the analysis of behavior required several innovations. One involved the design of an experimental chamber that facilitated the study of behavior. This chamber is commonly known as a "Skinner box." The chamber was designed to eliminate or reduce behavior that may compete with the behavior to be studied. Rats or pigeons are typically used as experimental subjects. There are some differences in the experimental chamber depending on which organism is being studied. When using rats, there is a bar that can be pressed by the rat and a tray into which food pellets can be delivered. With pigeons, one wall of the chamber contains a disk which can be pecked and a food tray that will allow the delivery of a mixed grain. The other innovation involved the measurement of behavior in terms of its rate or frequency.

As with Thorndike's experiment, a hungry or food-deprived organism is used. When the organism is first put into the chamber, it may react to the features of the experimental chamber in a variety of ways. A rat, for example, may wander around the chamber, stretch out on its hind legs to explore the top of the chamber, and engage in other behaviors. When a food pellet is first delivered by an investigator via a hand-held switch, it makes a rather distinctive sound, and the rat will discover the food fairly quickly. Since the rat is hungry, it hovers around the food tray and readily eats when a pellet is delivered. Once the rat is reliably eating from the food tray, the experimenter is then ready to make the food delivery contingent upon some given bit of behavior. In the rat's case, it is pressing the bar. Bar pressing for the rat, without specific training, is a low-probability event. The rat is not going to initially walk over to the bar, press it, and then go to the food tray to consume a food pellet. This given bit of behavior has to be developed or *shaped*.

During the shaping procedure, the experimenter carefully observes the rat. It will typically be hovering around the food tray. When it makes a slight movement toward the bar, which is located several inches to the left of the food tray, the experimenter delivers a food pellet. One finds that the rat will start making this "movement-toward-the-bar" on a more frequent basis. The experimenter then waits for an even more pronounced movement toward the bar and then delivers the food pellet. In this way, the experimenter can induce the rat to move progressively closer toward the bar. In a short time, the rat is now hovering around the bar instead of the food tray. This process of selectively reinforcing certain properties of behavior continues until the rat starts hitting the bar with its forepaws. When this shaping process is complete, the rat goes to the bar, quickly presses it with one if its forepaws and then goes directly to the food tray to obtain the food pellet. At this point the food is delivered automatically by the mechanical operations of the experimental chamber rather than by the experimenter.

GUIDELINE 3: OPERANT CONDITIONING

The above procedure is known as operant conditioning. Skinner, in his classic text *Science and Human Behavior*, noted that it is traditional to refer to a given bit of behavior as a response. In the above example, a shaping procedure was used to develop the response of bar pressing. Skinner reported, "A response which has already occurred cannot, of course, be predicted or controlled. We can only predict that similar responses will occur in the future. The unit of a predictive science is, therefore, not a response but a class of responses. The word "operant" will be used to describe this class." One bar press from a rat is a response. Bar pressing, regardless of when it occurs, would be an operant. To use an example from tennis, one serve would be considered a response. Serving would be an operant.

Reinforcement

Operant behavior acts or "operates" on the environment to produce consequences. When the consequences result in an increase in the frequency or probability of some response class, reinforcement has occurred. The presentation of a stimulus that results in an increase in the frequency of some response class is known as a positive reinforcer. The response-contingent removal of a stimulus that results in an increase in the frequency of some response class is known as a negative reinforcer. The distinction between these two reinforcement operations is not particularly relevant for the purposes of this book. What is relevant is that human behavior is vastly operant in nature. Individuals are constantly engaging the environment and generating consequences that are reinforcing in nature. Through operant conditioning, the environment builds a behavioral repertoire. This can include such basic behaviors such as standing and walking to highly skilled behaviors of elite performers in ballet, basketball, chess, and yes, tennis.

Was Thorndike's cat exhibiting intelligent, future-oriented behavior by escaping from the latched box? One can account for the cat's behavior as the result of operant conditioning. When the cat hit the button for the first time, the consequences included the opening of the door and access to the food. The food was a positive reinforcer that increased the frequency of "latch opening."[2] The cat's behavior did not involve any intelligent, purposive behavior. It only reflected a history of operant conditioning.

Shaping Operant Behavior

Skinner drew an analogy between operant conditioning and sculpting: "Operant conditioning shapes behavior as a sculptor shapes a lump of clay." A finished piece of sculpture may appear magnificent to others and reflect the genius and talent of the sculptor. But one could re-trace the process back to the original undifferentiated lump of clay to show how the sculpture developed.

It is the same process with any well-formed behavior. I am amazed with Roger Federer's topspin backhand return of serve. I find myself saying, "I can't do that. How can he do that?" I would be less amazed if I were able to see the development of Federer's return of serve from its original "undifferentiated lump." As with all tennis players, I'm sure that Federer initially struggled to produce a reliable service return. As a result of an extended history of operant conditioning, Federer's service return became more consistent and skillful. Viewed from this perspective, deliberate practice is nothing new or particularly innovative; it is the systematic application of operant shaping procedures.

Differential Reinforcement

The operation responsible for the shaping of behavior is known as differential reinforcement. Differential reinforcement is critical for the development of skillful behaviors. This is where one makes reinforcement contingent upon slight variations in the behavior to be developed over time. At every stage in the process of developing a skill, some responses are reinforced while others are not.

---

2 Negative reinforcement was also present in Thorndike's procedure in that escape from confinement reinforced latch opening.

Let's take a child learning how to volley. Prior to formal instruction, the child may make some rather haphazard and ineffective attempts at volleying. If the child has a prior athletic background, such as playing baseball, some of the volley attempts may be reasonable. In any case, it is the responsibility of the tennis instructor to arrange the contingencies for developing a skillful volley. The term contingency refers to the relationship between responding and the delivery of a reinforcer. Some of these reinforcers may involve verbal responses from the instructor such as "I like the way you made contact with the ball and punched through the shot." Fortunately, the reinforcement or feedback from the environment when developing a skillful response is often immediate. You see the outcome of your attempt at volleying. Some attempts may be good, others not. The goal for the novice volleyer is to produce a higher frequency of effective volleys. A process continues in which slight variations toward a more effective volley can be differentially reinforced. This is known as *differential reinforcement of successive approximations*.

There is an important property of behavior that allows one to apply differential reinforcement procedures to successively more skillful behavior - **behavior is variable**. No two volleys are identical. There are always some slight variations in the form, or to use some technical behavioral jargon, the topography of a response. The topography of each volley that the child hits will be different in some way. Some of these volley attempts will more closely approximate the desired volley to be developed. Thus, the reinforcement of one volley will produce a "spectrum" of volleys that differ in slight ways. If the tennis instructor is alert to this inherent property of behavior, he can then apply reinforcement to the more effective variation. A new spectrum or class of volleys, resulting from this latter reinforcement, will increase in frequency. Some of the volleys will even be more effective. Then reinforcement can be applied to these more effective variations. With sufficient training and instruction, the aspiring tennis player can develop a skilled or great volley.

Brad Gilbert, in his wonderful book *Winning Ugly*, noted that "John McEnroe's hands had the precision, soft touch, and dexterity of a brain surgeon's." McEnroe is considered to have one of the greatest volleys in the history of tennis. Gilbert noted that McEnroe would occasionally charge the net with a weak approach shot only to have his opponent crush the ball. "Four or five times a match," Gilbert noted, "John would desperately lunge at the passing shot and not only get his racket on it, but he'd hit a soft, drop-shot winner. This is not taught currently by any tennis coach in the world. Try it. Believe me, if you succeed in doing it it's an accident." Gilbert appears to be saying that it would be a waste of time attempting to either teach or execute this shot. And if, by some miracle, you were able to pull it off in a match it would be a fluke, an accident. There is an implication in Gilbert's statement that McEnroe possessed some special talent or gift that the rest of us don't have. What we don't have is *McEnroe's specific conditioning history with respect to the volley.* If it would be possible to trace back McEnroe's volley history to its original "undifferentiated" form and document its development over time, his magnificent volleys would be less mysterious. Some of his volley skills had to come from his extensive doubles play. Some may have come from his earlier athletic experiences such as playing stick ball. And, when he was young, he learned to volley from some of the best tennis instructors in the world. Behavior is behavior. It can be shaped and developed. If no coach in the world teaches this shot, it reflects their lack of understanding about how to arrange the relevant instructional contingencies. The more relevant question would be is it worth the time and commitment of both the instructor and the student to develop this shot?

TENNIS-PLAYING PIGEONS

Behavioral psychology has developed a rather powerful behavior change technology based on the principles articulated above. In their early endeavors, Skinner and his colleagues had fun demonstrating the continuity of human behavior with other organisms. One of their more entertaining projects involved training pigeons to play a version of tennis – table tennis.

The tennis table was 16 x 8 x 8 inches. The table did not have a net. Operant conditioning started with one pigeon at a time. Initially, the experimenters fastened a table tennis ball to the edge of the table. A hungry pigeon was reinforced with food whenever it pecked at the ball. Following this, the position of the ball was fastened to another location of the table edge. When the ball first changed position, the pigeon pecked the air where the ball had previously been. The ball did not possess, as the behaviorists would say, a strong controlling stimulus function at this point. With some skilled shaping by the experimenters, the pigeon reliably pecked at the ball regardless of where it was fastened to the edge of the table.

The next stage of this demonstration involved having the ball roll away free upon being pecked by the pigeon. The table was set, during this stage of the conditioning process, at a slight incline and the pigeon was reinforced with food if the ball traveled a certain distance from where the pigeon was standing. Over time, the distance that the ball had to travel in order for the bird to obtain food was gradually increased. Thus, the experimenters were training the pigeon to create greater depth on its shot so that eventually the ball traveled the length of the table. Food reinforcement was increasingly delayed so that the pigeon hit the ball multiple times without interruptions from eating. Another pigeon was trained in exactly the same way.

The conditions were set for the Novak Djokovic and Roger Federer of pigeons to have a spirited table tennis match. The experimenter placed the ball near the middle of the table. There was a slight angular deviation of the table's surface so the ball started moving toward one edge or other of the table. When the ball rolled to one edge of the table, the pigeon would be there to peck it, driving it back to the other side. When the ball approached the other pigeon, it returned the ball across the table. The pigeons routinely watched the ball as it crossed the table and put themselves in position to make the return shot. So, yes, footwork is also important in pigeon table tennis! If one of the pigeons missed the ball when it approached the edge of the table, the ball fell into a narrow trough and tripped a switch, activating a food dispenser to deliver a small amount of mixed grain to the opponent. In this way, the opponent won the point.

The pigeons became quite skilled at keeping the ball in play, routinely having five or six shot rallies before one of them won a point. This is particularly interesting because Arthur Ashe once proclaimed that if a club player were able to hit the ball in five times during every point, the player would never lose a match. Tennis coaches everywhere should be on notice. If pigeons can be trained to do this, aspiring human tennis players could do so as well.

Neither of the pigeons advanced to the stage of systematically varying shot placement or changing the pace of the ball in order to force its opponent to miss. I suppose this could be accomplished with a more refined shaping procedure. There was no mention of whether the birds threw a tantrum upon losing a point.

How does one account for the table tennis skills of these two pigeons? Did Skinner just happen to select two pigeons with an innate talent for table tennis? Or were these gifted pigeons that possessed a rage to master the game? No, the explanation for their behavior is to be found in the history of reinforcement and the use of specific shaping procedures by the experimenters.

SUPERSTITIOUS BEHAVIOR

There is something about athletic contests that create the conditions for the development of an interesting array of superstitious rituals among its various participants. Were you aware that the great Michael Jordan, during his six NBA championship seasons, wore his University of North Carolina shorts under his Chicago Bulls uniform in every game he played? He figured the shorts possessed some magical powers since wearing them during the Tar Heels' 1982 NCAA national championship run. Now, there's a little bit of March madness. Similarly, Jason Terry, point guard for the Dallas Mavericks, developed a particularly interesting superstition: upon going to bed for the evening, he wore the shorts of the opposing team he was about to face.

Tennis players are not immune to these superstitions either. Serena Williams brings her shower sandals to the court, ties her shoelaces in a certain way, and wears the same pair of socks, unwashed, as long as she continues to win in a given tournament. You can only imagine how those socks must have been at the end of one of her successful Grand Slam campaigns.

Andre Agassi had a version of the NBA shorts ritual during his successful run at the French Open in 1999. Five minutes prior to his first match at the Open, Andre realized that he forgot to pack underwear in his tennis bag. Andre proceeded, partially dressed, to win his first round match, defeating the Argentine, Franco Squillari 3-6, 7-5, 7-5, 6-3. Since Agassi had lost in the first round of the tournament in 1998, he attributed his first round victory over Squillari to his altered attire. He played the remainder of the French Open without underwear and, undoubtedly due to the freedom he must have experienced, won the tournament.

And then there's Goran Ivanisevic, the hard-serving Croat, who was the runner-up at Wimbledon in 1992, 1994, and 1998. He entered the 2001 championships as a wild card but this time he had a secret weapon – Teletubbies! Goran rigorously followed the same off-court routine for the duration of the tournament which involved watching Teletubbies in the morning, eating the same breakfast, packing his tennis bag at precisely the same time, using the same parking space at Wimbledon and showering in the same locker-room stall. He ate dinner at the same London restaurant and sat at the same table and ordered the same meal – fish soup, lamb with chips, and ice cream with chocolate sauce. These rituals obviously worked because Goran defeated Patrick Rafter in a thrilling five-set final 6-3, 3-6, 6-3, 2-6, 9-7.

Jack Sock requires that each ball boy or girl attending to his side of the net carry three tennis balls. During one tournament, while serving, Sock noticed that one of the ball handlers was carrying four balls and the other, two. Of course, Sock immediately lost the game. He had a quick conference with the ball handlers to correct this rather egregious error.

There are many players who, following a winning point, want to use the same ball for the next point. I have to admit, I do this on occasion. Other tennis rituals include drinking the same amount of water during the change-over, not shaving for the duration of a tournament, refusing to step on lines between points, and displaying of a variety of body ticks, gestures, and other bizarre motoric behaviors.

Rafael Nadal has a preoccupation with his courtside water bottles. He will arrange two bottles of water – one chilled and the other at room temperature – with labels facing the same way. During a match, he drinks from them in a certain order. John Lloyd, a former professional player, once suggested that someone should knock the water bottles over to "see what happens." Nadal also has this curious habit of not crossing the net before his opponent at the end of the changeover. Brad Gilbert expressed surprise that "no one has tried to wait him out."

The King of Quirk title, at least for elite tennis players, probably belongs to Bjorn Borg. Lennart Bergelin, Borg's coach, drove to the All England Lawn Tennis and Croquet Club by the same route every day during the Wimbledon Championships. When Borg arrived at Wimbledon, he insisted on having the same chair in which he sat the previous year. Borg never stepped on any of the court lines prior to serving. He used only two towels during a match. His last training session before the first round of Wimbledon was always with Bergelin. His parents were only allowed to come to Wimbledon on alternate years. With his parents in attendance, Borg lost in 1975 but won the Wimbledon title in 1976. Borg made the connection and insisted that his parents only attend during the even years – 1978, 1980. His parents also had to wear the same clothes they wore on the first day throughout the tournament. As Borg noted, "A productive stereotype must not be changed."

How is it that these otherwise seemingly rational human beings fall prey to these rather amazing sets of superstitious behaviors? We turn again to the pigeon for, at least, a partial explanation. In 1948, Skinner published an article, "'Superstition' in the Pigeon," in *The Journal of Experimental Psychology*. With the standard operant conditioning procedure, an organism is placed into the experimental chamber (Skinner box), and a bit of food is made contingent upon the occurrence of some designated behavior of the organism. As discussed above, a hungry rat will typically have to press a bar to receive some food. A hungry pigeon will peck a key to receive mixed grain. The receipt of food will result in an increase in the rate of bar pressing for the rat or key pecking for the pigeon.

Skinner wanted to know what would happen if food was delivered to a pigeon *without any designated reference to the bird's behavior*. That is, would conditioning take place if food was delivered to the animal based only on the passage of time, in this case every fifteen seconds? The results were startling, and the behavior of the birds appeared "superstitious" in nature. A conditioning effect took place with respect to whatever behavior the bird happened to be exhibiting at the time of the delivery of food. One pigeon was conditioned to turn about the experimental chamber in a counter-clockwise manner and did so two to three times between food reinforcements (that is, two to three times every fifteen seconds). A second pigeon repeatedly stretched its head into one of the upper corners of the experimental chamber. Skinner reported a "third developed a "tossing" response, as if placing its head beneath an invisible bar and lifting it repeatedly." Finally, two birds developed a pendulum-like motion of the head and body. With the exception of the pigeon conditioned to display the counter-clockwise turns, the other birds were conditioned to exhibit their responses to some specific part of the experimental chamber – that is, each bird repeated their "superstitious" response in a particular part of the chamber.

So, despite the fact that the behavior of the birds had nothing to do with the delivery of the food, the birds persisted in this rather strange behavior. And once conditioned, these behaviors can be quite durable. One pigeon, exposed to a similar type of conditioning procedure, manifested 10,000 "superstitious" responses following the termination of food delivery before the behavior eventually subsided. I hope that Goran Ivanisevic did not watch 10,000 additional episodes of Teletubbies following his 2001 Wimbledon win.

The results of Skinner's experiment have direct relevance to the superstitious behavior of athletes. In both cases, the pigeons and the athletes were engaging in some behavior that had no causal relationship to the reinforcing event. For the pigeon, the reinforcing event was food. For the athlete, the reinforcing event was winning some athletic contest. Sorry guys, wearing a type of short (or no shorts at all), tying your shoes in a certain way, drinking from water bottles in some order, eating the same meal for several days in a row, or watching Teletubbies does not have a causal relationship to the outcome of a point, game or match.

Once established, if the superstitious behavior of the athlete were to be disrupted this could affect the athlete's concentration and subsequent performance. Perhaps someone *should* kick over Nadal's water bottles during one of his matches and see what happens. I have a feeling that this would make him even more determined to demolish his opponent. What do you think?

ENVIRONMENTAL CONTROL

Properly understood, behavior modification is environmental modification. Unless one has a sufficient degree of control over the relevant controlling variables, behavior change will be limited. In the infrahuman operant laboratories, researchers have a considerable amount of control over the relevant environmental variables, and the impact on the behavior of experimental subjects such as rats and pigeons is often dramatic.

The application of operant conditioning principles to human affairs is challenging because of the greater degree of complexity of the human organism and the vast range of controlling variables. The typical lament of the applied behavioral practitioner is that they do not have access to the relevant controlling variables to make a sufficient impact on the people with whom they may be working. Behavioral practitioners work in many arenas including hospitals, universities, prisons, industry, and private practice. There is even one credible establishment of a utopian behavioral community, Los Horcones ("The Pillars"), located approximately forty miles from Hermosillo, Mexico. Los Horcones is an experimental community that applies behavioral principles for the establishment of a culture based on "principles of cooperation, equality, pacifism (non-violence), solidarity, and environmental sustainability." This community is based on the novel *Walden Two* by B.F. Skinner.

There are many people, regardless of whether they are knowledgeable about operant conditioning principles, who recognize the great potential of the environment for shaping and developing highly skilled behavior. Again, it's the environment, stupid. Perhaps one of the best environments to exercise maximum control for the development of the elite performer is the family.

LASZLO AND EMMANUEL

Judith Polgar was "this cute little auburn-haired monster who crushed you."

Publications devoted to elite performers typically focus on, well, the elite performers. One area that does not receive sufficient attention is the individuals who establish the environments that produce the elite performers. Two such individuals will be highlighted here – Laszlo and Emmanuel.

Laszlo

Laszlo Polgar had an educational vision of sorts. He believed that geniuses were made and not born. Laszlo is a Hungarian educational psychologist who in his book, *Bring Up Genius!*, articulated the idea that one could develop any reasonably healthy and intelligent child into a prodigy given a highly specific and intensive training regimen.

In 1965, Laszlo met Klara Alberger, a foreign language teacher, in Budapest. Klara was not particularly enamored with Laszlo upon their first meeting, but she was fascinated with his ideas regarding genius creation. Laszlo informed her that it was his intention of having six children and creating a prodigy-developing environment for them. Following this initial meeting, Laszlo and Klara corresponded by mail for approximately two years. These letters initially focused on pedagogical issues but became more intimate over time. Laszlo eventually proposed marriage to Klara, and they were married on April 20, 1967. This marriage produced three children. Susan was born on April 19, 1969; Sofia on November 2, 1974; and Judith on July 23, 1976.

One of the hallmarks of any scientific investigation is replication. If one can repeat or replicate the results of some investigation with multiple "subjects," then one can have greater confidence that the interventions used are responsible for the results. Laszlo reasoned if he could produce three prodigies from the same family, then he could be confident that his teaching methods were successful in producing the desired effects.

Laszlo was all set for his experiment. He and Klara had three healthy children and, as educators, they had the skills to design the training environment. All they needed now was a training domain. When Susan was four years old, she found a chess set and began playing with the pieces. Klara, who was not particularly knowledgeable about chess, informed Susan that her father would teach her the fundamentals of the game.

The Polgars decided that chess provided the ideal vehicle for their family project. Participation in chess yields objective results – the player either wins, draws, or loses – and there are numerous competitions in which to demonstrate one's skills. Furthermore, Laszlo was intrigued that only a small number of accomplished chess players were women. Garry Kasparov, former world chess champion, described chess as "the most violent of all sports" and alleged that "women are weaker fighters." Nigel Short, chess prodigy, stated, "Women will never be great chess players. They just don't have the killer instinct." Laszlo probably thought these statements were inane. After all, he rejected the idea that innate talent was responsible for elite performance. Why should gender matter? A final reason for selecting chess as the training domain was that the Polgars did not have the financial wherewithal or time to allow each girl to engage in three different specialties. Another advantage of chess is that the majority of training could be conducted at home.

Laszlo and Klara quit their jobs as educators in order to conduct their family experiment and home-schooled the three girls. This decision placed the family under considerable financial strain and resulted in conflict with the Hungarian authorities for not enrolling their children in school. At one point, the Hungarian authorities considered placing Laszlo in a mental institution, considering him to be mentally unbalanced for conducting this rather bizarre family project. The Polgars reached an agreement with the authorities in which the girls would be required to go to school once per year to take examinations. So long as they showed satisfactory progress in their academic work, the Polgars could continue to provide home schooling.

Since Susan was the oldest child, the family project began with her. Laszlo worked with Susan at chess for several hours per day. After about six months of intensive training, Laszlo took the four-and-a-half-year-old Susan to the Budapest Chess Club. Hungarians are serious about chess, and the Budapest Chess Club was the premier chess venue in Hungary. The club was male-dominated, mostly middle-aged and older. The members were amused when Laszlo and little Susan entered the club. Laszlo approached one of the members and asked whether he would be willing to give Susan a game. The member looked incredulous and began to laugh at the prospect of playing this little girl. He didn't laugh for long; Susan won the game.

As you can imagine, this experience at the Budapest Chess Club provided initial confirmation of Laszlo's training methods and encouraged him to intensify his efforts. When the two other girls, Sofia and Judith, were old enough, they became curious about what their father and big sister were doing for all those hours together each day. Laszlo would not allow them to be in the room with Susan while she was studying chess. He informed the two girls that after they had learned the basics of the game, he would allow them to study chess with Susan. This was all the motivation they needed. Under Laszlo's separate tutelage, Sofia and Judith quickly learned the fundamentals of the game and then joined Susan for the intensive training regimen. Laszlo worked with the girls for eight to ten hours a day, focusing on many facets of chess including opening theory, endgames, and speed chess. For fun, the girls amused themselves with blindfolded speed chess! At eight to ten hours a day of training, this would result in 29,000 to 36,500 hours of deliberate practice over a ten-year period. I suppose one could call this the extreme 10,000 hour rule.

Laszlo was obsessive and driven about his family project. In addition to all the training he provided, he wrote several books on chess, not all of them published. He possessed an impressive collection of chess books. He often stayed up late into the night and catalogued the girls' games on file cards. He developed an index of possible competitors' tournament histories.

In addition to all this chess training, the Polgar sisters managed to do well in their academic subjects. Under the tutelage of their mother, the girls became proficient in multiple languages including Magyar, Russian, Esperanto, Dutch, English, French, Spanish, and Bulgarian.

The results of the Polgar family experiment were impressive. Susan followed up her win over the Budapest Chess Club patron by capturing the

Budapest Schoolchildren's 11-and-under chess championship in 1973. She was still only four and a half years old. Susan attained international master status by age fifteen. At sixteen, Susan took the New York Open chess competition by storm. She defeated several adult opponents and was featured on the front page of the New York Times. And, in a preview of what was to come, Sofia, age eleven, won most of the games in her section. But it was the nine-year-old Judith who garnered the most attention. She took on five players simultaneously in blindfold chess and defeated them all.

Susan became the first woman to qualify for the Men's World Championship when she was seventeen years old. Nevertheless, the world chess federation, the FIDE (Federation Internationale Des Echecs), would not allow Susan to compete. I suppose the federation didn't know what to do with this "chess übergirl." Although disappointing, this was probably not unexpected. Susan once famously stated, "When men lost against me, they always have a headache…or things of that kind. I have never beaten a completely healthy man!" Headaches, apparently, were not a concern for the participants during that year's world championships.

As the girls were emerging as chess powerhouses, the Hungarian chess federation was hesitant in letting them travel abroad for fear of them defecting. Hungary was one of the Soviet Bloc countries, and there was always a concern that its most accomplished members would defect to the West. In 1988, the Women's Chess Olympiad was held in Greece, and the Hungarian chess federation consented to having the Polgar sisters compete against the world's best women chess players. Playing as a team, the Polgar sisters, aged nineteen, fourteen, and twelve, won the event and engineered the first victory for Hungary over Soviet Russia. The sisters became instant national heroines. Susan attained grandmaster status at age twenty-two.

There is agreement among the Polgar family that Sofia, the middle child, was the most talented of the three. The family described her as a "chess artist," but she was not particularly interested in the analytical part of the game. Susan alleged that Sofia was "lazy." For the Polgars, lazy is a relative term. At her best, Sofia was the sixth-ranked woman in the world. In 1989, she famously defeated five grandmasters during an Italian tournament that has since become known as the "Sac of Rome."

In 1988, a British chess correspondent writing about the exploits of Judith Polgar stated, "It is clear that she is the best 11-year-old of either sex in the entire history of chess. This young Hungarian girl has the potential to achieve the highest limits of men's chess, perhaps even to be a genuine rival for Garry Kasparov around the year 2000." Another journalist described Judith as "this cute little auburn-haired monster who crushed you." The Laszlo prodigy-production machine was operating at maximum efficiency with Judith.

As the youngest in the family, Judith looked up to and was inspired by her two older sisters, particularly Susan. She was committed to being the best chess player of the Polgar sisters. Judith considered chess to be a sport and devoted countless hours to training. She was the personification of deliberate practice, and her results in chess competition were staggering. She was the highest-rated woman player of all time at the age of twelve and the greatest twelve-year-old player ever. She attained the rank of international master by age twelve.

One typically attains the title of grandmaster with three strong finishes in separate tournaments against competition of grandmaster or international-master ranking. The legendary Bobby Fischer became a grandmaster in 1958 at the age of fifteen. Judith Polgar attained grandmaster status at fifteen years and five months, one month earlier than Fischer.

Judith Polgar has been the top-ranked women's player from 1989, when she was only thirteen years old, to 2014 when she announced her retirement from competitive chess. In 2005, at age twenty-nine, Judith was the top-ranked woman *and* eighth overall best player in the world. She won a match against the then reigning world champion Garry Kasparov. She defeated a number of other former world chess champions during her career.

There are several things to consider when evaluating the success of the Polgar project. First, Laszlo was cognizant of the role of the environment in shaping behavior. Although Laszlo might not consider himself to be a behaviorist, he was adept applying behavioral principles for developing and maintaining highly skilled behavior. He was critical of the traditional school system because it did not provide a sufficiently structured learning environment. He knew that he would have to create an innovative, learning-intensive environment to produce exceptional results. And once his children began to demonstrate some expertise in chess, the environment became even more enriched, with chess players of international or grandmaster ranking regularly visiting the Polgar home. With a regular diet of high-level competition, the Polgar sisters' skills became even more proficient.

Consistent with the work of Anders Ericsson, Lazlo Polgar was a strong advocate of deliberate practice. Laszlo demystified the process of prodigy development. When someone is successful with this type of endeavor, ill-informed criticisms are bound to follow. Garry Kasparov once said that the Polgar sisters were "just like trained dogs." Putting aside the obvious sexist and patronizing overtones of Kasparov's remark, behaviorists such as John Watson, B.F. Skinner, and Laszlo Polgar would probably dismiss his comment and smile. Woof!

One final note on the Polgar project: In 1990, the girls were sponsored by the Dutch billionaire Joop van Oosterom. He was intrigued by Laszlo's ideas of genius creation and made a formal proposal to Laszlo and Klara. He would arrange and finance the adoption of three boys from a developing country and have the Polgars raise them as they had raised their girls. Laszlo was allegedly intrigued by the proposal but his wife, realizing that the demands of child rearing would fall on her, talked him out of it.

Emmanuel

During their off-duty time, several members of the British and the American armed forces stationed in Iran during World War II gravitated to the two dirt tennis courts housed at the American Mission Church compound in Tehran for a spirited game of singles or doubles. The soldiers were not particularly good players, but they played hard and had a lot of fun. The American Mission Church was where Emmanuel and his family faithfully attended services every Sunday. Emmanuel and his siblings attended Sunday school and sang in the choir.

One day, Emmanuel watched as the American and British soldiers battled it out on the courts. Emmanuel described his initial reaction to the game as "love at first sight." He stated, "I loved the thwack of the ball, the arc of a well-played stroke. I loved the sheen of the wooden racket, the twang of the steel-wire strings. I loved the almost infinite variety of the game, the way you rarely saw the *exact* same shot twice." Whenever Emmanuel had a spare moment, he watched the soldiers play. Since the courts were not enclosed by a fence, Emmanuel chased down errant shots of the soldiers and returned the ball to them. The soldiers paid Emmanuel for his ball-boy efforts with candy or chewing gum. Soon, Emmanuel assumed the responsibility of maintaining the tennis courts. This included sweeping, rolling, and watering the courts. And watering the courts took a lot of effort. Since there was no piped-in water in Tehran, Emmanuel took a bucket to a nearby reservoir, filled it up with water, and then returned to the courts for watering. As you can imagine, this took multiple trips to water both courts. The soldiers were impressed with his work ethic. One day, in appreciation for Emmanuel's efforts, one of the American G.I.s gave him a present. He handed Emmanuel Agassi his first tennis racket.

Like any aspiring tennis player, Emmanuel spent hours hitting tennis balls against a wall. In Emmanuel's case, it was one of the walls of the American Mission Church. Unfortunately, the environment of Tehran was not conducive to developing Emmanuel's tennis skills. He had no one to practice against, and if there were any tennis clubs to join, the Agassi family would not have been able to afford it. The Agassis were Christian-Armenians and, in Iran, they resided at the bottom rung of the economic ladder. The Agassi family included Emmanuel, his parents, and four siblings. They lived in one fifteen by twenty foot room that had a dirt floor. There was no electricity or running water, and they shared an outdoor toilet with several neighbors.

Emmanuel was quick, agile, and athletic. Although he had the potential to be an accomplished tennis player, the thirteen-year-old Emmanuel was good at something else: he was a street fighter. He began street fighting at an early age because he had speed, great footwork, and a really hard punch. In *The Agassi Story*, Emmanuel portrayed street fighting in Tehran as a community pastime. He fought kids from neighboring streets.

One day at age sixteen, after a particularly intense fight, Emmanuel was approached by a man who said that he could be an exceptional boxer. This man was a trainer at the Nerou Rastey Club, a private fitness center equipped with a boxing ring and punching bag. He invited Emmanuel to check it out. The trainer escorted Emmanuel to the club and laced on some gloves. Emmanuel knocked out his first opponent and then another. He then entered a bantamweight tournament two weeks later and won it.

One of the trainers at the club was Hans Ziglarski, a silver medalist at the 1932 Los Angeles Olympics in the bantamweight division. Taking Emmanuel under his wing, Ziglarski offered a piece of advice to Emmanuel that served him well in his boxing career and later when training his own children in tennis: "You don't win a fight in the ring; you win it during the months beforehand." In other words, train hard. Ziglarski was a deliberate-practice advocate.

Following several months of intense training, Emmanuel entered the Tehran City Championships and won the bantamweight division. He next won the Iranian national tournament as a bantamweight. Emmanuel then dominated his weight class at the Olympic trials and joined the 1948 Iranian Olympic team.

The 1948 Olympics were held in London. These games were significant for several reasons. Of primary importance, these were the first games held following a twelve-year hiatus because of the events of World War II. London was still recovering from the German aerial assault from several years earlier and was in the midst of a post-war economic depression. The 1948 games signaled to the world that, finally, some degree of normalcy had returned. These were also the first Olympic Games in which Iran competed. Finally, the games provided Emmanuel with a personal blueprint or vision for the future.

Emmanuel was presented with a series of fortuitous events – his early exposure to tennis, a trainer from the Nerou Rastey Club who witnessed one of Emmanuel's street fights, boxing instruction by a former Olympian, becoming a member of the first Iranian Olympic team, and participating in the 1948 London games – that changed his life. So, how did Emmanuel do at the 1948 games? Not well. He lost both bouts and contended that the judges were biased against him.

With his remaining few days in London, Emmanuel visited the All England Lawn Tennis and Croquet Club (aka Wimbledon). The security at the club was rather lax in those days so Emmanuel had the opportunity to visit Centre Court. Like Laszlo Polgar, Emmanuel had a vision of sorts. As Emmanuel was surveying Centre Court stadium, he experienced one of those powerful, life-changing moments. Emmanuel reported, "I knew that I'd never play at Wimbledon. I might someday develop into a decent player, but I'd never compete internationally. My social position, my family's financial position, had denied me my shot at tennis greatness. But as I pondered that hallowed court on that summer afternoon, I dreamt that someday, somehow, somebody from my family would win this tournament." Emmanuel pursued that dream with a vengeance.

Emmanuel participated in the 1952 Olympic Games in Helsinki, Finland, but fared no better than with his first Olympic experience. He lost both bouts and, again, believed the judges were biased against him.

Following his return to Iran, Emmanuel became restless. For a man with great ambitions, it was quite obvious that life in Iran was too restrictive with limited opportunities to succeed. Emmanuel believed he could build a better life for himself in the United States. Despite numerous obstacles, Emmanuel successfully left Iran for the USA in November 1952, spent sixteen days on Ellis Island, and then settled in Chicago on December 7, 1952.

In Chicago, Emmanuel adopted "Mike" as his Americanized name because he could spell it. He enrolled in an English course offered by the local YMCA and obtained a job as an elevator operator at the Conrad Hilton.

Mike got involved in the Chicago boxing scene through the Catholic Youth Organization Club. Given his experience with boxing, he came to the attention of Tony Zale, who won the world middleweight title in 1940 and again in 1946. Zale was quite impressed with the young Agassi, especially noting his quick hands and solid punches. Zale's only significant critique of Agassi was that he did not hit hard all the time.

Agassi won the Chicago Golden Gloves tournament in 1953 in the featherweight division. He then entered the professional ranks and a fight was arranged for him at Madison Square Garden. His opponent did not pass the pre-fight physical. Agassi's manager quickly arranged for a replacement fighter, a seasoned boxer who appeared to be a welterweight. Sensing imminent danger, Agassi stated, "This guy was going to beat the shit out of me."

He returned to the locker room and, with suitcase in hand, crawled out of the locker room window located above a toilet and returned to Chicago.

Fleeing Madison Square Garden that evening ended Mike Agassi's professional career. He returned to amateur boxing and won the Chicago Golden Gloves tournament in 1954 as a featherweight and as a lightweight in 1955.

After his boxing career ended, Mike directed his energies and passion to tennis. He *was*, after all, going to create that Wimbledon champion. He met and married Betty Dudley while living in Chicago. In September 1960, their daughter Rita was born.

Mike Agassi had a plan: he would teach Rita tennis "at an absurdly young age" and moved the family to Los Angeles to conduct his tennis experiment. Life in Los Angeles did not work out for the young Agassi family. They briefly returned to Chicago but eventually settled in Las Vegas.

In a weird way, Mike felt as though he was coming home when he arrived in Vegas. Minus the casinos, Elvis impersonators, and drive-in wedding chapels, the topography of Vegas and Tehran were quite similar.

Mike secured a job at the Tropicana Hotel. Fortuitously, the hotel had two tennis courts. Mike approached the hotel's entertainment director and inquired if he could use the courts to give lessons to hotel guests. The entertainment director agreed so long as Mike maintained the courts. For someone who lugged bucket after bucket of water to maintain the two dirt courts at the American Mission Church in Tehran, maintaining two hard courts would be no problem for the enterprising Agassi.

Working nights at the hotel, he returned home at 3 a.m., got up at 7 a.m. and took Rita to the courts for lessons. Mike also offered tennis lessons to hotel guests for $12 an hour, a bargain compared to the prevailing rate for tennis lessons on the Strip.

Mike saved enough money from his tennis lessons to purchase his first tennis-ball machine. He modified the machine to throw off different types of spin. He purchased several more machines and even modified one to simulate serving.

Whenever he had the opportunity, Mike trained the two-year-old Rita. Although initiating tennis instruction for a two-year-old may appear extreme even in this era, this was unheard of in 1962. Mike opined, "The earlier you start, the better. Tennis becomes part of the kids' lives. Their walk becomes a tennis walk. Their thinking becomes tennis thinking. You start them early, they become great." Like many arriving immigrants to this country, Mike saw and capitalized on the opportunities available to him. But there was something more personal for him – he wanted Rita and, later his other children, to realize the dream he never could.

Mike Agassi was a tennis visionary. He was aware of the similarities between tennis and boxing in that both involved footwork, balance, and hand-eye coordination. And, at least with respect to singles, both are contests between two combatants. One major difference between the two sports was that, in the early 1960s, tennis was not a particularly aggressive sport. If one views video clips from tennis matches of that era, it is striking how "slow" the game was. Mike believed that the game needed speeding up. Mike wanted to teach his children the game of the future. He believed that the game could become more exciting, popular, and lucrative.

When Mike Agassi boxed, he hit hard. He saw that the wrist snap that produced an effective punch could also be used to increase the speed of a tennis ball coming off the racket. Mike was an early advocate of hitting the ball on the rise and with great velocity.

Mike and Betty Agassi had four children – Rita, Phillip, Tami, and Andre. Four "subjects" for Mike's tennis experiment. His approach was to have his children initially focus on hitting the ball early and hard. Consistency would come later by having them hit thousands of balls delivered to them from one of his several tennis-ball machines. Andre, in his book, *Open: An Autobiography*, noted that his father believed in math. Mike had his first three children hit from 7000 to 8000 balls per week. Andre hit twice that number. Mike reasoned if his children were to hit hundreds of thousands of balls per year, they would be unbeatable.

For every stroke – forehands, backhands, volleys, approach shots, and overheads – Mike had his children hit multiple variations of the shots. Sometimes, they hit shorter, more angled shots. At other times, they focused on hitting the ball deep. They hit shots from the net, from the middle of the court, and from behind the baseline. For any conceived variation of a tennis shot, Mike had his children practice it thousands of times. Mike wanted his children's tennis strokes to be automatic. He reasoned that if the game were to involve more power, they would not have time to think about the next shot, only react. He stated, "Their bodies would need to respond automatically, without the intervention of thought."

When not working at the hotel or training his children, Mike studied all aspects of the game. He analyzed the games of the great players and was particularly observant of variations in shot making that was almost Darwinian in nature. That is, a player might hit a variation of a particular shot that produced a new "sub species" of successful shot making – a sort of natural selection in action on the tennis court. The goal was to teach his children the most successful elements of the game. Mike noted, "I thought I could take a little of Lendl, some Borg, and a dash of McEnroe to create an unbeatable Frankenplayer."

Like many who are motivated by an all-consuming passion, Mike was not aware of the damage he was doing to his children. He was domineering and a strict disciplinarian. He had significant anger-control issues. Andre described his father as "[v]iolent by nature." Mike kept an ax handle in his car. He had salt and pepper in each pocket just in case he was involved in a street fight so that he could blind his adversary. He was often observed shadowboxing. He was involved in several "road rage" incidents. In one, he got into a shouting match with another driver. Mike, wielding the ax handle, ordered the driver out of the car. When the driver refused to exit his car, Mike smashed the other driver's headlights and taillights. On another occasion, he pointed a gun at another driver for what Andre described as "the automotive equivalent of hitting into the net." Mike once got into a physical altercation with a truck driver over some minor traffic issue. During the fight, Mike threw "a blazingly fast combination" that dropped the truck driver to the pavement. Witnessing this event from the Agassi family car, Andre thought the truck driver was dead.

One can imagine that his children would have been intimidated by their father during their tennis training sessions. It is a testament to Rita's character that she rebelled against her father's rather draconian tennis program. Mike acknowledged that he ruined tennis for Rita. By age thirteen, she was headed toward tennis burnout. She intentionally tanked matches to annoy her dad. When Mike watched one of her matches, Rita would hit returns of serve over the fence. When focused on the game and not rebelling, Rita was a great player, possessing a prototype power game used later so effectively by Monica Seles and Serena Williams. Once, Rita attended a tennis clinic given by Pancho Gonzales at Caesars Palace. Pancho described her tennis skills as "unbelievable." Mike argued that Rita could have been the best ever, but she resented the tortuous tennis program he designed for her and quit the game in her early twenties.

Mike made the same mistake with Phillip by pushing him too hard during their training sessions. When it was evident that Phillip was not going to be a world-class player, Mike started referring to him as a "born loser." I view this as a grossly unfair and severe accusation. In reality, Phillip was an accomplished player. He attended the University of Las Vegas and played number one singles for two years from 1982-1983. He compiled a remarkable record of 55-6 with a winning percentage of .902. Phillip still has the highest winning percentage in the history of UNLV tennis. But perhaps I shouldn't be too harsh on Mike Agassi. After all, Sir Francis Galton, when having a particularly "bad patrician day" might have referred to someone as a "born loser" rather than the line about finding true moral repose in one's mediocrity.

Mike took a more balanced approach with his third child, Tami. He taught her the game but decided not to push her as he had Rita and Phillip. He described Tami as not "terribly competitive by nature."

Consistent with the Polgar chess experiment, the Agassi tennis-prodigy production machine operated at maximum efficiency with Andre. This was Mike's last chance to fulfill his dream of creating a Wimbledon champion, and he pulled out all the stops. He wrote, "By the time Andre was born on April 29, 1970, I was ready. I vowed that I wouldn't push him the way I had Rita and Phillip. I would, however, begin teaching him about tennis before he could walk, before he could talk, before he could even sit."

Mike implemented a program of environmental control that would have impressed John Watson and B.F. Skinner. He designed a special mobile for Andre's crib that involved a tennis ball dangling from a wood racket. When a family member passed by the crib, they tapped the racket to make the ball move. Andre watched the ball as it moved back and forth. When Andre was six to seven months old, Mike developed a game in which Andre, sitting in his high chair, hit a balloon with a ping-pong paddle. Once Andre learned to walk, he had a tennis racket in his hand and Mike would toss balls to him. By age three, Andre was hitting a two-handed backhand and a one-handed forehand. By age four, Andre could serve, volley, and return any shot delivered to him.

Mike's coaching style with Andre was something out of a Vince Lombardi training manual. He was rough, dictatorial, and, at times, verbally harsh. As noted earlier, Andre practiced against the tennis-ball machine twice as long as either Rita or Phillip. Andre hit approximately 2500 balls per day which results in an impressive 912,500 ball strikes per year. If one uses a standard ball machine feed rate of five seconds, this translates into three and a half hours of training per day. Over the course of a year, Andre logged in 1267 hours of tennis practice, and in ten years, he amassed 12,600 hours of intensive, deliberate practice.

Andre Agassi is considered to have one of the best service returns in the history of the game. Was he born with some extraordinary ability to hit return of serves? Was he in the superior range of visual acuity? Did he have faster reaction times than you or I? That is what most people believe. Even Andre believes some variant of this. Nevertheless, one needs to rule out all relevant environmental influences before speculating about some innate biological advantage.

Mike instructed Andre to attack the other man's strength. Mike asserted, "If the man is a server, take away his serve. If he is a power player, overpower him. If he has a big forehand, takes pride in his forehand, go after his forehand until he hates his forehand." Mike's name for this strategy was "putting a blister on the other man's brain." Mike was training Andre to become a boxer with a tennis racket. Since most players relied on their serve, Mike crafted Andre to become a counterpuncher.

Andre referred to the ball machine that his father had modified to simulate serving as "the dragon." Mike placed the machine on a base several feet high and moved it right up against the net. He attached an extra-long neck of aluminum tubing that allowed the machine to shoot balls down at Andre's feet "as if dropped from an airplane." The seven- year-old Andre had to hit every ball on the rise or else it bounced over his head. Since he was hitting thousands of balls during a given session, there were always tennis balls around his feet when he was returning the dragon's "serves." Sometimes the serve hit another ball on the ground prior to Andre returning it. Andre became skilled at making last-second adjustments in order to execute the return. So, was Andre's remarkable return of serve the result of some anomalous genetic condition or the product of thousands of hours of deliberate, intensive, and innovative practice? Even if there was evidence that Andre possessed superior visual acuity, this protracted training had to have a significant impact on his remarkable service returns. And from an early age Andre was "conditioned" by his father to visually focus on a tennis ball or some equivalent.

Mike stood behind Andre during his practice sessions and yelled, "Hit earlier. Damn it, Andre, hit earlier." Mike wanted Andre to crowd the ball and hit it harder and faster than the ball machine. Mike went into a rage whenever Andre hit the ball into the net. Whenever Andre diverted his attention for a moment, his father yelled, "What the hell are you looking at? Keep hitting! Keep hitting!" The ultimate tennis sin for Mike Agassi was thinking. If he believed Andre was thinking or daydreaming, Mike screamed, "What the f**k are you *doing*? Stop thinking. No f***ing thinking!"

And Little Albert thought he had it rough with John Watson. Poor Little Andre. No wonder Andre was conflicted about tennis for most of his career. He stated in his autobiography, "I hate tennis, hate it with all my heart, and still I keep playing, keep hitting all morning, and all afternoon, because I have no choice. No matter how much I want to stop, I don't. I keep begging myself to stop, and I keep playing, and this gap, this contradiction between what I want to do and what I actually do, feels like the core of my life."

For those interested in behavioral psychology, Andre's tennis development was, in part, the result of negative reinforcement. Negative reinforcement is the behavioral principle in which some behavior will increase in frequency contingent upon the removal of an aversive stimulus. Andre reported, "Though I hate tennis, I like the feeling of hitting a ball dead perfect. It's the only peace. When I do something perfect, I enjoy a split second of sanity and calm." This would make sense. Andre's father constituted the "aversive stimulus," yelling and screaming at him whenever he hit an errant shot. When Andre hit a shot perfectly, I'm sure that Mike just kept quiet. He does not appear to be the kind of guy who would say to Andre after a perfectly executed shot, "Great shot, Andre my boy. You hit the ball early and with great follow through." Andre's perfect shot making served to prevent Mike from yelling at him. Thus, Andre's shot making was, in essence, negatively reinforced.

Despite Mike Agassi's flaws, he was a master of environmental design and the application of deliberate practice. No wonder Andre became so damn good under his tutelage. If Mike had the capacity to provide a loving, supportive environment while instilling a growth mindset, I believe Andre could have become an even more effective player without the angst that plagued him throughout most of his career.

Mike was aware that Andre needed a more concentrated tennis experience, competing against players of equal or superior skills. The Agassi family traveled hundreds of miles on the weekends to play tournaments in Nevada, California, Arizona, and Utah in search of adequate competition. Andre dominated the junior tennis scene. Only two players – Pete Sampras and Michael Chang – were occasionally able to give Andre a match. But Sampras struggled in the juniors and Chang was two years younger than Andre.

At age eleven, Andre entered a tournament in San Diego and came to the attention of Pancho Segura. Segura was an exceptional player, a master tactician, and coach of Jimmy Connors during the 1970s. Segura offered to coach Andre for six days a month and wanted complete control over his tennis development and a 12% cut of his future earnings. At that point, Mike was unwilling to relinquish control as Andre's coach.

Interestingly, Mike asserted that he wasn't going to push Andre as he did Rita and Phillip. If what Mike was doing with Andre wasn't pushing, I can't imagine the treatment Rita and Phillip received. Somewhat like Rita, Andre, at age thirteen, rebelled against Mike's training regimen and stopped listening to him. Having gone through this with his two other children, Mike was wise enough at that point to search for another coach for Andre.

Around this time, Mike watched a *60 Minutes* feature titled "Tennis Boot Camp" about the Bollettieri Tennis Academy in Bradenton, Florida.

Mike dismissed Bollettieri personally as a little "slick" and "phony" and that "the guy didn't know jack about tennis." What intrigued Mike about the academy was the potential to provide Andre with a concentrated tennis experience not available in Las Vegas. Academy participants included Jim Courier, David Wheaton, Martin Blackman, and Mark Knowles. Mike reasoned that, with this level of competition, Andre's tennis skills could blossom.

Despite Andre's objections, off he went to Bradenton at age thirteen on a one-month trial basis. Recognizing Andre's considerable tennis skills and potential for further development, Bollettieri offered Andre a full-time scholarship to the academy and the rest, as they say, is history.

Andre's career was brilliant, yet erratic, reflecting the personal conflicts he had about the game and his upbringing. Regardless, Andre turned professional at age sixteen. His father noted, "After a decade of Lendl's and Borg's robotic demeanor, of McEnroe's petulant outbursts, of Connors's charismatic antagonism, Andre's Elvis-like showmanship was, for many, as refreshing as a breeze in the desert."

Andre's rise in the men's world rankings was dramatic, improving from 603 in 1986 to number three by 1988. He performed well in major tournaments, for example losing in the 1990 finals at Indian Wells, Roland Garros, and the U.S. Open. Andre made it to the finals of the French Open for a second time in 1991.

Meanwhile, the three players Andre had dominated in the juniors – Chang, Sampras, and Courier – secured a Grand Slam title before him. But this is not unusual. There have been many dominant junior players who do not have stellar professional careers. There were rumblings in the press that perhaps Andre could not win the big ones. Perhaps, in Andre's case, "image was not everything." This was not, however, going to be Andre's fate.

By the spring of 1992, Andre's ranking had fallen from the top ten. He had an impressive run at the French Open but fell to eventual champion Jim Courier in the semifinals 6-3, 6-2, 6-2. Andre defeated Sampras in the quarters 7-6, 6-2, 6-1.

Andre had his "break-out" tournament at Wimbledon in 1992. He was the twelfth seed, and London bookmakers had him as a 50-1 shot to win the title. The British tabloids referred to him as "Gagassi" because of his three prior losses in Grand Slam finals. But Andre was on a mission. He defeated Andrei Chesnokov, Eduardo Masso, journeyman Derrick Rostagno, and Christian Saceanu to reach the quarterfinals, where Andre defeated Boris Becker in a grueling five set match 4-6, 6-2, 6-2, 4-6, 6-3. Andre vanquished McEnroe in the semis 6-4, 6-2, 6-3.

The finals of Wimbledon that year pitted Agassi versus Goran Ivanisevic. This was an interesting match-up: the great serve of Ivanisevic versus the great return of Agassi. Prior to the match, most considered Ivanisevic to be the favorite. After all, the tournament was played on grass and Ivanisevic had a devastating serve. And common wisdom suggested that baseliner/counterpunchers do not win Wimbledon. Goran's serve was "on" that day. He fired thirty-seven aces over the course of five sets. Ivanisevic won the first set 7-6; Andre, the next two at 6-4. Ivanisevic came roaring back to take the fourth set 6-1. Both Andre and Goran were "on serve" until Andre was up 5-4 in the fifth set. One could see Goran beginning to crack under the pressure. He double faulted twice to go down 0-30. He managed to tie it up at 30-30 with some effective serving and shot making. At 30-30, Goran missed his first serve and hit the second serve to Agassi's forehand. Andre replied with a dipping forehand return to Goran's backhand. Goran responded by hitting a solid volley to Agassi's forehand. Agassi then passed Goran crosscourt to set up match point wherein Goran hit his first serve in the net. The pressure on Ivanisevic was immense - a second serve against the greatest returner in the game's history. Goran hit his second serve to Andre's backhand, and Andre replied with only an adequate return to Goran's backhand. Andre's return jammed Goran somewhat, and Goran hit his backhand volley into the net.

Agassi won his first Grand Slam, and it was the premier tournament of them all – Wimbledon. Andre telephoned his dad, who had watched the match in Las Vegas, and at some point during their conversation, Andre realized that Mike was choked up with emotion and unable to speak. Emotional reactions, apart from anger and rage, were out of character for Mike. But I'm sure on that day in 1992, Mike was not only thrilled at his son's victory but probably visualized himself standing at Centre Court stadium in 1948, re-experiencing that epiphany that someone from his family would win Wimbledon. That 1948 epiphany had been the primary motivating force in Mike's life for nearly forty-four years. He and Andre had done it.

Andre continued to have a remarkable, albeit mercurial, tennis career. He won the 1994 U.S. Open. In 1995, Andre played in his first Australian Open and won it defeating Sampras in a four-set final. In April of that year, Agassi was ranked number one in the world, a position he held for thirty weeks. 1996 was not a particularly stellar year for Agassi, but he won the Olympics in Atlanta, defeating the Spaniard Sergei Bruguera in the finals.

Andre won the Australian Open in 2000 and 2001, and he won his eighth and final Grand Slam in 2003, capturing his fourth Australian Open title. Andre retired from professional tennis following his defeat to Benjamin Becker in the third round of the 2006 U.S. Open. Andre was inducted into the International Tennis Hall of Fame on July 9, 2011.

So, what can we learn from the Laszlo and Emmanuel projects? There are several important and inter-related issues.

1. The underlying assumption for both men was that elite performance could be created through environmental design.
2. Laszlo and Emmanuel started training their children at early ages. Laszlo initiated formal chess training with Susan when she was four years old. Emmanuel began his tennis experiment with Rita when she was two. With Andre, tennis training began in the crib with a specially designed tennis-ball mobile. I suppose if Emmanuel had thought about it, he could have designed something for the pre-natal environment, attaching small microphones to his wife's abdomen that would gently play the sounds and rhythms of a tennis match.
3. Both men were strong advocates of deliberate practice. Andre Agassi and all of the Polgar sisters amassed thousands of hours of deliberate practice by their mid-teens.
4. Laszlo and Emmanuel used innovative training techniques. Laszlo had amassed an impressive collection of chess books and trained his children on the approaches used by chess masters. Emmanuel did something similar by studying the games of the tennis greats

and training his children on the most effective elements from each. Emmanuel also modified several tennis-ball machines to more effectively simulate match conditions. His modification of the ball machine to simulate serving was particularly innovative. The return of serve is a critical part of the game but insufficiently practiced. With his modified machine, Andre was able to hit literally tens, if not hundreds, of thousands of service returns.

5. Laszlo and Emmanuel were obsessive and driven individuals. What drove these men to do what they did? One common factor is that they are both from minority groups. The Polgars are Jewish and the Agassis Iranian-Americans. These two men clearly wanted to excel, consistent with many members of minority immigrant communities. Both were the product of a strong cultural and religious upbringing. Laszlo initially wanted to become a rabbi but was later influenced by materialistic philosophies. He became an atheist but identified with the shared Jewish values of a strong work ethic and intellectual rigor. As Christian-Armenians living in Tehran, the Agassis were raised within a tightly-knit cultural group. Emmanuel's father was a skilled artisan and perfectionist.

6. The youngest of the Polgar and Agassi children became the most skillful. Judith and Andre became international stars. It is possible that both had something to prove to their older siblings, and this provided additional motivation to succeed. A more important factor appears to be Anders Ericsson's contention that the development of an expert-level performer is enhanced through the use of optimal training conditions. By the time Judith and Andre had started their training regimen, Laszlo and Emmanuel had perfected their training techniques. And, in the case with Andre, he received significantly more training time than did his siblings.

7. With all of their early successes in their domains of interest, the Polgar and Agassi children had expanding opportunities available to them. Several Cornell University researchers have referred to this as the *multiplier effect*. This is the process by which some initial skill advantage exhibited by an individual leads to a series of events that

produces even greater advantages. For example, once the Polgar children demonstrated a certain degree of chess expertise, they were exposed to higher levels of competitive chess and more effective chess instruction. With the multiplier effect, there is a type of selection process in which perceived "talent" or actual skill level provides opportunities less available to others. One can imagine that the four-and-a-half-year-old Susan Polgar's defeat of the middle-aged patron at the Budapest Chess Club ignited a firestorm of interest in the Polgar experiment. International masters and grandmasters were regular visitors to the Polgar home. Susan, and later Sofia and Judith, were the recipients of this increased attention and opportunities for enhanced chess development that continued to the international arena.

Like chess, tennis has built-in competitive venues – local, regional, state, national, and international tournaments. For those players who are fortunate enough to start early in the hands of a skilled coach, they will have opportunities not available to others. These children, with their deliberate-practice history, will be perceived by many from the tennis establishment as having "talent." They will be the recipients of special resources that increase their deliberate practice and competitive tennis time. This effect results in multiplying their skill level. The Bollettieri Academy served this function for Andre Agassi. Andre had considerably more deliberate-practice time than his siblings and, no surprise, was a better player and perceived to be "more talented." When Mike Agassi had exhausted the tennis opportunities available to him in Nevada and neighboring states, he enrolled Andre at the Bollettieri Academy for a concentrated tennis experience. Once Andre turned professional, this process only accelerated. During this advanced stage in his career, Andre, like the Polgar sisters, was competing against the elite players of the world.

Geoff Colvin reported, "This multiplier effect accounts not just for improvement of skills over time but also for the motivation that drives the improvement." Andre Agassi is a prime example of this motivational process. There is no doubt that Mike Agassi pushed Andre hard to succeed on the tennis court. Andre was conflicted about the game for many years, often stating that he hated tennis. The motivation to succeed can have both negative and positive elements. Both elements operated for Andre that produced this enhanced motivational effect.

Andre was undefeated in competitive junior tennis until he reached the finals of a 10-and-under tournament against Jeff Tarango. The match came down to a "sudden-death," 9-point tie break. The score was 4-4 when Andre ripped a forehand for a winner. At first, Tarango appeared despondent and started to cry. But then, he quickly called the ball out and raised his arms in a victory gesture. These were the days in which each kid was on the honor system and required to call his own lines. In short, Tarango cheated and stole the match from Andre.

Andre's response was telling: "After years of hearing my father rant at my flaws, one loss has caused me to take up his rant. I've internalized my father – his impatience, his perfectionism, his rage – until his voice doesn't just feel like my own, it is my own. I no longer need my father to torture me. From this day on, I can do it all by myself." This puts a new twist on Ellen Winner's rage to master concept. The ten-year-old Andre was angry at the world. That anger provided motivation for his continued improvement.

An example of a positive experience that leads to further motivation to succeed came when the fifteen-year-old Andre played in a professional event at La Quinta. He won three matches in the qualifying draw and then defeated John Austin in the first round of the main draw. As Andre strolled around the tournament grounds, spectators pointed at him and said, "*There he is. That's the kid I was telling you about – the prodigy.*" Andre thought, "It's the prettiest word I've ever heard applied to me."

CHAPTER 6

THE MENTAL GAME

Connors was "an eating machine, driven by aggression and hunger
that I haven't seen before or since."

Muhammad Ali's legendary trainer, Angelo Dundee, reportedly said that if he could have lured Jimmy Connors away from tennis he would have made him the middleweight champion of the world. Why? Connors was clearly not the most versatile athlete of his generation. Bjorn Borg, John McEnroe, and Ilie Nastase possessed superior athletic skills. Then why was Connors so successful? Dundee noticed something important about Connors; he was mentally tough and intense. He was a fierce competitor.

When Connors started playing on the tour, several of his fellow competitors believed that he would burn himself out after a few years due the sheer intensity of his competitive zeal. By the end of his career, Connors had won 109 career ATP singles titles, including eight Grand Slams. He won more matches (1,253) than any other male professional player. He reached the world number one ranking in 1974 and held it for 160 consecutive weeks. And in 1991, at age 39, he made it to the semifinals of the U.S. Open - so much for burnout. Peter Bodo, in *The Courts of Babylon*, described Connors as "an eating machine, driven by aggression and hunger that I haven't seen before or since." Connors was the Jake LaMotta of tennis - the "Raging Bull" with a racket. Dundee was right; Connors would have made a great fighter.

What made Connors so mentally tough? A large part of Connors's toughness was attributable to his mother, Gloria. She reported to Bodo, "I taught him to be a tiger on the court. Even when he was really little, I would hit the ball down his throat if he gave me the opportunity. Then I would call him up to the net and tell him, 'See that, Jimmy? Your own mother will do that to you. Everybody will do that to you if they have the chance." Perhaps there is another way, besides hitting a ball down your child's throat, to produce that Connors-like intensity.

DOES SPORTS PSYCHOLOGY HAVE ANYTHING TO OFFER?

In short, yes. Sports psychology has experienced exponential growth during the past several decades. The sports psychologist has multiple professional roles including teaching, research, and consulting with athletes, coaches, corporate executives, and others. In working with athletes, the sports psychologist may function in a more traditional role by providing psychotherapy for a variety of emotional issues including depression, anxiety, eating disorders, and substance abuse.

The primary role of the sports psychologist is to apply specific psychological procedures to maximize the competitive performance of athletes. These procedures may include relaxation training, imaginal rehearsal, self-talk, and the establishment of pre-competitive routines. The majority of these procedures are designed to promote self-control of thoughts, emotions, and physical reactions.

A critical assumption of sports psychology is that the modification or control of maladaptive thoughts and negative emotions will promote enhanced competitive performance. Sports psychologists will encourage athletes to suppress negative feelings during competition; to eliminate negative self-talk (e.g., "I can't do this," "I'm choking," and "I don't have a chance against this guy"); and to promote positive self-talk (e.g., "bring it on," "fight through the last point," and "I love to compete").

This assumption of sports psychology is part of a larger tradition within applied psychology and psychiatry that views emotional disorders as a result of a characteristic set of maladaptive beliefs or "cognitive errors." A major tenet of cognitive or cognitive-behavior therapy is that thoughts can produce emotional distress. Environmental events, by themselves, have no emotional valence. It is the individual's interpretation of these events that is critical and can lead to a variety of emotional responses.

The nature of these interpretations or meanings assigned to these environmental events is key to understanding emotional disorders. If you observe your thinking closely, you will see that you are constantly describing events in the world to yourself and assigning labels for each event or experience. These labels are produced from an unrelenting private, verbal dialogue. Several authors have used a particular metaphor to describe this dialogue as a "waterfall of thoughts cascading down the back of your mind." Albert Ellis, of Rational Emotive Therapy fame, described this dialogue as "self-talk." Aaron Beck, known primarily for his development of cognitive therapy for depression, prefers the term "automatic thoughts."

Much of our internal dialogue is rather innocuous with no adverse consequences. Some of this dialogue, however, regularly precedes the occurrence of painful or problematic emotional states. Listening closely to your internal dialogue provides important clues as to how you are interpreting the world in a manner that may lead to emotions such as anxiety, depression, or anger. Aaron Beck and his colleagues contend that these problematic thoughts have two primary characteristics: (1) they appear automatic, and (2) they contain specific predictions of some given situation. Automatic thoughts are difficult to discern because they occur quickly and are often outside of the individual's awareness.

CHARACTERISTICS OF AUTOMATIC THOUGHTS

1. **Automatic thoughts are experienced as spontaneous**. They seem to come out of nowhere, just popping into consciousness.

2. **Automatic thoughts may contain highly specific, negative messages**. A tennis player who is sensitive about performing well may think, "I suck," "I'm a loser," or "My backhand is terrible."

3. **Automatic thoughts are often framed in terms of *should or must***. A tennis player who finds himself in a tight match may think, "I must win this match" or "I should be able to beat this idiot."

4. **Automatic thoughts may involve only a few key words or some discrete visual imagery.** Words such as "bad," "no good," or "lousy" may just pop into your mind during a match. These specific thoughts are frequently shorthand for a larger group of problematic memories or concerns. Sometimes you may notice discrete visual imagery.

Allow me to elaborate on this imagery issue with a personal example. Eddie was gunning for me. I met Eddie in 1961. We went to the same elementary school, were friends, and played tennis on a regular basis. We were two of the better junior tennis players in our area. For about a three-year period I never lost a match to him, and we probably played about thirty times. We played doubles together for about two years in various tournaments but then I switched to another partner. When I was fourteen years old, Eddie and I played in the finals of our club tournament, and I was favored to win. I was aware that Eddie had been working hard on his game for several months prior to our match. He was focusing all of his energies on defeating me. The match was held in September 1964, and during the first set I was surprised at how much he had improved. His groundstrokes were more consistent, and his serve had some power. Eddie played his heart out during that first set but came up short, losing 6-4. You could see his confidence disappear. His physical presentation – slumped shoulders and minimal eye contact – communicated defeat. Despite months of training and playing a solid first set, he didn't have quite enough game to stay with me.

I raced out to a second set lead of 5-1 and was serving for the match at 40-15. I lost the 40-15 point and, just prior to serving at 40-30, a friend of mine, who happened to walk by the court, asked when I would be finished. With incredible hubris, I said, "This will be over in a few seconds." I may have said it loud enough for Eddie to hear. I then served out wide to Eddie's backhand and charged the net. He hit a "sitter" return to my backhand. I decided to hit a sharply angled crosscourt volley to end the match and to hit it with sufficient force to communicate to Eddie, "Don't you even think you will ever beat me." Well, you can probably see where this is going. I hit the volley, and it landed wide about half an inch left of the singles sideline near the service line. I could see a glimmer of hope return to Eddie's face, and he started to crawl back into the match. He broke me to go down 2-5 and then my game started to unravel. I started playing defensively, and Eddie became more aggressive. I was unable to stop the decline. I ended up losing the second set 7-5 and then Eddie closed out the third set 6-1. I was devastated at the time, although I probably deserved to lose the match. That was one of the few times on the tennis court when I acted in a rather conceited manner. I still consider this the worst loss of my tennis life.

I bring this up because I have occasionally over the years, when playing a tight match, had a brief visual image of that 40-30 shot going wide. I can still clearly see the mark the ball left. This brief, rapid image usually occurs just as I am about to serve and volley.

5. **Automatic thoughts are often believed**. They are experienced as automatic and appear natural. Individuals assign the same truth value to these thoughts as they do to events in the real world. These thoughts are rarely questioned or challenged because they reside in our private world of thinking. Only when we are able to identify these thoughts and share them with others can they be challenged or evaluated.

6. **Automatic thoughts often "catastrophize."** They predict the worst. A missed overhead means "I'm choking." An early loss in a tournament means "I'll never be any good." A headache surely means the early stages of brain cancer. This type of automatic thinking is quite common and constitutes a major source of anxiety.

7. **Automatic thoughts are hard to stop**. Since they are automatic and may appear plausible, they often go as an unnoticed part of one's internal dialogue. They seem to come and go on their own. They can also serve as "cues" for other problematic thoughts. All of us have had the experience of one worrying thought leading to a long chain of associated worries.

8. **Automatic thoughts are learned**. They are part of our verbal history and are impacted by others, including friends, family, teachers, and coaches. In essence, you have been "conditioned" by others to

interpret events in a particular way. This early conditioning history results in habitual patterns of automatic thinking that are often difficult to detect.

TEN TYPES OF PROBLEMATIC THINKING

Awareness is the first step in learning how to cope with problematic or limited thinking. Many individuals engage in one or more of the following cognitive distortions without any significant adverse consequences to their lives. As with other aspects of human functioning, these distortions lie on a continuum. It is only when the distortions become particularly pronounced or pervasive that significant emotional problems may develop. Here is a list with definitions of the ten most common forms of problematic thinking. I probably have engaged in all these forms of thinking at various points of my tennis career.

1. **Tunnel Vision**: This type of thinking is where you focus on only one part of a situation and ignore everything else. A coach praises a player at the end of a training session by noting his excellent footwork and great anticipation. The coach also adds that the player's backhand needs additional work. The player leaves the court feeling rather despondent, thinking that the coach didn't think much of his game. He selected the one comment about his backhand and didn't even hear the praise about the other parts of his game. When you use tunnel-vision thinking, you are essentially magnifying the negative thoughts while passing over positive comments and experiences.

2. **Dichotomous Thinking**: This is where you perceive events at the extremes, leaving out the vast middle ground. This is also known as polarized thinking. By engaging in this type of thinking, you are creating a black and white world while missing all of the greys. People are seen as good or bad, fabulous or horrible. Your emotional pendulum swings from one extreme to another. The one particularly problematic part of dichotomous thinking is the effect it has

on your self-evaluations. If you aren't perfect, then you must be a failure.

A great example of dichotomous thinking took place during a conversation between Bjorn Borg and John McEnroe. In 1985, Borg and McEnroe played six, one-night exhibition matches as part of a "Tennis Over America Tour." One night, after a match, they were having a drink and discussing Ivan Lendl's ascension to the number one world ranking. McEnroe informed Borg that perhaps he could be satisfied with being number two or that maybe he should just quit the professional tour. Borg responded, "Number one is the only thing that matters, John. "You know as well as I do. If you're number two, you might as well be number three or four – you're nobody." Borg's comment is a classic example of dichotomous thinking. If you are not number one in the world, Borg stated emphatically, then you're nothing. If that were the case, Rod Laver, Jimmy Connors, Roger Federer, and Rafael Nadal would be nobodies because they all lost their number one ranking at various points in their careers, but they continued competing. I seriously doubt that any of these players saw themselves as "nobodies" when their ranking slipped to number two or three in the world. Perhaps this type of thinking was partly responsible for Borg's sudden exit from the professional tour when he lost the number one ranking to McEnroe.

3. **Overgeneralization**: In this type of thinking, you reach a general conclusion based on a single piece of evidence. One badly played overhead means "I will never learn how to hit this shot." If you lose to a pusher, this means "I will always lose to pushers." One negative outcome means that, when you encounter a similar situation again, the same outcome will occur. Specific words that indicate you may be overgeneralizing include absolutes such as never, always, none, and all.

4. **Catastrophizing**: This type of thinking is where you imagine the worst possible outcome. If you lose a tennis match, this means "I will never win another match." If you have a stomachache, then you must have stomach cancer. Before traveling on an airplane, you

may catastrophize that it surely will crash. These types of statements are almost endless and only limited by the creativity of the catastrophizer.

5. **Personalization**: This type of thinking is where you relate events around you to yourself. When one of your teammates discusses how to deal with anger on the court, you are convinced that he is talking about your anger. When someone mentions cheating, you think it's a comment about you. If you notice players laughing on an adjacent court, you conclude, "They're laughing at me." Another problem with personalization is that it places you in a position of comparing yourself to others (e.g., "He plays tennis so much better than I do"; "He is mentally tougher than I am"; or "He is not very smart, I am"). With personalized thinking, you are interpreting each experience as it relates to your own self-worth.

6. **Distortions Involving Control**: There are two control distortions. One is where you see yourself as being controlled by external events. When you feel externally controlled, you believe that you can't impact events around you (e.g., "I can't win this match because they put me on the hard court with cracks in it" or "I don't have a chance at winning today, it's too hot." Something external to you is responsible for your losses or failures. And because you believe that you are externally controlled, you would not look for solutions as they are not likely to work.

   The other type of control distortion involves omnipotence. This is the belief that you are responsible for everyone and everything around you. Everyone on your team depends on you. You are responsible for others' happiness and good fortune. You have to correct all wrongs and take care of everyone's needs. And, if you can't do this, you become guilty.

7. **Emotional Reasoning**: Emotional reasoning involves the belief that what you feel must be the truth. If you feel inept, then you are inept. If you feel like a loser, then you are a loser. If you feel great, then you must be great. If you are feeling upset or angry, then someone must have taken advantage of you. You believe that these things

must be true because they *feel* true. The problem is that feelings, by themselves, have questionable truth value. Feelings are often the result of our thoughts and, if we are engaging in distorted thinking, our feelings will mirror those distorted thoughts.

8. **Global Attributions**: An opponent who gives you one bad call is a "total asshole." A member of a particular political party is a "complete moron." Your supervisor at work is "completely insensitive." You get the point. Global attributions, even if containing some truth value, distort reality. This type of labeling ignores contradictory evidence, producing a rather uni-dimensional world view.

9. **The Blame Game**: This is a classic one for tennis players. I lost the match because "it was too hot," "my opponent was too tall," "there was too much noise," "the linesman was a jerk," and so forth. There is comfort in knowing who or what to blame when losing a match. By blaming others, you absolve yourself of responsibility for your own behavior.

    There are other people, however, who exclusively assign blame to themselves. They denigrate themselves for being incompetent, stupid, or inept. They always seem prepared to be wrong.

10. **Shoulds**: With this type of maladaptive thinking, you are operating from inflexible mandates about how you and other people should behave (e.g., "My coach *should* be more sensitive to my needs"; "My doubles partner should be more supportive of me on the court"; "I should *always* be in peak physical condition"; "I *must* never get angry on the court"; "I should *never* make mistakes"; "I must always control my feelings"). Notice the key words here: should, always, must, never.

Once an individual's problematic thinking has been identified along with its causal role in producing emotional disturbance, the psychologist's task is to use various strategies to promote change in these thoughts and beliefs. These strategies typically include analyzing logical errors in thinking, questioning the validity of dysfunctional thoughts or beliefs, and using evidence to challenge these beliefs. Over time, the therapist assists the individual in developing more accurate thoughts and beliefs to supplant the inaccurate ones. One may then "test out" these new beliefs in one's daily life to see if they are an effective and useful way to view things. A change in these negative cognitions or dysfunctional beliefs, so the assumption goes, should promote greater psychological well-being and adjustment.

Is this assumption accurate? Yes, to a certain degree. Data from applied clinical research clearly indicate that cognitive and cognitive-behavioral therapies have a positive impact on a wide array of emotional problems. Unfortunately some fail to benefit from these treatments, and there are others who do not attain what would be considered a "clinically significant" level of change. And although it is reasonably straightforward to observe the connection between our thoughts and emotional reactions, it is often quite challenging to modify these thoughts to change how we feel.

The same situation holds true for sports psychology. Data suggest that the control or modification of negative thoughts and emotions do not consistently produce an increase in athletic performance. So, where does the tennis player turn to develop that Jimmy Connors tenacity?

GUIDELINE 4: THE THIRD WAVE PSYCHOTHERAPIES

ACCEPT, COMMIT, AND BE MINDFUL

During the past twenty years, there have been a number of important developments in the field of psychotherapy that can have a positive impact on athletic performance. Contemporary therapies, referred to as the "third wave," have names such as Dialectical Behavior Therapy, Mindfulness-Based Cognitive Therapy, and Acceptance and Commitment Therapy. These therapies emphasize values clarification, rule-governed behavior, acceptance, and mindfulness.

VALUES CLARIFICATION

Your tennis epitaph: Do you recall that chapter in Mark Twain's *The Adventures of Tom Sawyer* in which Tom, Huck, and Joe were hiding in the church and listening to their own funeral service? What would people say at your "tennis funeral?" More important, what would you like to have as your tennis epitaph? The latter question is a critical one. Think about it. Your answer to this question provides the key to successful development of your tennis game and clarifies what's important about your tennis life. Once these values are clarified, specific and achievable process-oriented goals can be formulated that are consistent with these values. For the competitive tennis player, these value-oriented goals would include rigorous training or deliberate practice, adoption of a lifestyle to promote optimum health and well-being, aggressive play, the formulation and execution of strategic plans, and the development of select skills to promote sustained concentration. Specific action steps can then be formulated to meet each of these value-oriented goals. The articulated values provide a framework for developing an increasing array of effective tennis behaviors, on an off the court. There is an emphasis on making a *passionate* commitment to the development of these effective behaviors.

Formulating values is an "action-oriented" activity that provides a directional path for your tennis behavior. Formulating a tennis epitaph provides you with important information about what you *currently* value about your tennis life. The way you want your tennis life to be remembered provides you with information about what you value right now. These articulated values are for you and you alone. Although these values may be consistent with those of your parents or coach, they ought to reflect *your* core beliefs. If for some reason you have generated values that do not mirror your true self, change them to reflect what is really important for you. If you value competition, then the articulated values should reflect this. On the other hand, if you play tennis for social reasons, formulate values commensurate with "having fun."

Examples of Tennis Epitaphs: Here lies Jack, he

* gave his best effort during matches.
* gave his best effort during practice.
* was an effective, strategic thinker.

* maintained a healthy lifestyle.
* handled victories and defeats with dignity.
* developed many friends through tennis.

COMMIT TO ACTION

This leads us to several important questions: *Are you ready to passionately commit to actions that will lead you in the direction of your chosen tennis values? Can you begin doing these actions today? What steps can you take right now?* This is where you formulate specific and achievable goals that can facilitate movement in the direction of your tennis values. Values give you direction; goals provide the means through which you can stay true to your values. Goals also provide a way to measure your progress with respect to your chosen values.

As formulated here, goals are used in the service of values. Goals are not an end in themselves. If they were, progress would stop. There is an important distinction between "goals as process" versus "goals as outcome." A common experience among athletes is a feeling of loss or depression following the achievement of some coveted goal. For example, winning a tournament or becoming the number one tennis player in the world should be a joyous experience. For some, however, there is a sense of bereavement or simply a loss of motivation after reaching some goal. For instance, having attained the number one ranking in 1988, Mats Wilander appeared disheartened with little desire to compete. Goals may be attained, but the "values path" continues. Goals may be seen as a process in the service of values rather than as an end product; this approach is consistent with establishing and maintaining a growth mindset. There are always ways to pursue your values to keep you motivated, excited, and energized.

So, let's assume that you value competition, have "bought in" to the deliberate-practice model, and want to set up a tennis-training regimen. Below is an example of the process from the articulation of a tennis value to the formulation of specific action steps.

1. **A competitive tennis value**: "I give my best effort during practice sessions."

2. **Set Goals:** Now that you have a valued direction or path, you take steps to move along that path. Here is where goals come into play. In order to put forth your best effort, you need to design and implement a deliberate-practice regimen; maintain a healthy lifestyle that includes eating nutritious foods and getting a sufficient amount of rest; stretch; do weight training; run (or some equivalent) with fartlek training; and improve your capacity for sustained concentration.

3. **Formulate Specific Action Steps:** This is where you formulate, with specific behavioral referents, the action steps required to achieve your tennis goals. Because a deliberate-practice regimen involves many components, it will be helpful to focus on one area, breaking it down into its component parts. One obvious area involves tennis strokes – forehands, backhands, approach shots, half-volleys, volleys, drop shots, overheads, serves, and service returns. For a given training session, you will need to determine on which strokes to focus. For example, if a typical training session lasts eighty minutes, you could spend forty minutes hitting topspin backhands and another forty minutes practicing serves. There are multiple variations of training sessions. A teaching professional can be a great resource in designing a detailed training regimen. You can then design a training plan for the other components that contribute to effective practice sessions such as healthy eating and improvements in your level of concentration.

RULE-GOVERNED BEHAVIOR

Look around you. Rules are everywhere - the Golden Rule, rules of grammar, rules of engagement, and rules of the game. Rules are routinely impacting and guiding our behavior. Each of us also has a set of personal rules of conduct that have a strong regulatory effect on our behavior.

Although some rules are functional and lead to effective forms of behavior, others are not and can produce all sorts of emotional and behavioral difficulties.

For example, individuals who are anxious and prone to worry have certain rules that lead to anxiety and worry in situations that are not realistically dangerous. When these individuals worry, they lose contact with the present moment and focus their attention on some preconceived conceptualized future.

There is a psychiatric condition known as Social Anxiety Disorder in which the defining feature involves a pronounced fear of social situations because of concerns regarding being scrutinized by others. Exposure to situations such as public speaking, parties, and even eating or writing in public may generate excessive, crippling anxiety. These individuals are convinced that others will notice their trembling hands or quivering voice. There is often avoidance of social situations that can be problematic for their social and occupational functioning. Their anxiety is anticipatory about some possible future event and related to their personal rules regarding scrutiny or evaluation by others. These individual rules or beliefs reshape experience; they distort experience in a way supportive of the personal rules. The fears of Social Anxiety Disorder individuals are "out of proportion to the actual threat posed by the social situation." Thus, these individuals are not accurately responding to the real world but to their own private, mental creations.

There are also rules that govern tennis players' behavior. If these rules are based on an accurate and thorough analysis of one's own and an opponent's game, they can lead to effective on-court behavior. If not, there may be problems. Playing a pusher or retriever, for instance, can be a challenging and frustrating experience. A dysfunctional personal rule may go something like this: "Well, I know I can't outsteady this guy, so I'm going to go for winners, hit for the lines." What's going to happen? The player will go for more angled and difficult shots in an attempt to "shorten" the points. The pusher will eat this up. He will keep the ball in play until the opponent makes an error. This dysfunctional tennis rule pulls one into the pusher's trap. If one maintains this rule throughout the match, the only way out is with a loss.

The tennis player needs to be aware of the personal rules that he brings into a particular match. The major criterion advocated in this book for the tennis player is *effective* behavior. Adopt a flexible set of rules that leads to effective tennis behavior. Personal rules are not literal truths. They are truthful only to the extent that they lead to effective tennis play. If you can develop a passionate commitment to live according to your tennis values and formulate rules consistent with these values, you will have taken a big step toward developing that Connors-like intensity. There is, however, more to consider.

Acceptance

Attempts to suppress negative thoughts and feelings during competitive play do not consistently result in enhanced athletic performance. Data from psychological studies indicate that conscious attempts to suppress thoughts and feelings can have the paradoxical effect of increasing their occurrence and disruptive impact upon ongoing behavior. Control is actually the problem. To repeat, thoughts are not literal truths. Forcing negative thoughts out of consciousness is giving them way too much importance. The problem is that our thoughts are quite powerful; they can in a very real way "re-create" the past or conjure up a conceptualized future, bringing them into the here-and-now and often for an entire lifetime.

Contemporary psychological interventions emphasize acceptance rather than suppression or control. Classic negative thinking on the tennis court includes, "My backhand sucks today," "I can't return this guy's serve," "There is no way I can beat this guy," and so on. When these thoughts invariably occur during competition, acknowledge that they are not literal truths and let them pass through your consciousness.

Defusion is a key concept in Acceptance and Commitment Therapy that borrows from the Buddhist practice of observing and distancing from the mind. This practice changes the relationship between you and your thoughts and can be helpful in dealing with negative thinking. There is an important distinction between *being* your thought and *having* a thought. An example of being a thought would be "I am a loser." With defusion, however, you merely describe the thought, for example, "I am having a thought that I'm a loser." *Being* a thought appears as though it is true, an absolute. *Having* a thought allows you to recognize that it is just a thought, one of thousands that you will have during the day. So, rather than identifying or "fusing" with your thoughts, defusion allows you to detach from and let go of these thoughts. Defusion is "the process of holding *all* of your thoughts lightly enough to be able to do what you need to do in your life."

Several types of specific imagery may prove helpful in letting go of these negative thoughts. Experiment with the following and select the one that is most helpful to you. Imagine each thought as a cloud moving across the sky on a windy day, and allow each cloud to pass out of sight. Another image to use involves leaves falling into a swiftly moving stream. With this image, each thought is a leaf that falls into the stream and quickly disappears downstream. If you're partial to trains, you can imagine yourself at a railroad crossing with a freight train passing by. Assign a thought to one of the boxcars and watch it move down the track out of sight.

Acceptance and Commitment Therapy encourages individuals to dispense with the belief in the literal truth of their own thoughts while advocating a passionate commitment to living according to their articulated values. The major shift in emphasis is this: move away from attempts to control negative thoughts and emotions and, instead, move toward a passionate commitment to valued tennis behaviors such as quality practice, focused play, strategic planning, and sustained concentration. By doing this, you are directing your energies toward developing a larger repertoire of effective tennis behavior. Neutralize negative thoughts and emotions by distancing from and letting them go.

MINDFULNESS

Take a moment to reflect upon your thinking. How much time do you spend ruminating or thinking about events that happened in the past or speculating about what might happen in the future? If you're like most people, this happens frequently. Tennis players do this often. The prospect of playing a serve-volley player may generate a series of thoughts about past matches with these players and how much pressure they exerted on your game. A future-oriented example is where you are serving to stay in a match and the thought occurs, "It's going to be embarrassing if I lose to this guy. I'll probably be pissed off for the next couple of days."

Then there's the problem with nerves and choking. Every tennis player has been there. Several years ago, my partner and I were playing in the finals of a local NTRP 4.5 doubles tournament. We lost the first set 7-6 and were down 4-5 in the second. I was serving to even the set. At 15-30 I distinctly recall my gut becoming tense and anxious. My first serve went long. Just prior to the second serve, I thought, "Man, I'm going to choke." I seemed to lose all motor control of my left arm. I dumped the second serve in the bottom of the net. On match point, the opponent on the deuce court hit a screaming return for a winner. This was a classic choke job on my part. I apologized to my partner and returned home a little despondent. Double faulting at 15-30 by dumping it into the net?" In fact, the ball barely made it to the net. I later thought, "If I'm going to double fault, at least go down swinging and hit it long."

Tom Borkovec, a psychology professor and anxiety disorders researcher at Penn State University, raised an important question. What would reality be like if we *fully* lived in the present moment? Borkovec noted that anxiety would not be present because the future does not yet exist. And there would be no depression because the past no longer exists. Only the strong primary emotions, like surprise, anger, fear, and joy, would remain.

Living in the present moment or "here-and-now" is a powerful concept and deserves some discussion. Borkovec argued that there is an advantage in focusing on process (here-and-now) versus the outcome of some activity. When one focuses on outcome, there is always the possibility of failure. This is exactly what is happening to the tennis player who chokes. The focus is on outcome. There is the anticipation of failure. Attending to the outcome of an activity is conducive to anxiety and other negative emotions that, in turn, can have a disruptive effect on behavior.

So, what does this mean for the tennis player? In a bizarre and paradoxical way, the pursuit of some extrinsic outcome (e.g., winning a match) may result in failure to achieve that outcome. Borkovec noted, "So seeking the extrinsic outcome makes the failure to achieve that outcome more likely. A focus on the process and intrinsic qualities of an activity reduce the likelihood of anxiety and depression (thus eliminating their negative impact on performance), increase the pleasure or joy during the process, and thus increase the likelihood of achieving the extrinsic outcome. I have to let go of the desired outcome in order to acquire it."

This approach appears to fly in the face of traditional approaches to competitive play. After all, aren't you supposed to set and achieve training goals? Aren't you supposed to win tennis matches? So, what's the deal with letting go of desired outcomes? The deal is this: instead of focusing on some outcome, make a passionate commitment to behaviors consistent with your tennis values - rigorous training and practice; aggressive, competitive play; incisive, strategic planning; and sustained concentration. If you can be true to these values and do so with a here-and-now focus, you are likely to win more matches. This means that during a match you are fully engaged during the present point. You are not thinking about what just happened or what might transpire during the next point. After all, the illusory past and illusory future are only that - illusory. All we have to work with is the present moment. I suspect that the great tennis players throughout history – Bill Tilden, Don Budge, Rod Laver, Roger Federer, Chris Evert, Steffi Graff, and others - were masters at maintaining this sustained here-and-now focus.

Fortunately, one can develop this "being in the present moment." A key component to contemporary forms of psychotherapy involves "mindfulness." Mindfulness has its origins in Eastern meditation practices. It involves a particular way of paying attention. The molecular biologist, Jon Kabat-Zinn defines mindfulness as "the awareness that emerges through paying attention on purpose, in the present moment, and nonjudgmentally to the unfolding of experience moment by moment." There are a number of techniques designed to develop mindfulness skills. Some involve meditation; others do not.

The most widely cited psychology-based mindfulness training is Jon Kabat-Zinn's Mindfulness-Based Stress Reduction (MBSR) Program at the University of Massachusetts Medical School. This program was designed to help medical patients who were suffering from chronic pain and stress. A guiding principle of this program is that when individuals experience physiological or psychological pain, they will attempt to escape from or avoid their own distressing feelings and thoughts. Although this appears to be a rational response, avoidance often results in a narrowing of behavioral options. For example, socially anxious individuals who avoid social events because of their belief that they will experience crippling anxiety, deprive themselves of the opportunity for establishing fulfilling interpersonal relationships.

Mindfulness teaches us to observe and experience thoughts, feelings, and sensations without becoming enmeshed in them.

An important feature of mindfulness is acceptance. You can only be fully present in the here-and-now if you accept the present moment as it is. Acceptance does not mean that you approve of the way things are, particularly if you are experiencing physical or psychological pain. Acceptance does not mean resigning yourself to some aversive situation. But you must accept reality as it is before it can be changed. You need to be aware of where you are before you can move forward. There is this interesting paradox regarding mindfulness and acceptance. You practice mindfulness to change things, but the essence of mindfulness is accepting things as they are.

To promote acceptance of present reality, the MBSR and other mindfulness programs have participants attend to bodily sensations occurring on a moment-to-moment basis. Another aspect involves paying attention to environmental features such as sights, sounds, and touch. A core feature of mindfulness involves nonjudgmental acceptance. Phenomena that enter into one's awareness are carefully observed without any type of evaluation. Thus, any thought, emotion, or sensation a person may have is noted and then allowed to pass by without judgment.

Mindfulness should be a core skill for the competitive tennis player. There are many events unfolding on a moment-to-moment basis during a tennis match. You and your opponent are attempting to outmaneuver one another during each point. You're running, getting your racket back, and attempting to execute a variety of shots on any given point. You are experiencing numerous thoughts, emotions, and sensations.

A mindful, here-and-now focus allows for maximum flexibility to the numerous demands of a tennis match. The ultimate criterion of this approach to the game is *effectiveness*. If you can be more effective than your opponent, you will win. If not, your opponent will win. And if you want to change your game, you need to know and accept where it is at this present moment. Playing tennis mindfully allows for maximum effectiveness. Note that acceptance and mindfulness disrupt the control exerted by dysfunctional self-rules and beliefs and allows more flexible and adaptive tennis behavior to emerge. So play mindfully.

Staying in the moment with full concentration is quite challenging. We actually miss much of what is going on in the present moment because our minds are often wandering, preoccupied with past events or expected future events.

Question: When is the best time to practice mindfulness?

Answer: Anytime.

If you would like to bring your attention to the many moments of your life in an accepting and nonjudgmental way, mindfulness is for you. But this takes practice and lots of it. There are many specific exercises to promote mindful attention.

The most established way to practice mindfulness is with meditation. Many erroneously believe meditation to be a rather esoteric activity reserved for those living in some cloistered, religious setting. At its core, meditation is merely a form of paying attention.

Mindful Breathing: Mindfulness-based training programs use various exercises to promote mindfulness. The most common involves observing one's breathing. The MBSR program introduces meditation to program participants with a three-minute breathing exercise. Now, this sounds rather straightforward. All you have to do is sit and attend to your breathing. As you will see, there is a lot happening when you just sit and breathe. One of the major misconceptions about meditation is that you attain some centered place without any thoughts or feelings. On the contrary, many thoughts, sensations, and emotions may occur during this, and other, meditation exercises.

To do this three-minute exercise, find a place where you can sit without many distractions. I recommend setting an alarm to free you from having to look at your watch several times to see when the three minutes have elapsed. Assume a sitting position on the floor with a straight but not rigid posture. Close your eyes and observe your breathing as you inhale and exhale. Remain in the present moment during each breath. Allow your breathing to happen without trying to control it. You may find your mind wandering during this exercise to various thoughts, emotions, or sensations. Do not attempt to suppress these experiences; observe them and then gently bring your attention back to your breathing. This may occur several times during this exercise. These wandering thoughts are not a problem and should be expected as part of the process. At the end of the three minutes, note how often your mind wandered from your breathing.

As you perform this exercise, particularly for the first time, you may experience judgmental thoughts about the exercise being a waste of time, worthless, or perhaps fun or relaxing. If these thoughts occur, note them and then bring your attention back to your breathing. By doing this, you become a *neutral observer* to your own experience.

For those interested in practicing mindful breathing for longer periods, you could gradually increase the meditation time in small increments until your meditation time reaches, for example, thirty minutes per day. Find a time period that is comfortable for you.

Mindfulness in Threes: This exercise, an adaptation from one of Dr. Marsha Linehan's professional training workshops, is a way to expand mindful attention. The exercise begins with one minute of mindful breathing described in the previous section. Pay close attention to all of the sensations involved in breathing: notice the cool air as it enters your nostrils, the rising of your abdomen, the pressure in your lungs, and the sensations involved in exhalation. Following approximately one minute, don't shift, but *expand* your awareness to your hands. In addition to focusing on your breathing, you are now also paying attention to any sensations from your hands. If your hands are on your lap, notice the tactile sensations of your hands resting on your clothing. If your hands are on the arms of a chair, be aware of these sensations. After another minute, expand your mindful attention further by noticing any sounds in your immediate environment. You are now paying close attention to your breathing, hands, and any sounds that may be present. If you cough, notice the sounds involved in coughing. If your cell phone rings, don't answer it but observe the sounds while still attending to your breathing and the sensations of your hands. With this exercise, sounds do not have a distracting function because it is specifically what you want to be aware of, in addition to your breathing and hands.

This exercise is a particularly good one to expand your awareness to multiple features of your environment. You may notice, when first doing this exercise, that you quickly shift your attention in some pattern from your breathing to your hands and then to the sounds present near you. With practice you will be able to simultaneously expand your awareness to all three areas for longer periods of time.

Mindful Eating: Eating, or drinking, offers a great opportunity to practice mindfulness. Because we all eat or drink on some regular basis, doing so mindfully is a way to practice staying in the here-and-now.

For most of my life, consistent with many people, I engaged in mindless eating. There were times, particularly when I was younger, when I stopped by a drive-thru fast-food restaurant after work and ordered several double cheese burgers and a large order of fries. By the time I made it home, I had consumed most of the food, barely aware of what I was eating. And, strangely enough, I was still hungry.

Mindful eating is a totally different experience. One exercise to practice mindful eating used in the MBSR and other programs involves eating raisins. I suppose any food item would work, but I would stay away from those Zebra cakes. Raisins are a great choice because they are portable, reasonably nutritious, and have great texture. With this exercise, you eat one raisin at a time, but in a special way – mindfully. First, take out a raisin and put it in front of you on a napkin or paper towel. Bring your attention to the raisin, observing it carefully. Notice the wrinkles on the raisin's skin with its various shapes. Do you realize that no two raisins, like snowflakes, are identical? Take out another raisin and notice the differences. Next, hold one raisin between two fingers, notice its colors, and experience its textures. Be aware of any thoughts you may have about raisins if, for instance, you like them or not. The next step involves smelling the raisin. Then slowly bring the raisin to your lips, being aware of your arm moving your hand to your mouth. Place the raisin in your mouth and slowly move it around to various parts of the inside of your mouth. Then begin to chew the raisin until it reaches a mushy consistency. Pay close attention to the taste of the raisin with its various flavors. Then be consciously aware as you swallow the raisin.

Once you become proficient with this rather "simple" exercise, expand your mindfulness practice to an entire meal. Carefully observe the actions involved in consuming a meal. Notice the flavors, textures, and temperature of the food and whatever beverage you may be consuming.

Kabat-Zinn noted that when you engage in this type of mindful attention, you are changing your relationship to things. You will actually see and become more conscious of your experience because you are no longer doing things on "automatic pilot." Practicing mindfulness is "being in the present on purpose."

Mindful meditation is a way to stabilize your mind and to promote sustained focus and attention. With mindfulness exercises, such as the ones described above, you may find your attention wandering multiple times. You do not attempt to force these thoughts out of consciousness. Instead, you accept them as they are and then bring your attention back to whatever you are observing. Through this process of systematically bringing your attention back from your "wandering mind," you are training yourself to become less reactive to your environment, regardless of whether external or internal, *and to enhance your ability to concentrate for greater periods of time.*

This issue with your thinking is an important one. A seemingly endless stream of thoughts goes through our minds. Some thoughts may be rather ridiculous, silly, or judgmental; others may be quite sublime or profound. Some may contain a significant emotional charge. Regardless of which thought occurs or how emotionally charged or important the thoughts may be, during mindfulness exercises, you treat them with equal value. By bringing your attention back to the specific mindfulness exercise in which you are engaged, you are practicing letting go of these thoughts as they enter your consciousness.

With mindful practice, you will find that these various thoughts come into your awareness and then depart. Once you realize that thoughts are just thoughts, this can be quite a liberating experience. You are not your thoughts. They are only thoughts. And mindfulness can prevent the establishment of dysfunctional personal rules or distorted beliefs that are often the cause of considerable emotional distress. Kabat-Zinn referred to this as "liberation from the tyranny of the thinking mind."

White Room Meditation: A critical element to mindfulness involves nonjudgmental awareness. The following exercise, a composite from two mindfulness exercises presented in *Thoughts and Feelings* by McKay, Davis, and Fanning (2011), may prove helpful to neutralize judgmental thoughts. Begin this exercise by closing your eyes and taking several slow, deep breaths. Imagine that you are in an empty, white room. Place yourself anywhere in the room and imagine an open doorway to your left and another open doorway to your right. Past each doorway is only darkness; you are unable to see anything beyond the open door. Imagine now that your thoughts are emerging from the open doorway on your left. As a thought enters your visual field, label it as either judgmental or nonjudgmental. Pay close attention to each thought until it exits the room through the right doorway. All you have to do is to acknowledge it as a thought, judgmental or not. You may find that the thoughts you label as judgmental may try to "hook" you and linger in the room for some time.

The main point of this mindfulness exercise is to be aware of how tenacious judgmental thoughts can be. You can be sure that you are dealing with a difficult, judgmental thought if it remains in the white room or if you find yourself becoming emotional about the thought. Attend to your breathing while you are observing and labeling your thoughts. Be aware that a thought is only a thought. You have had millions of them during your lifetime that are no longer present, but you are still here. Continue to observe your thoughts as they pass through the white room and through the right doorway. Acknowledge each thought as it is and, after it passes, be prepared to observe the next thought. Continue with this process until you feel detached from your thoughts. Keep at it until the judgmental thoughts readily pass through the room.

On-Court Mindfulness Exercises: The "mental aerobic" exercises that Ivan Lendl used during his rise to the top of the tennis world were essentially mindful in nature. Recall that Alexis Castori, in one of the exercises, had Lendl concentrate on a common household object for an increasingly greater period of time in order to develop his powers of concentration. There is one potential limitation of this exercise. Does practice concentrating on some object at home generalize or transfer to where you want it to occur – on the tennis court? This generalization or transfer-of-training issue has plagued researchers in psychological treatment outcome studies for decades. Fortunately, there is an effective way to deal with this: *Do your mindfulness training at the tennis court.*

I have done several variations of this "on-court" training. I went to one of the public tennis courts in Tallahassee during a time when the courts were not in use. I recommend this if you are particularly sensitive to the reactions of others. One time, I assumed a sitting position just behind the center marker on the baseline. I focused my attention, which included touching the area, on an approximately two square inch area of the tennis court, noting its multiple features – color, size, shape, and texture. I was amazed at the variations of color contained in this small segment of the court. I initially did this for one minute and then, over time, increased it to three. Several times, I experienced various thoughts that diverted my attention from the tennis-court segment. I acknowledged these thoughts, allowed them to pass, and then directed my attention back to the court.

I would not, as Castori recommended, describe the features of the observed object out loud. This would appear to have a suppressive effect on the distracting thoughts that invariably occur. It is the process of returning your attention to the object of interest that stabilizes your mind and enhances your powers of concentration.

Another time, I did the same mindfulness exercise with a tennis ball, noting the multiple features of the ball. To more closely simulate the experiences of a tennis match, I stood a foot or two behind the baseline and mindfully observed several aspects of the tennis court in my visual field.

The M-Drill in Threes: The M-Drill, discussed on page 22, involves a warm-up exercise to promote enhanced mobility and footwork. This expanded version also helps with your footwork but is specifically designed to promote greater awareness and concentration. This is how you do it: First, go back and review the details of the M-Drill. Then go to a tennis court and execute the drill while directing your awareness to your breathing. Be aware of the changes in your breathing as you perform all aspects of this drill. Observe if you are breathing through your nose or mouth. Allow yourself several minutes rest after this first round. Perform the M-Drill a second time, but now expand your awareness to include both your breathing and your feet. That is, you are now being aware of your breathing and to the experience of your feet moving through all aspects of this drill. Take another break and then execute the M-Drill a third time, but extend your awareness to include your breathing, feet, and hands. Be aware of the sensations involved with your breathing, feet, and hands as you progress through this exercise. By doing this expanded drill, you are training yourself to be mindful while going through many of the movements that you will execute during an actual tennis match.

Because this drill is physically intense, you may not experience distracting thoughts. If you do, acknowledge the thoughts and let them pass through your consciousness.

Mindfulness is constant awareness. With training, this mindfulness will begin to flow naturally and smoothly. I suspect that when tennis players speak of being in the "zone," they may be referring to playing tennis mindfully.

The typical point of a tennis match rarely lasts more than a minute. If you can train yourself to mindfully pay attention for several minutes on court with the above-noted exercises, you will be ready to concentrate well and effectively during a match.

THE MOST IMPORTANT POINT

"The emperor was not pleased with any of the answers, and no reward was given."

What is the most important point of a tennis match? This appears to be an absurd question. How could anyone specify one particularly crucial point of a match? Several tennis theorists posit a hierarchy of important points. The great Arthur Ashe believed that the first point of a game was critical. He then suggested that the points on the ad side of the court have more importance than those on the deuce side because the players are either in the process of building a lead, getting even, or having an ad or break point.

Brad Gilbert, in his classic book, *Winning Ugly*, advocates a "percentage" approach to the game. He suggests that players need to be aware of those critical, dynamic situations that position them to win a game or set. Every tennis player knows the importance of ad points. Both you and your opponent know this and will (or should) be fully engaged in competitive play. Gilbert persuasively argues that there are key moments during a match that are typically overlooked or under-appreciated by tennis players. These situations, if approached wisely, can have a significant impact on the outcome of a match. Gilbert labels one class of these dynamic situations as "set-up" points. He suggests that you need to be keenly aware of these situations and to focus and concentrate well. The "set-up" points are those (e.g., 30-love, 30-30) that can get you to an ad point. If you can win enough of these "set-up" points, you are positioning yourself to win more games and, ultimately, the match.

Both Ashe's and Gilbert's observations merit serious consideration but they do not help answer the question, "What is *the* most important point of a match?" There appears to be no answer to this question. And yet perhaps there is, and it comes from an unexpected source – Leo Tolstoy, the great Russian writer and author of *War and Peace*, *Anna Karenina*, and other literary classics. In one of his lesser known works, *The Emperor's Three Questions*, Tolstoy provides the answer to this important tennis question. Allow me to retell this short story:

One day it occurred to a certain emperor that if he only knew the answers to three questions, he would never stray in any matter.

What is the best time to do each thing?
Who are the most important people to work with?
What is the most important thing to do at all times?

The emperor issued a decree throughout his kingdom announcing that whoever could answer the questions would receive a great reward. Many who read the decree made their way to the palace at once, each person with a different answer.

In reply to the first question, one person advised that the emperor make up a thorough time schedule, consecrating every hour, day, month, and year for certain tasks and then follow the schedule to the letter. Only then could he hope to do every task at the right time.

Another person replied that it was impossible to plan in advance and that the emperor should put all vain amusements aside and remain attentive to everything in order to know what to do at what time.

Someone else insisted that, by himself, the emperor could never hope to have all the foresight and competence necessary to decide when to do each and every task and what he really needed was to set up a Council of the Wise and then act according to their advice.

Someone else said that certain matters required immediate decision and could not wait for consultation, but if he wanted to know in advance what was going to happen he should consult magicians and soothsayers.

The responses to the second question also lacked accord.

One person said that the emperor needed to place all his trust in administrators, another urged reliance on priests and monks, while others recommended physicians. Still others put their faith in warriors.

The third question drew a similar variety of answers.

Some said science was the most important pursuit. Others insisted on religion. Yet others claimed the most important thing was military skill.

The emperor was not pleased with any of the answers, and no reward was given.

After several nights of reflection, the emperor resolved to visit a hermit who lived up on the mountain and was said to be an enlightened man. The emperor wished to find the hermit to ask him the three questions, though he knew the hermit never left the mountains and was known to receive only the poor, refusing to have anything to do with persons of wealth or power. So the emperor disguised himself as a simple peasant and ordered his attendants to wait for him at the foot of the mountain while he climbed the slope alone to seek the hermit.

Reaching the holy man's dwelling place, the emperor found the hermit digging a garden in front of his hut. When the hermit saw the stranger, he nodded his head in greeting and continued to dig. The labor was obviously hard on him. He was an old man, and each time he thrust his spade into the ground to turn the earth, he heaved heavily.

The emperor approached him and said, "I have come here to ask your help with three questions: What is the best time to do each thing? Who are the most important people to work with? What is the most important thing to do at all times?"

The hermit listened attentively but only patted the emperor on the shoulder and continued digging. The emperor said, "You must be tired. Here, let me give you a hand with that." The hermit thanked him, handed the emperor the spade, and then sat down on the ground to rest.

After he had dug two rows, the emperor stopped and turned to the hermit and repeated his three questions. The hermit still did not answer, but instead stood up and pointed to the spade and said, "Why don't you rest now? I can take over again." But the emperor continued to dig. One hour passed, then two. Finally the sun began to set behind the mountain. The emperor put down the spade and said to the hermit, "I came here to ask if you could answer my three questions. But if you can't give me any answer, please let me know so that I can get on my way home."

The hermit lifted his head and asked the emperor, "Do you hear someone running over there?" The emperor turned his head. They both saw a man with a long white beard emerge from the woods. He ran wildly, pressing his hands against a bloody wound in the stomach. The man ran toward the emperor before falling unconscious to the ground, where he lay groaning. Opening the man's clothing, the emperor and hermit saw that the man received a deep gash. The emperor cleaned the wound thoroughly and then used his own shirt to bandage it, but the blood completely soaked it within minutes. He rinsed the shirt out and bandaged the wound a second time and continued to do so until the flow of blood had stopped.

At last the wounded man regained consciousness and asked for a drink of water. The emperor ran down to the stream and brought back a jug of fresh water. Meanwhile, the sun had disappeared and the night air had begun to turn cold. The hermit gave the emperor a hand in carrying the man into the hut where they laid him down on the hermit's bed. The man closed his eyes and lay quietly. The emperor was worn out from a long day of climbing the mountain and digging the garden. Leaning against the doorway, he fell asleep. When he rose, the sun had already risen over the mountain. For a moment he forgot where he was and what he had come here for. He looked over to the bed and saw the wounded man also looking around him in confusion. When he saw the emperor, he stared at him intently and then said in a faint whisper, "Please forgive me."

"But what have you done that I should forgive you?" the emperor asked.

"You don't know me, your majesty, but I know you. I was your sworn enemy, and I had vowed to take vengeance on you, for during the last war you killed my brother and seized my property. When I learned that you were coming alone to the mountain to meet the hermit, I resolved to surprise you on your way back and kill you. But after waiting a long time there was still no sign of you, and so I left my ambush in order to seek you out. But instead of finding you, I came across your attendants, who recognized me, giving me this wound. Luckily, I escaped and ran here. If I hadn't met you I would surely be dead by now. I had intended to kill you, but instead you saved my life! I am ashamed and grateful beyond words. If I live, I vow to be your servant for the rest of my life, and

I will bid my children and grandchildren to do the same. Please grant me your forgiveness."

The emperor was overjoyed to see that he was so easily reconciled with a former enemy. He not only forgave the man but promised to return all the man's property and to send his own physician and servants to wait on the man until he was completely healed. After ordering his attendants to take the man home, the emperor returned to see the hermit. Before returning to the palace the emperor wanted to repeat his three questions one last time. He found the hermit sowing seeds in the earth they had dug the day before.

The hermit stood up and looked at the emperor. "But your questions have already been answered."

"How's that?" the emperor asked, puzzled.

"Yesterday, if you had not taken pity on my age and given me a hand with digging these beds, you would have been attacked by that man on your way home. Then you would have deeply regretted not staying with me. Therefore the most important time was the time you were digging in the beds, the most important person was myself, and the most important pursuit was to help me. Later, when the wounded man ran up here, the most important time was the time you spent dressing his wound, for if you had not cared for him he would have died and you would have lost the chance to be reconciled with him. Likewise, he was the most important person, and the most important pursuit was taking care of his wound. Remember that there is only one important time and that is now. The present moment is the only time over which we have dominion. The most important person is always the person you are with, who is right before you, for who knows if you will have dealings with any other person in the future? The most important pursuit is making the person standing at your side happy, for that alone is the pursuit of life."

As I transcribe Tolstoy's words, I am filled with awe at the power and simplicity of his message. *The Emperor's Three Questions* is a truly remarkable story. So, returning to tennis, what is *the* most important point of a match? It is the point currently being played. This is the only point, as Tolstoy would say, over which we have dominion. One must be fully engaged and concentrating well for Ashe's critical first point. Likewise, in order to reach Gilbert's "set up" point, you have to win the earlier points. Each point ought to be played well and effectively. But can this be done? Can tennis players focus and concentrate well on each and every point? Ashe and Gilbert are saying that certain points have more value than others, and it is during these key points that one must really concentrate. These writers appear to subscribe to a "reservoir theory" of concentration, suggesting that your supply of concentration is finite and that you need to save some of it for critical points. I would argue that *all* points are critical and need to be approached with maximum concentration. Is this possible?

Before we return to this issue of tennis concentration, I would like to present some little known information about Tolstoy's history. He was the first Russian novelist to mention the game of tennis in one of his works, *Anna Karenina*, first published in 1878. The description of tennis played in Tolstoy's novel suggests that he had at least a rudimentary understanding of the game in that he mentioned rallies and groundstrokes but failed to note other aspects of the game such as serving and scoring. Yale professor Vladimir E. Alexandrov, in an article titled "Tolstoy and Tennis," reported that "it is hard to think of another great writer who was as capable of grand contradictions as Tolstoy." For instance, Tolstoy became a passionate tennis player yet also dismissed the game "as a pastime of the idle rich." It appears that Tolstoy began playing tennis in 1896 when he was sixty-eight years old. One can almost imagine a family member or friend saying the Russian equivalent of "Hey Leo, wanna hit some?" Upon the first strike of the ball, Tolstoy was hooked. He was a tennis convert. According to entries in his wife's diary and from reports of select visitors to his estate during the summer of 1897, Tolstoy often played tennis for two to three hours per day. No opponent could rival his enthusiasm for the game. Tolstoy's guests and family members took turns facing him across the net. With his long beard and searing gaze, he would have been a formidable-looking opponent. He might have given Reginald Doherty, the 1897 Wimbledon champion, a match. And you can bet that Tolstoy would have been fully in the moment, concentrating well on each and every point.

HOW LONG CAN YOU CONCENTRATE?

How many times have you heard these lines? "He won the match because he was mentally stronger than his opponent"; He had a mental edge over the rest of the players"; or "Matches all come down to the mental part of the game." Now, what exactly is this mental part of the game, and does it reside in some non-physical world of consciousness? It seems to me that when tennis players talk about the mental aspects, they are typically referring to two primary areas. One involves the capacity to control negative thoughts and emotions to promote sustained attention and concentration. The other involves the formulation and execution of strategic plans.

Some suggest that the tennis greats have the capacity to concentrate at maximum intensity for hours at a time. Allen Fox stated, "All the great professionals have tremendous willpower and concentration. They can play every point at 100 percent efficiency for four or five hours." Do select tennis players have some innate ability to concentrate more effectively than others? Is this another one of those Galton you've either got-it-or-you-don't issues? Perhaps their concentration "reservoir" is larger than that of the weekend hacker.

In my view, concentration is another form of behavior that can be shaped and improved. With practice and training, one can learn to concentrate well. But, *and this is a key point*, the training must take into consideration the structure of a tennis match involving alternating periods of vigorous activity and rest.

Tennis players are aware that the duration of a match can be long, with some professional matches lasting in excess of five hours. And even at the club level, matches are occasionally played for three hours or longer. That is a significant amount of time to maintain one hundred percent concentration.

Here is the good news. Tennis players rarely have to concentrate for more than forty-five minutes. Jeff Greenwald, author of *The Best Tennis of Your Life: 50 Mental Strategies for Fearless Performance*, noted that in a typical two-set match, the ball is in play for only *eighteen minutes*. If you think about this for a minute, Greenwald's observation has revolutionary implications for mental and physical training. Although this will be discussed in more detail below, the basic idea is to gear one's mental training for these critical eighteen or so minutes.

I tested Greenwald's assertion by taking data from five matches. The Florida State University men's and women's tennis team provided data for three matches. The collegiate matches used a 10-point tie break in lieu of a third set. A fourth match was observed at the 10th Annual Rosemary Beach Open (2014) in Rosemary Beach, Florida, involving the semifinals of the men's open division. Finally, I took data from the 2014 French Open men's final between Rafael Nadal and Novak Djokovic.

So off I went, stopwatch in hand, to observe the five matches. One, of course, only involved sitting in front of the television set. I recorded the duration of time that the ball was actually in play. Here are the data from the five matches:

1. The first match was held on February 28, 2014 and involved a women's match between Florida State University (FSU) and Georgia Tech (GT). Megan Kurey of GT defeated Daniela Schippers of FSU 6-3, 7-5. The ball was in play for *19 minutes and 46 seconds.*

2. The second match occurred on March 1, 2014 that involved a men's match between Florida State University and University of South Florida (USF). Marco Nunez of FSU defeated Vadym Kalyuzhnyy of USF 6-1, 6-4. The ball was in play for *13 minutes and 26 seconds.*

3. The Florida State Women's tennis team played the University of Pittsburgh (Pitt) on April 13, 2014. Amanda Wickman of Pitt defeated Majlena Pedersen of FSU 3-6, 6-3, 1-0. The ball was in play for *19 minutes and 15 seconds.*

4. A semifinal match between Tyler Marengo and Michael Matisons at the Rosemary Beach Open in Rosemary Beach, Florida occurred on May 3, 2014. Marengo defeated Matisons 6-7, 6-1, 6-0. The ball was in play for *19 minutes and 18 seconds.*

5. The most grueling tournament in the world is the French Open. To win this event, you have to prevail, over a two-week period, against some of the best "dirt" players in the world. And the best dirt player in history is, undoubtedly, Rafael Nadal. The 2014 French Open final pitted Nadal against Novak Djokovic, who was gunning for his first French Open title. Nadal defeated Djokovic in four sets 3-6,

7-5, 6-2, 6-4 to secure his ninth title at Roland Garros. Although the match lasted three hours and thirty minutes, the ball was in play for only *27 minutes and 23 seconds.*

Data from these five matches supported Greenwald's position. There is only a limited amount of time during which the ball is actually in play. Given this reality, what is the most effective way to approach this concentration issue? Sustaining maximum concentration is challenging even on a time-limited basis. Fortunately, we are only talking about brief periods of concentration lasting a few seconds to, at most, several minutes. There are, of course, some outlier situations. For instance, during a women's professional match played in 1984 between Vicky Nelson and Jean Hepner, one point lasted 29 minutes and involved the ball passing over the net 643 times. Nelson won the match 6-4, 7-6.

The typical point, fortunately, is relatively short, and the tennis player needs to be acutely aware of and prepared for three distinct phases of a tennis match—the point itself, the 25-second period between points, and the 90-second changeover. With sufficient mindfulness practice, the player will be equipped to concentrate well, effectively, and non-judgmentally for every point. But how do you handle the time period between points and during the changeover?

TAKE A CAT NAP

Recall that the most skilled performers in the "Great Violin Study" took a 20-minute restorative afternoon nap to maintain their deliberate-practice regimen. Ivan Lendl was also a dedicated practitioner of the restorative nap to recover from his austere training program. Now, is it possible to take a nap during a match? I can see it now. Inform your opponent that you are going to take a quick, 20-minute nap and then drag a mattress out to the court for a snooze. By the time you're finished, you will be refreshed and ready for the next point. Alright, so this is a little impractical. But the concept is a good one and has been discussed in the sports psychology literature as "*periodization*," which involves alternating periods of intense, focused activity with periods of rest.

Jim Loehr and Tony Schwartz (2003) reported that periodization was first articulated by Flavius Philostratus in his work with Greek athletes approximately 2,000 years ago. The Russian sports establishment used the concept to great success with their Olympic athletes in the 1960s.

The 20-minute nap for the violinists in Ericsson's 1993 study allowed them to recover in order to return to their intense training regimen. Lendl applied the same principle for his training program. Periodization is also routinely used for longer periods of time to allow athletes to recover from months of intensive training. Some suggest a recovery period of two to four weeks in which athletes would not engage in competitive play or training in order to sufficiently recover in preparation for their next phase of competitive activity. The capacity to balance high performance with sufficient rest is critical for the competitive athlete, but few do this well.

Jim Loehr, noted sports psychologist, wanted to discern the factors that differentiated the elite professional tennis players from the rest of the field. Despite spending hundreds of hours watching the various tour players, he was unable to detect any differences in how they comported themselves during points. It was only when he studied the interval *between* points that it became clear how the elite tennis players were different from the others. He found that the elites used a personalized recovery ritual between points. Part of this involved their physical posture, breathing patterns, how they focused their attention, and their self-talk. The lower-ranked players had no such routines. The best players, in short, were maximizing their recovery between points. When Dr. Loehr took some physiological data of the best players during the time period between points, he found that their heart rates dropped substantially by twenty beats per minute. The heart rates of lesser players often remained high during the same period. Thus, the elites were able to experience a brief period of physiological "rest" between points played whereas the others did not experience such a recovery. Over the course of a match, players who are able to experience these multiple, brief recovery periods will have a distinct competitive advantage.

I propose extending Jim Loehr's pioneering work by specifying how to induce this recovery period between tennis points. Thus, you will be able to maximize the capacity for sustained concentration during a point by taking a brief "nap" during the 25-second period between points. In this case, the "nap" will involve a brief period of relaxation. This allows you to sufficiently recover from the previous point and be fully engaged for the next point. I refer to this as "*micro-periodization*." The concept is the same: alternate periods of intense, focused activity with periods of rest.

Continued practice with the mindfulness exercises discussed earlier will equip you with a powerful tool for sustained concentration during a particular point. Because the ball is typically in play for no longer than a *total* of twenty minutes, you will be able to maintain this optimum level of concentration during actual match play.

There are several ways to induce the relaxation response during the 25 seconds between points. I recommend two methods: diaphragmatic breathing and progressive relaxation.

1. **Diaphragmatic Breathing**: This type of breathing can be mastered with relatively limited training and is readily portable to any situation, including a tennis match. You can breathe in two ways – one involves breathing from the chest and the other from the diaphragm. With chest breathing, the chest and rib cage will expand and contract with each inhalation and exhalation. Diaphragmatic breathing involves the expansion and contraction of the abdomen. The distinction between these two types of breathing is important. One type (chest breathing) is associated with stress, tension, and anxiety. In contrast, the other (diaphragmatic breathing) induces a state of *attentive relaxation.*

    When you breathe from the chest you are stimulating the sympathetic branch of the autonomic nervous system. This is the branch stimulated during threatening, "fight-or-flight" situations and can produce many of the common symptoms of anxiety including pounding heart, sweating, feeling unsteady or dizzy, shortness of breath, restlessness, and *difficulty concentrating*. Rapid, shallow chest breathing also occurs when hyperventilating.

If you want to maintain your "cool," breathe from the diaphragm. With diaphragmatic, abdominal breathing you are stimulating the parasympathetic branch of the autonomic nervous system. This is the branch that produces the bodily sensations associated with relaxation.

The diaphragm is a rather large piece of muscle that is attached to the lower part of the rib cage. The diaphragm separates the chest from the abdomen. The overall process of breathing involves air entering the lungs as the diaphragm contracts (inhalation) and is expelled as the diaphragm relaxes (exhalation). Whenever the muscles in your abdomen are taut, the diaphragm will meet a considerable amount of resistance when it contracts; this results in shallow, chest breathing.

An excellent way to experience diaphragmatic breathing is to assume a comfortable sitting position. Place one hand on your abdomen and the other on your chest. Begin breathing from the abdomen. The hand on your abdomen should rise when you inhale and fall as you exhale. The hand on your chest should be motionless. Gradually slow the pace of your inhalations and exhalations while also deepening your breaths until you reach a comfortable level.

At select times during the day, become aware of your breathing and practice breathing diaphragmatically. Do this while you are sitting or walking. I have practiced diaphragmatic breathing during slow jogging. Once you become proficient at inducing diaphragmatic breathing, you are ready to apply it during the "resting" moments of a tennis match.

At the conclusion of a given point, implement diaphragmatic breathing. This will allow you to attain a state of focused relaxation, thus providing maximal recovery from the previous point. You are relaxed, attentive, and focused for the next point. Use this time wisely and productively. Let your opponent breathe from the chest and remain stressed and tense. After a particularly vigorous point, I find myself breathing primarily from the chest. After a few seconds I can productively shift to diaphragmatic breathing and achieve a state of attentive relaxation prior to the next point.

2. **Progressive Relaxation**: This is probably the most effective and well-researched method of inducing relaxation. I recommend this approach for those who have the time to commit to the process, which typically involves ten weekly sessions. The primary goal of progressive relaxation, as it relates tennis, is to develop the ability to induce relaxation following each point. In this way, the player experiences a brief recovery period between points.

The material presented in this section of the book is only an introduction and is abstracted from a guidebook written by Bernstein, Borkovec, and Hazlett-Stevens (2000). This section is not intended as a "how-to" manual. To be done well and effectively, progressive relaxation requires the guidance and expertise of a skilled behavioral or cognitive-behavioral therapist.

The development of the progressive relaxation procedure dates back to 1908 with the work of the eminent Harvard physiologist, Dr. Edmund Jacobson. Jacobson noted that tension and anxiety were the result of muscle fiber contractions. He reasoned that one could reduce tension and anxiety by relaxing muscle fibers. His technique for achieving this involved sequentially tensing and then relaxing dozens of muscle groups throughout the body.

As with any skill, learning to relax requires practice. The more you practice, the better you will become at relaxing. Everyone has some level of tension during their waking hours. Each of us has a specific tension "adaptation level," which refers to the degree of tension that we experience during the day. For some, this adaptation level may be relatively low; for others, it can be quite high.

Lowering muscle tension has multiple benefits including the reduction in heart rate, breathing rate, and other sensations that occur when one becomes tense or anxious. Another benefit, of particular importance to tennis players, is that inducing relaxation allows their thoughts to slow down and become clear and rational. This is particularly important for players who want to maintain optimal concentration during point play.

The primary goal of progressive muscle relaxation is to produce large and noticeable reductions in tension level. This is accomplished by initially creating a significant amount of tension in a particular muscle group and then by releasing the tension all at once. By systematically doing so, the amount of tension drops well below one's adaptation level.

Progressive relaxation begins with sixteen muscle groups to be tensed and relaxed. The sixteen muscle groups are, for a right-hand dominant person, listed below:

1. Right hand and forearm
2. Right biceps
3. Left hand and forearm
4. Left biceps
5. Forehead
6. Eyes and nose
7. Mouth, jaw, and cheeks
8. Neck
9. Chest, back, and shoulders
10. Abdomen
11. Right upper leg
12. Right calf
13. Right foot
14. Left upper leg
15. Left calf
16. Left foot

The basic procedure for the tense-relax cycle is as follows: The therapist directs the trainee's attention to the muscle group to be tensed. The trainee then tenses the muscle group for a period of 5-7 seconds. During the tensing period, the therapist directs the trainee to attend to the sensations associated with tensing the muscle group. The therapist then directs the trainee to release the tension and to notice the sensations as the muscle group relaxes. The therapist continues making comments for approximately 30 seconds directing the trainee's attention to the unfolding relaxation process. The same muscle group is then tensed and relaxed a second time. Thus, each of the sixteen muscle groups goes through the above process two times.

As the trainee becomes proficient with this tensing and relaxing procedure, the number of muscle groups is reduced to seven and then four. Progressing from the sixteen to the four muscle group procedure takes approximately seven sessions.

The therapist then proceeds to *relaxation by recall* where the trainee is directed to recall what the relaxed state was like and attempts to achieve that state for the four muscle group unit without the tense-relax cycle.

Once the trainee achieves recall proficiency, the therapist adds a counting procedure during which the therapist counts from one to ten while the trainee is instructed to become even more relaxed as the count proceeds.

The next stage involves relaxation by counting alone. At this point, the therapist counts from one to ten, instructing the trainee to become more relaxed on each count. The trainee should now be able to achieve a state of deep relaxation within approximately one minute.

One important goal of progressive relaxation is to make the procedure portable, for use in daily life, and this involves two additional procedures – differential relaxation and conditioned relaxation. With differential relaxation, the goal is to remain relaxed in those muscles *not* required for some ongoing activity. This is achieved in a step-wise manner, progressing from relatively quiet, solitary activities to situations involving more active behaviors. Even during match play, there are some muscles that do not need to be tense. If you can remain relaxed in those select muscle groups while playing, you can more effectively direct your energies to the task at hand.

Conditioned relaxation is particularly important for the micro-periodization issue. The goal of conditioned relaxation is to produce a relaxed state to a self-produced cue. You can do this by pairing a word such as "relax" or "calm" as you exhale during diaphragmatic breathing. Conditioned relaxation is typically introduced early in the progressive relaxation process to allow the individual sufficient practice in pairing this sub-vocalized cue with a relaxed state.

Diaphragmatic breathing alone or in combination with progressive relaxation allows for a powerful way to apply the periodization issue during a tennis match. There is no need to be intensely focused during the total duration of a match. The goal is to focus and concentrate well *while the ball is in play.* At the conclusion of a point, use these relaxation skills to recover in preparation for the next point. I also recommend using relaxation skills during the changeover to continue this recovery process. In this way, you are saving your energies for optimal concentration during actual match play.

USE YOUR IMAGINATION

Walter Isaacson, in his celebrated 2007 biography, *Einstein: His life and Universe,* chronicled that the sixteen-year-old Albert Einstein enrolled in a school in the village of Aarau, Switzerland. This school emphasized creative thinking by using intuition and visual imagery. The students were encouraged to visualize images to understand the laws of physics and math. This school was a perfect fit for the rebellious Einstein, who once asserted, "Blind respect for authority is the greatest enemy of truth." While at this school, Einstein began his quest to discern the laws of the universe by imagining the experience of riding alongside a light beam. His general theory of relativity was developed, in part, through visual imagery.

Einstein was apparently onto something. Visual imagery can be helpful to tennis players as well. After all, tennis players are a pretty intelligent bunch. A review of the sports psychology literature on visual imagery indicates that rehearsing a visual image, known as *imaginal rehearsal,* can boost athletic performance.

Imagery is typically viewed as a mental process. I prefer to view imagery as another form of behavior, albeit private in nature. To borrow a phrase from Tom Borkovec, imagery is *incipient action.* Imagery is action in development. That is, when you imagine a particular athletic skill, you are engaging in private behavior toward the overt performance of that skill. And because imagery is private, it is readily portable.

Here is a wonderful story that captures the power of imaginal rehearsal. Major James Nesmith was an American prisoner of war in Vietnam, held in solitary confinement for seven years. In order to cope with the tedium and stress of confinement, he played a complete round of golf in his mind every day, incorporating as much detail as possible into his imaginal round. Each "mental" round took approximately five hours. He imagined taking his golf clubs from the closet, counting the number of clubs in his bag, checking his golf balls, and doing all the things necessary to play a round of golf. He imagined the smallest detail with as much clarity as possible. He imagined various weather conditions, the manicured greens, the types of trees and other vegetation on the course, and the feel of the grip of the clubs. Following a drive, he watched the trajectory of the ball and how it would bounce down the fairway. He heard the chirping of birds and insects. He imagined and felt every step as he progressed along the course. And he did this five hours a day, seven days a week, for seven years - a tribute to human ingenuity and survival.

Following his release from captivity and return to the United States, Nesmith returned to his home course to play an "actual" round of golf. Before his prisoner of war experience, and extensive imaginal rehearsal, his typical golf score was in the low 90s. Can you guess what happened when he played his first real round of golf in over seven years? He went out and shot a 74.

Jack Nicklaus, widely recognized as the greatest golfer in the history of the game, was a strong advocate of imaginal rehearsal. He stated, "I never hit a shot, even in practice, without having a very sharp, in-focus picture of it in my head. It's like a color movie. First I 'see' the ball where I want to finish. Then the scene quickly changes and I 'see' the ball going there. Then there's a sort of fade-out, and the next scene shows me making the kind of swing that will turn the previous images into reality."

Imaginal rehearsal involves the use of imagery to rehearse or practice a particular skill. Sports psychologists have delineated two broad types of imaginal rehearsal. One involves **external imagery**. This is where an athlete views himself performing a particular athletic skill as though watching the performance on a YouTube video clip. Consider the following: The score is 4-4 in the third set. You are serving at 30-30. Now, you see yourself walking to the baseline and positioning yourself about a yard to the right of the center marker. You are wearing black tennis shorts, a white t-shirt, white socks, white tennis shoes with a red trim, and a blue sweatband on your right wrist. You place your left foot just behind the baseline. Your right foot is approximately 24 inches behind at about a 45 degree angle to the baseline. You briefly glance at your opponent and then begin your service motion. You see yourself executing a perfect toss with the racket head going into the "back scratch" position. You bend your knees and then uncoil your body while extending the racket to hit a heavily sliced ball to the corner of the deuce court and singles sideline.

The other type of imaginal rehearsal involves **internal imagery**. This is where you imagine being inside your body and experiencing the sensations that most likely will occur while executing a particular sports skill. Now, consider this imaginal scene: The score is 4-4 in the third set. You are serving at 30-30. Initially you are breathing heavily and your heart is still pounding from the effort exerted during the previous point. You quickly shift to diaphragmatic breathing and, as you feel your abdomen rising and falling, your heart rate begins to slow. The air is hot and humid. You feel your sweat-soaked t-shirt sticking to your body. You can feel the texture of the only dry spot on your shorts as you attempt to wipe the sweat from your right hand. You approach the baseline and position yourself about a yard to the right of the center marker. You feel the leathery grain of the racket grip in your hand. You briefly glance at your opponent, who has assumed the ready position to return serve. As you begin your service motion, you can feel the tension in your right thigh as you transfer your weight to your right leg. You feel the ball leaving your left hand as you execute a perfect toss. You feel the tension in your right shoulder as your racket assumes the "back scratch" position. You experience the bending of your knees. You again feel the tension in your right shoulder as you uncoil your body and extend your racket to hit a heavily sliced ball. You hear a "ping" as your racket makes contact with the ball. You watch the ball strike at the corner of the deuce court and singles sideline and continue its wide-left trajectory.

As you read these two imaginal scenes, which seemed more "real," as though you were actually on the court serving? If you are like most people, it was the second scene. There appears to be a preference among top athletes to use internal imagery. Sports psychologists suggest that internal imagery may lead to enhanced performance results because it generates kinesthetic feedback for the athlete. Kinesthetic awareness, or getting the feel, appears to be important for the acquisition or execution of a particular sports skill. So, imagine the feel of a perfectly hit serve.

There are two dimensions of imaginal rehearsal that merit some discussion – **vividness and controllability**. Vividness refers to the clarity of the image. I suspect that some readers of this book are able to create vivid images that seem life-like. Others may only be able to initially create a rather vague image with few details. With focused practice, most can develop a clear and vivid image. Incorporating as many of the five senses – seeing, hearing, kinesthesis or "feel," taste, and smell – into your imagery can improve the quality of your imaginal rehearsal. Seeing, hearing, and kinesthesis are typically used in tennis imagery but, if you are creative enough, all five senses could be used.

One of my most salient tennis memories involved the sense of smell. Prior to the 1970s, tennis balls were packed in pressurized metal cans. There was a small "key" soldered to the bottom of the can. You had to tear off the key and use it to open the can as though you were opening an old tin of sardines. As you began to turn the key, there was this wonderful hissing noise and pungent odor of Dacron, nylon, and wool. You just don't get the same thrill with modern-day tennis balls.

The other dimension of imagery rehearsal is controllability, which refers to the ability to control the outcome of the image. Returning to the tennis serve imagery, an example of low controllability would be imagining dumping the serve in the net or hitting it long. A service image with high controllability would be imagining a well-executed and effective serve.

I suggest the following for developing your tennis imagery. Tennis is not like golf, where you could, as in the Major Nesmith account, imagine a sequence of shots for an entire round. Tennis involves a reciprocal relationship with your opponent. During rallies, your next shot is, in part, dependent on your opponent's previous shot. It is difficult to use imaginal rehearsal in this situation because you cannot regularly anticipate your opponent's next shot. It might be a crosscourt to your backhand, a moonball to your forehand, or a drop shot.

The two areas in tennis where imaginal rehearsal can be used to great effectiveness involve the serve and footwork. Serving is obvious. This is the one area in which you are in total control. Nobody is rushing you. You have part of the twenty-five-second "inter-point interval" in which to productively use imagery. I recommend two types of service imagery: (1) a detailed scene that you can use off-court, while at home or during a particularly boring meeting at work. Practice these at your leisure and use different types of serves – slice, flat, or kick; and (2) an abbreviated version of the image for use on the court. Focus on the salient features of the serve for on-court use including a well-executed toss, fluid service motion, explosive power at contact, and the service target – out wide, down the middle, or jamming your opponent. The image can be brief. For instance, I will use service imagery a few seconds before I begin my service motion.

The other area for imaginal rehearsal is footwork. Again, have a detailed version for use off-court and an abbreviated on-court version. Use part of the changeover to use imaginal footwork.

Take some time to develop a well-crafted image for the serve and footwork. Go to the court and bring something with which to take notes. Hit a few serves. Be mindful of the components and physical sensations involved in hitting a serve. Take detailed notes. Then craft your imaginal scene. Practice imagining the off-court and on-court scenes until you achieve a high level of vividness and controllability. Repeat this process for imaginal footwork.

THE iPLAN

"The emphasis is on process, not outcome."

What's your iPlan? The individualized plan, or iPlan, is the formulation of a strategic plan for a particular opponent; it is a set of strategic guidelines. The iPlan is flexible because changes may be necessary as a match progresses. It can be simple or relatively complex given your current skill level. If you are a beginner, your iPlan could be as simple as "Keep the ball in play." These plans can increase in complexity as your skill level improves.

Probably the most entertaining and succinct iPlan in tennis history belongs to John Sadri. Sadri played for the North Carolina State Wolfpack during the latter part of the 1970s. He sported a Mohawk haircut, which gave him a rather intimidating on-court presence. Sadri was scheduled to play John McEnroe in the finals of the 1978 NCAA tennis championships.

I recall reading a newspaper article in which the reporter asked Sadri what plan he had for McEnroe. Sadri replied, "Boom, boom. I'm going to boom my serve and boom my return." Not exactly a nuanced plan - the cave man approach to tennis. And it almost worked. McEnroe won 7-6, 7-6, 5-7, 7-6. The total point differential was one (McEnroe, 144; Sadri, 143). Some contend that this was the greatest match in NCAA history. Sadri went on to play professional tennis and achieved a career-high ranking of fourteen in the world in 1980. He lost to Guillermo Vilas in the finals of the 1979 Australian Open.

The iPlan incorporates the concepts of acceptance and mindfulness. It is flexible and subject to change. The player maintains a here-and-now focus during a match. The emphasis is on process, not outcome.

Ideally, develop an iPlan following an analysis of your opponent's game. If your opponent is someone you play on a regular basis, this is easy to do. With someone you have never played before, do some scouting. Note the player's strengths and weaknesses and think about how you can use your game to neutralize your opponent's strengths and exploit their weaknesses. If you are playing someone for the first time and have not had the opportunity to see them play, your initial scouting will be limited to the warm-up. Observe which stroke they prefer, backhand or forehand. Observe their footwork and court movement. Some players move well side-to-side but are not particularly facile moving forward or backward. Note for any "quirks" in their game - ground-strokes, overheads, or volleys. Keep a mental note on these and exploit during critical stages of the match.

Fortunately, the majority of tennis players may be classified into one of these categories: the pusher, the serve-volley player, the basher, and the all-court player. A generic iPlan can be formulated for these types of players until you can obtain some on-court data to customize your plan to a specific opponent.

THE PUSHER

A sadist is one who derives pleasure from the suffering of others. A pusher is the tennis equivalent of a sadist. Every competitive tennis player has had the wonderful experience of playing a pusher. A pusher is the tennis player who camps out at or behind the baseline and hits everything back. A variant of the pusher is the moonballer, who hits high-arcing balls deep into the court with heavy topspin. The pusher or moonballer conveys the attitude that he will be on the court for hours, if necessary, in order to win. Like the sadist, the pusher enjoys watching his opponents suffer.

It is important to be mindful of what's happening on the court when playing a pusher. There are two serious mistakes you can make. One is to become lulled into the pusher's style of play. Since there is so little variation in the pusher's game, one experiences a narrowing of attention like that of driving on a long, boring stretch of highway. Before you know it, you are pushing with the pusher. The problem is the pusher is better at pushing than you are. The other mistake is to go for too good of a shot. Although you may actually make a few of these, the odds of doing this on a sustained basis are low. The pusher knows that you will increase your unforced error rate with this strategy. It's almost as if the pusher is challenging you to hit more angled and difficult shots.

There is a variant of the pusher that requires some discussion before going into the details of the iPlan - the junkballer. These guys are mutant pushers. There is nothing orthodox about their game. Their grips are weird. Their groundstrokes are weird. They have weird serves. They probably even sleep weird. They slice, dink, chop, lob, and occasionally hit these strangely angled, slithering shots that die on contact with the court surface. And not only does the ball keep coming back to you, it routinely comes back with a weird spin. The junkballer is rarely seen in the professional ranks, but you will see them at the club level.

In 1996, I played in a tournament in San Luis Obispo, California and had just won my quarterfinal match. As my opponent, a former mayor of Paso Robles and a good tennis player, and I were walking off the court, we briefly observed the other quarterfinal contestants. The former mayor looked at one of the players and said, "If you play that guy tomorrow, you are going to kill him." I watched him for a few minutes and then started to experience a queasy feeling in my stomach. All of his strokes were unorthodox, he was extremely fast, and he kept the ball in play. He won most of the points I watched. Well, he won his quarterfinal match easily, and I played him the next day. And it was a long one. He sliced, diced, and chopped. He ran down almost all of my shots. He was a great lobber. He also had this irritating habit of shouting out "Yes!" when I made a mistake. I became stubborn and decided that if I needed four hours to beat him, I would do it. The match ended up taking over three and a half hours. I served and volleyed and chipped and charged the net on his serve. I hit numerous overheads and ran down many lobs. I finally prevailed 7-5, 4-6, 7-5, but I was exhausted. I distinctly remember thinking at one point during the third set, "What am I doing out here? I'm not sure this is worth it." Between my opponent's game and his gamesmanship, I was not having fun. So, this is what you contend with when playing a pusher or junkballer. It can be an extremely frustrating experience.

iPlan # 1: The Pusher

1. Recognize that there is no easy way to defeat the pusher. Be prepared to play for several hours.
2. Be mindful of your emotional reactions. If you become frustrated or irritated, note these emotional responses and let them pass. Focus on your iPlan.
3. Pushers enjoy playing at a slow, steady pace. Selectively speed up play. Take less time between points without disrupting your own rhythm. Disrupt the pusher's rhythm.
4. Maneuver the pusher to hit shots they don't enjoy. Getting to the net is another form of speeding-up play. This forces the pusher to have to make quick decisions about which shot to hit - a passing shot or lob. Take the pusher's serve and attack the net. Do this on the second serve and sometimes on the first.
5. Bring the pusher to net with drop shots or with low, sliced balls that land in front of the service line. Pushers don't enjoy volleying, and they don't want to generate their own pace. By doing this, you have placed the pusher in foreign territory. The pusher's volley is often comical. Occasionally return the pusher's serve with a drop shot.
6. Finally, as a surprise maneuver, lob off the pusher's serve. This is another way to throw the pusher out of synch and afford you the opportunity to approach the net just as the pusher is returning the lob.

This particular iPlan maximizes your control on the court. Enjoy watching the pusher suffer.

THE SERVE-VOLLEY PLAYER

The serve-volley player introduces a whole different set of dynamics. He is approaching the net and placing pressure on you to make quick decisions with respect to shot selection. His goal is to quickly finish the point. Most serve-volley players will look for opportunities to approach the net on your serve as well. They tend to play at a fast pace.

iPlan # 2: The serve-volley player

1. Be mindful of your emotional reactions to the serve-volley player. Standard reactions are feeling rushed and pressured. Alter the dynamics of the match by slowing down the pace of play.

2. Hit low, soft returns at his feet. This forces the serve-volley player to hit up on the ball. Don't rush the return of serve or passing shots. Relax and take a good swing at the ball. Direct your attention to the ball and not to the opponent.

3. Vary your service returns. Hit the majority crosscourt to limit the serve-volley player's angle but occasionally hit the return down-the-line.

4. Take the serve and sporadically chip and charge the net.

5. If you are able to execute this, hit a lob return of serve. Do this only selectively. This presents another "look" to the serve-volley player and prevents him from closing the net too tightly. Lob over his backhand side.

This particular iPlan maximizes the control you have on the court against this type of player. Instead of being under constant pressure from this attacking style of play, you are forcing the serve-volley player out of his "comfort zone."

Drill, Baby, Drill: There are three traditional options when your opponent is at the net. You can pass down the line, pass crosscourt, or lob. In addition, there is a fourth option. Some contend that it is legitimate to "drill" a shot right at the net man. By doing this you give the net player another thing to think about. It is difficult to execute a volley off of one's navel. And, more often than not, the net man will attempt to hit an out ball drilled right at him due to some "reflexive" action.

Ivan Lendl was a proponent and dedicated practitioner of this fourth option. When Ivan was playing in the early 1980s, he realized that he was losing too many points because the net man was anticipating where Ivan was going to hit the passing shot. During one point of a match, Ivan mishit a crosscourt shot that went right at the net man. He jammed his opponent with this shot and won the point. This was, fortuitously for Lendl, one of those Darwinian, natural-selection-in-action issues on the tennis court. Ivan had created a highly effective tennis "mutation" that he used to great effectiveness. This shot had a prominent place in his tennis arsenal. When one of his opponent's took the net, Ivan would occasionally aim the shot at the right side of the opponent's stomach and then hit the ball with great velocity. As every net player knows, this is a very difficult shot to handle. And this strategy had interesting consequences on several occasions. Lendl actually physically "decked" John McEnroe and Vitas Gerulaitis with this type of play.

Select players may argue that this approach violates some aspect of tennis etiquette. I don't think so. Lendl is correct about this issue. If an opponent takes the net, he should be prepared to deal with this very effective reply. My advice to you is this: drill, baby, drill.

THE BASHER

This is the player who is either on speed or brings a large cup of Starbucks coffee to the court. The basher talks fast, moves fast, and usually won't sit during the changeover. His goal is to complete the match in record time. He loves to "bash" his groundstrokes and move his opponent from one side of the court to another. If you hit hard, the basher will hit harder. Some bashers will use the "quick serve," forcing the opponent to return the serve before they are fully prepared to do so.

I played a basher during a 4.5 flex singles league in Tallahassee. My opponent was an excellent player and probably flirting with a NTRP 5.0 rating. He had a Nadal-type forehand and loved to pound it. And he did so with great regularity. Fortunately, I was able to do some scouting before I was scheduled to play him the following week. His opponent was a good player with solid groundstrokes and a penetrating serve. Curiously, he directed many groundstrokes to the basher's forehand. They got locked into this slugfest, which was distinctly to the basher's advantage. The basher destroyed his opponent 6-1, 6-1.

Several key elements emerged from this scouting session. The basher hit some of his backhands with a slice that had a tendency to float. One point proved especially helpful in developing my iPlan for the basher. During a rally, the basher's opponent mishit a forehand. It was this low-paced, sliced junk ball that landed approximately three feet in front of the service line to the basher's forehand side. The basher netted the ball because he had difficulty handling the slice and slow pace.

This is the key to defeating the basher. The basher does not like to move forward and generate pace. I incorporated this into my iPlan for the following week's match. Even though I lost the match 6-3, 6-4, the strategy was correct. The basher became frustrated with the low-paced junk to his forehand. I attacked his backhand whenever possible. I served and volleyed on occasion. The basher had, however, too much speed, power, and youth. After all, he was thirty years younger than I.

The 1975 Wimbledon final between Jimmy Connors and Arthur Ashe proves instructive in how to play the basher. Jimmy Connors, the "brash basher from Belleville," was a tennis juggernaut in 1974. He won three Grand Slams that year and most likely would have won a fourth had he not been prevented from playing in the French Open. Because he had signed a contract to play World Team Tennis, both the Association of Tennis Professionals (ATP) and the French Tennis Federation opposed his playing at the French Open. In fact, all entries to the French Open from World Team Tennis players were rejected that year. Had Connors been allowed to play, he probably would have joined Don Budge and Rod Laver in winning all four slams in a calendar year. Interestingly, Bjorn Borg won the first of his six French Open titles in 1974. Could Borg have defeated Connors that year? I don't think so. Connors had a definite edge on Borg until 1977.

Connors's tennis dominance continued into 1975. He had little trouble reaching the 1975 Wimbledon final. He destroyed Roscoe Tanner in the semis 6-4, 6-1, 6-4. It was looking bleak for Ashe. With the assistance of Donald Dell and Dennis Ralston, the cerebral Ashe formulated a game plan to neutralize Connors's game. And effective it was. Connors, I believe, never knew what hit him. Ashe served and volleyed extremely well. But it was the strategy of hitting low-paced junk to Connors's forehand that was particularly effective. Ashe gave Connors few balls to bash. Connors was forced to move forward and generate his own pace. Connors made many errors. Ashe triumphed 6-1, 6-1, 5-7, 6-3. For anyone interested in developing strategic tennis plans, this match is a must to watch. Ashe executed the plan brilliantly. Connors continued with his remarkable career, but Ashe had found the chink in Connors's tennis armor. Connors never recaptured the degree of dominance he had over the other players following this Wimbledon final.

iPlan # 3: The Basher

1. The player's typical emotional response to the basher is one of feeling overwhelmed. The basher is playing fast and crushing the ball. There is a pull to "bash back," to hit the ball harder than the basher. This is exactly what the basher wants you to do. Don't do this.

2. Slow down. Take the allotted amount of time between points and during the changeover. This can aggravate the basher. He will give you this look, conveying the message, "Are you ready yet?"

3. Hit short, low-paced balls at or in front of the service line, preferably toward the middle of the court. Bashers do not enjoy generating their own power. They prefer to feed off your power.

4. Keep the basher off balance with a variety of shots, like serve and volley, short-angled balls, and lobs. Throw in a lob during a rally. Give the basher everything he hates to hit. Finesse is the key to defeating the basher.

The All-Court Player

The all-court player presents with no apparent weaknesses. He can play steady from the baseline. He can serve and volley. His overheads are solid. His game is nuanced and flexible. The all-court player typically resides at the upper echelon of his particular age group. There are no easy solutions when playing an all-court player. Fortunately, every player can be beaten. If you've trained well and work hard during a match, you have a chance to win. All players have vulnerable points to their game, although these vulnerabilities may be subtle and not readily apparent. You need to pinpoint and determine how to exploit these weaknesses. This particular iPlan is designed to initially probe for weaknesses in the all-court player's game. Once these are evident, solidify your plan and be prepared for a long match.

iPlan # 4: The all-court player

1. Focus on the basics. Make sure your footwork is good, and get your racket back early.
2. Stay steady. Keep the ball in play
3. Attack the all-court player's weaker groundstroke, particularly on key points.
4. Alter the pace of play. Sometimes fast, sometimes slow.
5. Throw in some moonballs during rallies.
6. Attack the net on occasion. Selectively serve and volley.
7. Use the changeover to review your iPlan and make changes according to how the match is progressing. Be flexible. Stay tough.

The Senior Player

Seniors may present with any of the aforementioned styles of play. Determine which style of play they have and formulate your iPlan accordingly. In addition, be mindful of several issues unique to senior tennis players. They are repositories of tennis wisdom. They are skilled and crafty. They would enjoy nothing more than to defeat you 6-0, 6-0.

There are several important issues to consider when playing senior tennis. First, stay in good shape. Be physically prepared to play three hard sets of tennis. And keep your weight down. As noted earlier, mobility is the key. Many senior players will tire during the third set. Don't be one of them. Keep the ball in play. Be steady. Use the lob and drop shot; keep your senior opponent running.

ATTACK YOUR OPPONENT'S STRENGTH

A high-risk strategy to consider when playing an opponent is to go right at his strength. If you can break down an opponent's primary strength, he will be left with no viable options. Take away his big weapon, and his game is destroyed. This is the Mike Agassi "put a blister on their brain" strategy.

There was a classic match played seventy-seven years ago that illustrates the approach of breaking down the opponent's strength; it involved the final match of the 1939 Davis Cup between the United States and Australia. The members of the U.S. team included Joe Hunt, Jack Kramer, Frank Parker, and Bobby Riggs. The members of the Australian team were John Bromwich, Jack Crawford, player/coach Harry Hopman, and Adrian Quist.

The United States had won the Davis Cup the two preceding years, largely attributable to the efforts of J. Donald Budge. Budge turned professional in 1939 and the Australians were confident that, without Budge on the U.S. roster, they could unseat the Americans.

The 1939 Davis Cup was played on grass at the Merion Cricket Club in Haverford, Pennsylvania. The competition did not start out well for the Aussies. The twenty-three-year-old Parker surprised the veteran Quist in the opening match 6-3, 2-6, 6-4, 1-6, 7-5. Riggs disposed of Bromwich with an impressive display of strategic tennis in the next match 6-4, 6-0, 7-5. On the second day, Quist and Bromwich, the world's premier doubles team, defeated Hunt and Kramer 5-7, 6-2, 7-5, 6-2. On the final day of the competition, Riggs lost a grueling 5-set match to Quist 6-1, 6-4, 3-6, 3-6, 6-4. The Cup was now tied 2-2. The showdown was on: Parker vs. Bromwich for the 1939 Davis Cup title.

Frank Parker: He was born Francisek Andrzej Paikowski on January 31, 1916, in Milwaukee, Wisconsin, to immigrant Polish parents. His father died when he was two years old. His mother supported the family by laundering clothes. Cynthia Beardsley in her book, *Frank Parker: Champion in the Golden Age of Tennis,* provided a loving tribute to this remarkable tennis player. Although Frank did not have the economic advantages of many aspiring tennis players of that era, he did have an older brother who worked as the manager at an exclusive Milwaukee country club. It was there that Frank Parker was introduced to the game of tennis. He fell in love with the sport and spent three hours a day after school developing his game.

At age ten, Frank came to the attention of local tennis luminaries and was soon introduced to Mercer Beasley, the internationally-renowned tennis coach. Under Beasley's tutelage, Frank became known as the "Boy Wonder of Tennis." He won his first tournament in July 1927 at the Wisconsin Open Championships. After that, there was no stopping him. He won his first national singles title at the U.S. Boys Championships in 1931. He became the number one junior player in 1932 and made the first of his nineteen appearances at the U.S. National Championships in Forest Hills, winning the title in 1944 and 1945. In 1933, at age seventeen, he was ranked in the top ten of the men's division and remained in this elite group for the next seventeen years. He won the men's singles title at the U.S. Clay Court Championships five times between 1933 and 1947. He won the French Championships in 1948 and 1949; he is one of only three Americans to have won this title twice.

John Bromwich: John Bromwich (the "Brom") was born on November 14, 1918 in Sydney, New South Wales, Australia. The press referred to him as the "Melancholy Dane" because of his rather dour and sometimes angry on-court demeanor. He was one of those players who never appeared to have fun on the court. He approached the game with a fierce intensity, only matched in the modern era by Jimmy Connors. To miss one in fifty shots was "nothing less than a stark Shakespearean tragedy for the most self-exacting perfectionist to wield a racket." He despised losing and would give a linesman the "death stare" when he disagreed with a line call.

Bromwich was ambidextrous. Although a natural left-hander, Bromwich served with his right. When he started playing the game as a kid, he used two hands on both his backhand and forehand. He eventually gave up the two-handed forehand. His strokes, as well as his temperament, were similar to Connors.

Bromwich was an accomplished singles player, but he was even better at doubles. In his autobiography, Jack Kramer opined, "If Earth were playing in the all-time Universe Davis Cup, I'd play Budge and Vines (Ellsworth Vines) in my singles, and Budge and Bromwich in the doubles. That's what I think of Johnny as a doubles player." Bromwich and his partner, Adrian Quist, won eleven Grand Slam championships. He won two more with other partners. He won the singles title at the 1939 and 1946 Australian Championships (now the Australian Open). He lost in the singles final at Wimbledon in 1948.

The "Brom" vs. the "Boy Wonder of Tennis": The final match of the 1939 Davis Cup serves as a classic example of how to break down an opponent's strength. The match was played on September 5 before a packed crowd. The excitement and tension in the stadium were palpable. Frank Parker was the human backboard, the player who, allegedly, could not be defeated from the baseline. The "Brom" challenged Parker's strength: his steadiness. Surely, the American-dominated audience and Parker's teammates were thrilled as the first point began. After all, no one had the temerity, or apparent ability, to outsteady Parker. The first point involved one hundred exchanges. The initial fifty were forehand to forehand. The next fifty involved backhand to backhand. The spectators were entranced by the display of steadiness. As the point unfolded, there were "titters of amusement, then chuckles and finally roars of mirth and an explosive cheer as Parker knocked the ball out of court."

The match was won on that first point. One can only imagine what was going on inside Parker's head. Parker was adept at keeping an on-court "poker face." He was drilled by his coach, Mercer Beasley, to remain affectively neutral. Nevertheless, on the inside, Parker's emotions probably fluctuated from elation ("You mean this guy is actually attempting to outsteady me?") to near panic ("This guy is never going to miss!"). After all, this was the finals of the Davis Cup. The pressure was huge. Parker was unable or unwilling to change tactics. His steadiness, his major strength, was failing him. Bromwich won the match 6-1, 6-0, 6-3 and shattered the myth of Parker, the invincible tennis machine.

GAMESMANSHIP

"Nice shot, dearie."

The bad line calls; the head games; the psych jobs. It all happens on the tennis court. You need to be prepared to effectively handle these on-court irritations. Junior tennis is a wonderful arena for early exposure to tennis gamesmanship. During my junior tennis years, an opponent would occasionally yell, "How could I possibly be losing to *this* guy? He sucks."

But it was a match in 1964 that introduced me to real tennis gamesmanship. I, along with two of my junior high classmates, was invited to participate in the spring high school invitation tournament. This tournament included all members of our local high school team plus some promising junior high school players. This was a big deal to the three of us. Our high school team was a perennial powerhouse in New Jersey and won several state championships during the 1960s. The team had great quality and depth.

This was an interesting tournament because one of the junior high participants was an exceptional player. He was a physically large kid with good groundstrokes and a big kick serve. He attained a high ranking in the Eastern Section during his junior career and achieved some prominence on the national stage. He also was rather arrogant and had this uncanny sense for how to intimidate and diminish his opponent. Several of the high school players were dreading playing him. He validated that dread by easily winning the first two rounds and making it to the semifinals.

I was thrilled just to be invited to play and expected to lose in the first round. The format of the tournament was one 8-game pro set. My first-round opponent was a high school senior and the fifth-rated player on the team. He had a steady backcourt game. At age fourteen, my game was beginning to gel. I was good from the backcourt and managed to prevail in this first-round match 8-6.

My opponent in the quarterfinals was the third-rated player on the team. He had a big serve-volley game and wanted to avenge my victory over his teammate and friend. My opponent was hitting big serves and volleying well. I thought my only chance was to remain in the backcourt and lob him every time he approached the net. He had a 4-0 lead but then my lobbing strategy unnerved him. He missed several overheads, began to play tentatively, and retreated to the backcourt. I knew I had him at that point because I was the steadier player. I won the match 12-10.

There was no way I was supposed to be in the semifinals of this high school tournament but there I was. And I had to play my high-achieving junior high classmate. I had played him on two prior occasions and was only able to win a couple of games each set. He just had too much game for me. During this semifinal match, however, I was playing well. I had a great deal of confidence after defeating two of the high school players and figured I had nothing to lose. At one point in the match, I believed I had a legitimate shot at winning.

The match was tight. I was serving at 6-6, but my opponent had a break point. Fortunately, he hit the return into the net. He then confidently strolled to the net to retrieve the ball. I waited on the baseline, expecting him to throw the ball to me so that we could resume play. Well, was I wrong! As noted above, my opponent knew how to intimidate others and would pull these classic psychological maneuvers during key points of a match. In this particular instance, he picked up the ball, shot me a contemptuous and dismissive look, and merely dropped it on the other side of the net. He then sauntered over to the deuce side of the court to return my next serve.

I hesitated for a few seconds, not knowing what to do. I felt cornered. I then submissively walked to the net to retrieve the ball. I don't recall where the third ball was, but I didn't have it. The point at which I walked to the net was when my opponent owned me. It had been a competitive match up until that moment. Once I allowed myself to be put into a "one down" position, I was history. My opponent had control; he won the match 8-6.

Several years ago, I decided to pull this dropping-the-ball-on-the-other-side-of-the-net maneuver on a tennis friend during a tight, competitive match just to see what would happen. He got rather upset and called me a prick. I immediately explained the genesis of this psychological ploy and my friend replied, "Man, that's brilliant. How did that fourteen-year-old come up with it?" "Yeah," I said, "He was rather creative in that way."

There are many facets to tennis gamesmanship – cheating, quick serving, and an almost endless array of verbal and behavioral "mind games." At some point in your tennis career, you will have to deal with some type of gamesmanship issue. The best way to deal with these situations is to have an effective response ready to go.

1. **Cheating:** The score is 4-4 in the third set. Your opponent is serving and is down 15-30. You return the next serve with a deep reply to your opponent's backhand. You smell blood and are ready to attack. Your opponent cries out, "Long!" "You've got to be kidding," you say to yourself. You are positive that the ball landed either on or just in front of the baseline. This is a situation that requires an immediate response. If not, it can throw you off your game. I recommend confidently walking toward the net and saying, "You know, I thought that ball was in. Are you sure about that call?" Be direct but not angry. This allows your opponent to reverse the call - and if that happens, great. If your opponent sticks to the call, I would say, "Well, I don't agree" and proceed to play. Let it go, and focus on the here-and-now. Stick to your iPlan. Should your opponent give you another bad call and, if it's during a tournament, stop play, inform your opponent you no longer can trust his calls, and ask a tournament official to observe the match. If this situation occurs during social tennis, write that person off your list of tennis partners. Life is too short to deal with a tennis jerk.

2. **Quick Serving:** The quick serve is when your opponent begins the service motion before you are in the ready position to return serve. The result is that you either miss or hit a weak return of serve. Fortunately, there is an easy way to deal with this. Once you see that you are about to be "quick-served," take one step back, hold up your hand and say, "I'm not ready." Take control of this situation early. Be effective. Should your opponent again attempt the quick serve, repeat the above suggestion but this time take ten seconds and walk toward the back of the court before returning to the area of the court where you feel comfortable returning serve. Then say to your opponent, "I'm ready now." They'll get the hint and stop quick serving. Another approach I use for the quick server is to have the third ball in my possession. I take the ball with me as I'm setting up to return serve. Just prior to assuming the ready position, I will hit the third ball to my opponent. This "environmental" solution prevents the opponent from using the quick serve.

3. **Tennis Mind Games:** Tennis mind games are designed to disrupt your rhythm or get you angry. They come in many forms and are limited only by the creativity of your opponent.

The Rogue Ball Routine: During the finals of a NTRP 4.5 doubles tournament, one of our opponents, Jimmy, made some questionable calls and, during his return of serve, made multiple and exaggerated on-court movements designed to disrupt our serves. Now, Jimmy was well known to us and the local tennis community as a classic tennis "scam artist." He had many endearing qualities, but he could be incredibly aggravating on the court. Sound familiar? You probably have your own version of Jimmy at your local club. The match was competitive. My partner and I were up 4-3 in the third set. During the changeover and, unknown to us at the time, Jimmy deliberately took a "rogue" ball from his tennis bag to use in the match. Well, this particular ball was well-worn and had seen its better days. He elected to use this ball to serve to me, probably sensing that I was becoming irritated with him and about to "lose it." I missed the return by hitting it into the net. As soon as I hit it, the ball switch was obvious. I glared at Jimmy and yelled, "I'm tired of your f***ing sh*t," and slammed the ball over the fence. I probably should have included the Gonzales snot-blowing routine, but I didn't think of it. My partner attempted to calm me down and then said, "I don't think you realize this, but a local television crew has been recording our match for the last couple of minutes." I looked up and it was our local CBS affiliate recording some of the matches, presumably to televise on the local evening news. I was mortified, thinking, "Great, my first tennis tantrum in over twenty-five years and it makes it on T.V." It was not quite a McEnroe tantrum, but it was close. And I was forty years old at the time. Now that I'm older and presumably wiser, I hope that I would handle a similar situation in a more mindful and effective manner.

Jimmy was a master of tennis gamesmanship. Bernie Madoff would have admired him. During one tournament, I saw Jimmy approach the tournament assignment desk. There were players milling around, getting their assigned court number and a can of new balls. Well, Jimmy got his court assignment and a can of balls for his match. He then walked away, saw me, and said, "Watch this." He then took out a used can of balls identical to the ones being used in the tournament, returned to the tournament desk, and said to one of the officials, "Hey, you gave me a used can." The official apologized and gave him another can of new balls. Jimmy pocketed those and went out to play his match.

Nice Shot, Dearie: One of the more interesting practitioners of tennis mind games was Herbert B., Jr., who played tennis during my dad's era. Everybody dreaded playing Herbert. He was an accomplished pusher, but his gamesmanship was particularly unique. According to my dad, Herbert had designed this tennis belt that held three tennis balls. So, he had this rather large belt fastened to his tennis shorts that resembled some cheesy prop from a Buck Rogers movie. During his service games, he would pop one of the balls from the belt and go into his service motion. The belt was just strange enough to be distracting. Herbert also referred to his opponent as "dear" or "dearie." If his opponent hit a winning shot, Herbert replied, "Nice shot, dearie." Or if his opponent missed, Herbert said, "I'm sorry dear, the ball was long." After a while, these comments got to be quite grating, especially in a tight, competitive match. So, go make a tennis-ball holding belt and endear yourself to the tennis world.

Give Me A Break: I have to give credit to my dad for this maneuver. It was 1966, and my dad, age 46, was playing in the annual Bergen County, New Jersey tennis championships. His second-round opponent was Warren Lucas, a top-ranked junior in the 18-and-under Eastern boys' division. Warren was not a particularly versatile athlete, but he had this Ivan Lendl work ethic. He had punishing groundstrokes, was steady, and fast. My dad won the first set 6-3 and Lucas took the second, 7-5. The players were allowed a ten-minute break before starting the third set. And my dad needed it because he was tired. After the ten-minute break, my dad was nowhere to be found. People were asking me where he was, but I didn't have a clue. The tennis club had no locker room facilities, and people thought he might have gone off to some nearby wooded lots to take care of some personal business. Lucas was looking increasingly distracted waiting for the match to resume.

Twenty minutes later, my dad came strolling back to the court looking refreshed and relaxed. He had walked home, which was several blocks from the courts, taken a shower, changed clothes, and had a light snack. Ordinarily, he would have been defaulted, but this was his home club and he was a well-liked and established member of the community. There was no way that Lucas, age seventeen, would have been awarded with a default. By the time they resumed play, Lucas had lost his focus and momentum. He lost the third set 6-2, done in by a long senior tennis moment.

Gamesmanship will always be a part of tennis. Commensurate with having a strategic plan for a particular opponent, you also need to have an effective response for dealing with gamesmanship issues. Your goal is to remain effective on court. By dealing productively with your opponent's antics, you remain in control and can direct your energies to playing each point well. I acknowledge that some types of gamesmanship are easier to deal with than others. There are straightforward ways to deal with bad line calls and quick serving, as discussed above. Others may be quite challenging, with no obvious effective response available. In these situations, such as with a Herbert B., Jr., you have the opportunity to practice your mindfulness and acceptance skills. Observe your opponent's antics, appreciate them for what they are, and let them go. Direct your energies into aggressive, competitive play.

CHAPTER 7

THE TENNIS COMMUNITY

"Living and practicing with champions created the conditions for
the younger players to become champions."

One definition of community involves a group of people sharing common interests. In this sense, there are many types of tennis communities. A small community would be two people playing singles or a foursome who meet for a regular doubles match. For example, in Tallahassee a group of senior players, ages sixty and older, refer to themselves as the "golden boys." They meet three times per week at 10 a.m. and have a spirited game of doubles on the clay courts of one of Tallahassee's more popular public tennis venues. There is a corresponding group for the women called the "golden belles." Other tennis communities include the various USTA leagues and tournaments, tennis clubs, high school and college teams, tennis camps and academies, and, of course, the Association of Tennis Professionals (ATP) and the Women's Tennis Association (WTA).

If we were to look at these communities from a behavioral perspective, each has imbedded within its structure *the capacity to shape the tennis behavior of its individual members*. For some communities, the tennis skills of their members will remain relatively static, with limited change over many years. This would include the various informal groups who meet for an enjoyable morning or afternoon of social tennis.

Other groups may have a more competitive, dynamic format with the primary purpose of increasing the skill level of its members. Some of this is intrinsic to the structure of the particular community. Playing in a USTA singles league, for instance, allows one to compete against others of a comparable level. For those who do well, they may advance to the next level and compete against more experienced players. Thus, in competing against increasingly skilled opponents, the player undergoes a continual shaping process.

LADDERS OF SUCCESS

Access to competition is critically important in any stage of skill development. In October 2011, Fred Palmer and I had just completed a 3-set match. As we were engaging in the obligatory post-match processing, I asked Fred if he was ever involved in a tennis ladder as a kid. His face lit up, and he said he had fond childhood memories of playing on a ladder in Alabama. I also had similar experiences with tennis ladders in New Jersey. For those who are not familiar with this format, a tennis ladder is a way to rank a group of players. Each player is essentially a "rung" on the ladder. The best player resides at the top rung. Players challenge one another to a match according to the rules developed for a particular ladder. A player may change his position on the ladder depending on the outcome of a match. In this way, the ladder provides players with a continual source of competition and potential for skill development.

When Fred and I had this conversation, there was no such ladder available in Tallahassee. Historically, ladders were operated by and limited to a particular tennis club. Fred and I explored setting up a ladder through a public tennis club in Tallahassee.

Tallahassee is a good tennis town. The local tennis association is active in arranging a variety of USTA leagues at different skill levels. Unfortunately, these leagues are typically held during the weekdays, usually in the early evening hours. For those with work and family responsibilities, this poses scheduling challenges. In contrast, a tennis ladder is extremely flexible. Matches are held at the convenience of the participants. All you need is a tennis court, a can of balls, and an agreed upon time to play.

I spoke with the head pro of one of Tallahassee's public tennis clubs and proposed the idea of setting up a ladder through the club. The pro was against it, explaining that a ladder had been tried several years ago and there just wasn't sufficient member interest. So I informed him that I would explore other options; he wished me luck.

Upon returning home, I checked on-line regarding how to structure a tennis ladder. A Google search led me to the Global Tennis Network (GTN). GTN was developed by Trevor Meier, a Utah-based web designer and avid tennis player. Trevor initially designed an internet-based site to organize some small, local tennis tournaments. A tennis ladder was added to the site shortly thereafter. GTN evolved from these modest beginnings to a worldwide network, a sort of Facebook for tennis. At this writing, GTN has over 60,000 members from more than one hundred countries. Over 600 active ladders are operating through GTN across the globe. For the international traveler, you could find a match through GTN in places as diverse as Brazil, China, Croatia, Cyprus, Hong Kong, Indonesia, Qatar, and Singapore. In the United States, there are GTN ladders operating in all fifty states. Since its inception, over 150,000 matches have been played through the GTN site.

The GTN site is convenient and flexible. Because it is internet-based, there is no need for a tennis bureaucracy to organize leagues and tournaments. Besides tennis ladders, GTN can organize leagues, tournaments, tennis partner and court searches, message boards, and classified advertisements. Additional features include a tennis forum and blog.

Because Fred's work schedule was somewhat more flexible than mine, he became the first Tallahassee-based GTN ladder administrator. We called our ladder the "2012 Tallahassee Men's Open Top 100 Tennis Ladder." We contacted a couple of our tennis buddies, and five of us were the original participants. Fred and I weren't sure what response the ladder would receive, but it struck a major chord in the Tallahassee tennis community. Within two months, over 100 people registered for the ladder. One of the great things about the ladder is that it brings tennis players together who, under usual circumstances, would never meet.

The ladders can be organized according to a number of different criteria. Fred and I limited our ladder to players with a NTRP rating of 3.5 to 6.0. Additional criteria included:

1. A ladder participant can only challenge up ten positions on the ladder. This allows for considerable movement on the ladder with the opportunity to play someone of greater skill level. It also typically prevents someone with a low NTRP rating from challenging a highly skilled player. This rule is important because it allows the ladder to be fluid and dynamic in character.

2. A challenge match is canceled if the participants have not played their match within twenty-five days.

3. A participant has three days to accept or decline a challenge before it is automatically declined.

4. Each time a participant declines a challenge, he drops three positions on the ladder.

5. Both participants bring a new can of balls. The winner keeps the unopened can.

6. When challenged, the higher ranked player has the choice of court surface and location.

7. The ladder is free to join.

To start the challenge process, log on to the GTN site, go to the particular ladder for which you are registered, and submit a challenge. An electronic message is sent to the opponent regarding either accepting or rejecting the challenge. It is a simple and efficient process.

For those members who are regular participants on the ladder, there has been a noticeable increase in their skill level. Ladder participants, in essence, are shaping each other's behavior in a more skillful direction. And with the number of people involved in a ladder, one can experience a wide variety of tennis "styles," which is important for continued skill development.

EFFECTIVE TENNIS COMMUNITIES

It is interesting to observe how certain areas of the world dominate international tennis for a time before fading to some level of mediocrity. During the past several decades, several nations have produced accomplished tennis players who dominated their particular era. Australia, Czechoslovakia (now the Czech Republic), Spain, Sweden, Switzerland, and the United States are the most notable among the dominant tennis nations. What were the conditions in these nations that facilitated this tennis excellence? Is there perhaps a natural ebb-and-flow to this process in that even the most successful tennis nations will eventually decline to some level of obscurity before rising again to tennis greatness? Would it be possible to implement a program of cultural design to produce a steady stream of effective players for a given nation?

The United States has had its moments of tennis supremacy. Names such as Bill Tilden, J. Donald Budge, Jack Kramer, Richard "Pancho" Gonzales, Stan Smith, Arthur Ashe, Jimmy Connors, John McEnroe, Pete Sampras, and Andre Agassi were part of a remarkable tennis tradition. They all had stellar individual careers and some, like McEnroe, were instrumental in engineering multiple Davis Cup victories.

But if you were to select one country to study the conditions under which tennis flourished, and subsequently declined, it would be Australia. Australia dominated international tennis from the 1950s to the early 1970s. Between 1950 and 1971, Australian men won the Wimbledon title fourteen times. During ten of those twenty-two years, both finalists at Wimbledon were Australian. The names are legendary – Frank Sedgman, Ken Rosewall, Lew Hoad, Neale Fraser, Rod Laver, Fred Stolle, Roy Emerson, Tony Roche, and John Newcombe.

Of all these Australian greats, who was the consensus pick among the players themselves as the single greatest player? If you guessed Laver, you would be wrong. The consensus among the Australians was Lew Hoad. When Hoad was "on," no one could defeat him. Jack Kramer reported, "Hoad has the loosest game of any good kid I ever saw. There was absolutely no pattern to his game. I'd marvel at the shots he could *think of*. He was the only player I ever saw who could stand six or seven feet behind the baseline and snap the ball back hard, crosscourt. He'd try for winners off everything, off great serves, off tricky short balls, off low volleys. He hit hard over spin drives, and there was no way you could ever get him to temporize on important points." When Hoad was playing his best tennis, it was as if his opponent wasn't even on the court with him.

Pancho Gonzales was the dominant player on the professional tour from the mid-1950s until approximately 1962, with the exception of a brief period in 1958 when Hoad had an 18-9 record against Gonzales in head-to-head play. Gonzales, whom some consider to be the greatest tennis player of all time, opined that Hoad was the toughest opponent he ever faced, adding, "He was the only guy who, if I was playing my best tennis, could still beat me. I think his game was the best game ever. Better than mine. He was capable of making more shots than anybody. His two volleys were great. His overhead was enormous. He had the most natural tennis mind with the most natural tennis physique."

The problem with Hoad was that he was not consistent in day-to-day competition and was plagued by an arthritic back that cut short his career in his late twenties. Nevertheless, if I could take any tennis player from history to play a match when that player and his opponent were playing at their absolute best, I would take Hoad.

It would be remiss of me to not mention two great Australian women players of that era– Margaret Smith Court and Evonne Goolagong Cawley. Court still leads the list of women Grand Slam titles with twenty-four. Cawley secured seven Grand Slam titles. And in 1980, at age twenty-eight, Cawley was the first mother to win the singles title at Wimbledon.

The fortunes of Australian men's tennis took a precipitous decline after 1971. If we look at the data from the Wimbledon Championships from 1972-93, an Australian made it to the men's final round of Wimbledon only twice and one of those was by a member of the old guard, Ken Rosewall. Pat Cash won the title in 1987, defeating Ivan Lendl.

There appear to be several reasons for Australia's tennis dominance during the 1950s to the 1970s. Australia has always been a sports-crazed nation but it was particularly so during that era. Peter Bodo commented, "[B]ack in the 1950s, the two things you could find in even the smallest of Australian towns were a pub and a tennis court, of which the pub can be said to be an intellectual institution." Fraternalism and camaraderie were critical elements of Australian tennis. The Australian tennis stars were, in the truest sense of the word, "mates."

John Newcombe articulated two important reasons why Australian men dominated the tennis world during the 1950s and 1960s. First of all, the players, with some exceptions, were extremely fit. They engaged in a considerable amount of off-court physical training, something unheard of during that era. A second, and more important reason, involved the players' travel schedule. Because Australia was located so far from many of the major tournaments, the Australian national team traveled together. They stayed in the same hotels and ate, drank beer, and practiced together. This created an environment in which the younger players were, to a considerable extent, *in an apprentice relationship* to the older, more established players. Living and practicing with champions created the conditions for the younger players to become champions. Thus, the Australian national team followed the great tradition of those periods in history in which guild-like, apprenticeship systems produced a flurry of artistic and scientific achievements, with the Renaissance period in Florence, Italy, being a great example. The advent of Open-era tennis in 1968 created a new set of dynamics for the players, ending the apprenticeship system that had worked so well for Australia and its dominance of tennis.

And then there was Harry Hopman, whose accomplishments in tennis are equivalent to those of John Wooden in college basketball. Harry was born on August 12, 1906, in Glebe, Sydney, New South Wales. He was an enthusiastic soccer player during his grade school years. At age thirteen, he took up tennis and won, playing barefoot, an open tournament held on the grounds of Rosehill Public School, where his father worked as headmaster. His tennis successes continued during high school and, at age seventeen, he represented New South Wales in a national junior-team competition.

Hopman was a doubles specialist. He and Jack Crawford won the Australian Junior Doubles Championships for three consecutive years beginning in 1925. He and Crawford also won the Australian Doubles Championships in 1929 and 1930. Hopman was runner-up to Crawford in the Australian Singles Championships in 1931 and 1932. Hopman was quick and agile with good volleying skills.

On March 19, 1934, Hopman married Nell Hall, who was also an accomplished tennis player. Together, they won four Australian Mixed Doubles Championships and, in 1935, were the first married couple to reach the finals at Wimbledon.

Hopman assumed the captaincy of the Australian Davis Cup team in 1938. He is widely acknowledged as the greatest Davis Cup captain in history.

In his first year as captain, Australia reached the final round for the first time in fourteen years, losing 3-2 to the United States led by the great J. Donald Budge. In 1939, Australia prevailed in the final round against the United States with Bromwich defeating Parker in a match detailed in chapter six.

Davis Cup competition resumed in 1946 following a six-year hiatus resulting from the events of World War II. Hopman was not the Davis Cup captain in 1946 and he watched, with dismay, as Jack Kramer and Ted Schroeder demolished the Australian team. The American team continued their domination of Australia through 1949.

Hopman was recalled as captain in 1950, ushering in the "Hopman era." From 1950 to 1967, Australia won the Davis Cup a remarkable fifteen times. Hopman was a brilliant strategist and motivator. He stressed the importance of physical conditioning and focused, deliberate practice. He exhorted his players to hit thousands of balls.

Hopman orchestrated an ongoing program of player development. His approach was seen by some as creating a tennis "assembly line," and he assembled some of the greatest players in the game's history. His first crop of Davis Cup stars included Frank Sedgman and Ken McGregor. Next included Lew Hoad and Ken Rosewall followed by Ashley Cooper, Neale Fraser, Rod Laver, Roy Emerson, and Mal Anderson. His final group included John Newcombe, Fred Stolle, and Tony Roche.

Hopman was a strict disciplinarian who instituted a system of fining his players for minor transgressions, such as poor table manners and curfew violations. He professed to abhor professional tennis, and he resisted the establishment of Open-era tennis. He withdrew his support for any of his players who joined the professional ranks. Ken Rosewall stated Hopman reacted, once his players left amateur tennis, "as if we never existed." One of the lesser known Australian Davis Cup players, Mervyn Rose, allegedly named his dog after Hopman so that he could occasionally kick it.

FORK IN THE ROAD

Yogi Berra once famously quipped, "If you come to a fork in the road, take it." Life comes down to a series of choices. You have to decide how much time and energy you are going to allocate to various pursuits. Imagine, for a minute, that you are given 100 "life units" to use. For the aspiring professional tennis player, 80 to 85 of these units may be allocated toward their developing tennis career. This leaves only 15 or 20 units to devote to other areas such as personal relationships, education, recreational pursuits, personal growth, and so forth. Professional tennis players are not, for the most part, well-rounded individuals. The combination of hard-driving and, for some players, dysfunctional parents, rigorous training schedules, constant travel, and living in hotels for a substantial part of the year does not promote a well-rounded life. The allure of big money and fame are an inherent part of contemporary professional tennis and can have a deleterious impact on a young person's development. It is the rare individual who can cope with the demands of competitive tennis with dignity and grace.

Others may elect to allocate their life units on a more equitable basis on areas such as career, family, friends, recreational interests, and finances. The trade-off for these individuals is that they may sacrifice eminence, to hijack a line from Sir Francis Galton, for balance.

Which is the better course? It all depends on which fork in the road you are willing to take. Bobby Fischer would say the first type is better. He once stated, "Chess is life." For him, it was. He probably devoted 95 or more of his life units to the game. Other areas of his life were problematic. Pancho Gonzales experienced six failed marriages and could be a rather angry and difficult individual – but he was one of the greatest tennis players in history. Others may be happy with a rather balanced, somewhat anonymous life.

GUIDELINE 5: ENVIRONMENTAL DESIGN

I'm unable to resist the temptation to paraphrase the words of John Watson:

> *Give me a dozen healthy infants, well-formed, and my own specified world to bring them up in and I'll guarantee to take any one at random and train him to become any type of tennis player I might select - pusher, moonballer, net rusher, basher and, yes, even Grand Slam winner, and cheat, regardless of his talents, penchants, tendencies,*

abilities, vocations, and race of his ancestors. I am going beyond my
facts and I admit it, but so have the advocates of innate ability and they
have been doing it for many thousands of years.

Given the above, I need to make clear that I am not a strict environmental-
ist. We are all biological organisms and genetic determinants of elite athletic
performance may ultimately prove to be of some importance. Nevertheless,
there are dangers in promoting the innate talent hypothesis. If you buy the
contention that performance thresholds are some rigidly determined entities,
then you are at risk for developing a fixed mindset with respect to athletic
development and practice.

And then there is the issue of accessibility. Even if genetic research speci-
fies certain biological markers for expert-level performance, there is no readily available technology to directly change one's genetic make-up to promote
enhanced athletic skills. And I doubt that anyone would seriously promote a
program of "athletic eugenics." There would be implications for the identification and management of talent should reliable biological markers be found
that contribute to athletic success, but biological performance thresholds
appear quite malleable and susceptible to a program of deliberate practice.
Selecting individuals for enhanced training programs based upon biological
markers could leave out athletes who could benefit from such training programs and ultimately excel as elite athletes.

Enough of speculating about some imagined future. With respect to
the present moment, instead of waiting for the emergence of the next great
tennis talent, arrange for its creation through environmental design. During
the last several decades, the field of psychology has generated a systematic
account of the relationship between elite performance and the environment.
Two questions must be addressed: How can expert-level performance be
generated and maintained? How can members of the tennis community
support this process? A related issue is whether this proposal can be accomplished while promoting the psychological well-being of the designated
trainee.

This proposal will involve multiple supports ranging from parents and
coaches to tennis academies and national tennis organizations. There will

be a different combination of these supports depending on the particular circumstances of the aspiring tennis player.

The following proposal involves several issues to consider when designing a tennis development program:

1. **The Decision:** One parent or both will play a determinative role during the early years of a tennis player's life. Mike Agassi planned to produce a championship tennis player before his children were born. Others, perceiving some level of athletic "talent" in their offspring, pursue focused tennis training at a later point. This decision is a critically important one for both the parents and the child. The parents are, in essence, making a major decision for the child and for themselves regarding the allocation of those "life units" discussed above. By investing heavily in a child's tennis future, other areas of development for the child and parents could suffer.

2. **Deliberate Practice:** Whether or not one begins focused tennis development at ages two or eight, the data from Anders Ericsson and his colleagues are clear: the critical variable in producing an elite performer involves a considerable amount of deliberate practice. The more deliberate practice you do, the more skillful you will become. The group of elite violinists in the great violin study *averaged* approximately 10,000 hours of deliberate practice by age twenty. To accumulate this amount of deliberate practice over a ten-year time span you would have to spend over 2.7 hours per day. Logging in 15,000 hours over the same time frame will involve slightly over 4 hours per day. That is a huge investment of time and energy for the child as well as time and resources for the parent(s).

3. **Establish Progressively Competitive Environments:** The reciprocal relationship inherent in a tennis match allows for "shaping" or operant conditioning to occur. Each participant is attempting to outmaneuver the other, and the one with the greater skill set will

generally prevail. By competing against superior opponents, you have the opportunity to improve your skills.

It is no accident that the best tennis players in this country typically emerge from areas with rich tennis traditions. Florida, Southern California, and the New York metropolitan area historically have produced a disproportionate number of skilled players. USTA sanctioned junior tournaments provide valuable competitive arenas for the players.

In his autobiography, *You Cannot Be Serious*, John McEnroe expressed surprise over how three world-class players could have emerged from the same, small area in Queens, New York – himself, his brother Patrick, and Mary Carillo. If one buys into the innate talent hypothesis, this *would* be rather remarkable. Could it be that some weird distribution of tennis DNA found its way to this small corner in Queens to produce these three international performers? No. They all were trained at the same academy run by tennis luminaries such as Harry Hopman and Antonio Palafox. Furthermore, there were many top-level juniors training at the academy allowing for a high-level of tennis shaping to occur.

Ivan Lendl made an important observation with respect to his early tennis development. He noted that during the summer months in Czechoslovakia all top junior players competed in the same tournaments. This involved an intensive experience of two tournaments a week in both singles and doubles over a span of eight weeks. By contrast, in the United States, the junior tournaments were fragmented into seventeen sections, thus establishing the conditions for a diluted competitive environment.

Jack Kramer understood this competitive dynamic. When he was learning the game in the latter part of the 1930s, he often played at the Los Angeles Tennis Club where he competed against some of the best players of that era – Ellsworth Vines, Bill Tilden, Bobby Riggs, Gene Mako, Joe Hunt, Ted Schroeder, and Frank Shields. Kramer was aware that superior competition was crucial for the continued development of his game, and he took full advantage of the opportunities available at the club. He also noted that as "soon as the L.A. Tennis Club began to decline in power, so did American tennis." Kramer argued for a central tennis training site in the United States to promote player development, adding, "Competition is crucial to the player, because no matter how good you are technically, you cannot improve unless you play against somebody better."

Tennis environmental programming takes many forms. The standard approach, within junior tennis, is to train at some tennis facility, involving varying degrees of technical expertise of the staff and to play sanctioned USTA junior tournaments. The more successful members play national and international tournaments. The "elite" of the junior players may join the professional tour. This type of system allows for a steady progression of competition but may not be a particularly efficient way to maximize player development.

Tennis academies offer a concentrated competitive experience. These are often construed as "tennis factories," with the International Management Group (IMG) Academy (formerly the Nick Bollettieri Tennis Academy) being the most well-known. The Academy's record has been impressive with select Academy alumni including Andre Agassi, Jim Courier, David Wheaton, Tommy Haas, Maria Sharapova, Jelena Jankovic, and Monica Seles. From a behavioral perspective, this approach makes a lot of sense. These academies are often well-designed, "experimental communities" with the express purpose of developing expert-level tennis players. These communities provide for a concentrated version of the Ivan Lendl junior tennis experience. I suspect that there is less emphasis on tennis development at some of these academies than on identifying the next "great talent" to fast track to the sports industrial complex with its many lucrative corporate sponsorships and endorsements. And with the IMG - a global sports, media, consultant, and fashion conglomerate leading the way - this corporate emphasis should continue to unduly influence the operations of these academies.

There have been many tennis players who have attained expert-level status without enrolling in one of these academies. The critical variables involved in producing an elite performer include the requisite number of deliberate-practice hours under the guidance of a skilled and innovative teacher or coach and a sufficiently concentrated competitive environment. Although the golden era of Australian tennis is long past, I believe the apprentice system they had in place could be established within a small, dedicated, and innovative tennis training community.

There has always been a vibrant, pragmatic streak running through the history of the United States. Innovations in basic science and technology, creative entrepreneurship, and even political experimentation embedded in Louis Brandeis's popularization of the phrase "laboratories of democracies," have always been dynamic features of this country. I believe it is time to develop and implement "experimental tennis communities." These communities could range from only a few select individuals, as in the development of a Jimmy Connors, to an organized community dedicated to tennis excellence. Let the experimentation begin.

4. **Instill A Growth Mind Set:** This is a critical issue and, if done well, will preclude the burnout and other unnecessary emotional stresses experienced by many young, aspiring tennis players. With all the challenges involved in a regimen of deliberate practice, a child's emotional life may go unattended, thus setting the conditions for future problematic consequences.

Most tennis parents would assert that they have their children's best interests at heart and hope they would develop into productive, happy, and emotionally stable adults. The practices of some of these tennis parents do not, however, match this professed rhetoric.

I experienced a minor version of this when I was playing junior tennis in the 14-and-under division. In one tournament, I had just won the first set of a quarterfinal match. The second set was competitive. I noticed a man anxiously watching the match and assumed he was my opponent's father. During the changeover with me leading 4-3 in the second set, he approached his son and offered a ten dollar bill if his son could pull out the match. My opponent appeared rather embarrassed and chagrined following this brief conversation with his father. I was rather bemused by the whole affair and managed to win the second set 7-5. I remember experiencing mixed emotions upon shaking my opponent's hand following the match. I was happy that I won, but I also felt sorry for my opponent regarding the ten-dollar bribe. I also recall experiencing some level of pride. After all, if a parent was offering monetary inducements to defeat me, I figured my tennis game must be improving. I also briefly considered asking the dad if he would give me the ten dollars but, in one of my rare moments of teenage good judgment, decided against it.

The rise of the tennis father is a particularly interesting, contemporary phenomenon among a select group of professional tennis players. Peter Bodo characterized these individuals quite well, stating, "These fathers tend to be a funny and predictable lot. For instance, I've yet to meet one who didn't claim to have been some kind of world class jock who just didn't happen to make the Olympics or Wimbledon because of blah-blah-blah. Furthermore, when you ask why they're walking around at tennis tournaments in short pants eating ice cream cones instead of working, they come up with tennis's version of the Twinkies defense: The sheer talent of their kids, combined with their need for guidance, unfortunately forced them to abandon the glowing prospects of their former lives." To give Mike Agassi great credit, unlike other well-known tennis fathers, he did participate in the Olympics and maintained his employment throughout Andre's tennis career.

Undoubtedly an aspiring tennis player's significant others – parents, coaches, and others involved in their support network – can play a primary role in the development of the growth mindset. The essence of this mindset involves defining success in the learning process, through sustained effort. To a considerable degree, the development of mindsets is a social product. The development of "character" and "heart" is, from this perspective, a function of the messages we primarily receive from our significant others. Messages regarding sustained effort, the here-and-now appreciation in the process of development, and persistence and maintaining optimism when faced with challenges can only enhance one's emotional and character development.

TENNISVILLE, U.S.A.

From the 1940s to the 1960s, one city in the United States earned the title, "Tennisville, U.S.A." What city was it? Los Angeles? Fort Lauderdale? Atlanta? Well, of all places, it was Hamtramck, Michigan. How in the world could a small, working-class city near Detroit where the tennis season was only six months long, become the dominant junior tennis development center in the world?

The story of the Hamtramck tennis program is a fascinating one and ought to be studied by those interested in establishing effective tennis communities. Hamtramck was a tough, working-class community populated by immigrants from Germany, Ireland, and Poland. In 1930, there was no tennis tradition or infrastructure in Hamtramck. There were no country clubs or teaching professionals. There were only two cracked and uneven courts at the local high school. Tennis was not even on the radar screen in Hamtramck – that is, until Jean Hammond arrived to take a teaching position with the Hamtramck school system. Hammond was a dynamic individual, combining the energy, commitment, determination, and toughness of a Margaret Thatcher with the public relations savvy of a P.T. Barnum.

Public county records indicate that Jean Hammond was born on March 13, 1899, near the town of Gladwin, a small farming community north of Detroit. Hammond graduated from high school in 1917 and secured a teaching position at Hamtramck in 1921. Initially, she worked as a physical education teacher in an elementary school. She enjoyed the challenge of working with the children from immigrant families, most of whom encouraged their sons and daughters to quit school early to obtain employment.

An event took place in the summer of 1923 that would lead to dramatic changes not only in Jean's life, but also the life of Hamtramck. Hammond enrolled at Columbia University to enhance her teaching credentials. She was offered a choice of either swimming or tennis to fulfill the physical education requirement. Because she didn't know how to swim and was deathly afraid of water, she took the tennis class. When she returned to Hamtramck, she started playing tennis at the Detroit Club, where she met Jerry Hoxie, a regular at the club. They became an "item," eventually marrying on October 10, 1926.

Jean Hoxie worked hard on her game and won the Detroit women's singles title in 1931 and 1932. At age thirty-four, Hoxie realized that she was not going to become a world-class tennis player so she set her sights on becoming a coach to develop world-class players. She approached the Hamtramck High School principal with a proposal to develop a boys' tennis program at the school. After some initial reluctance, the principal approved the project.

As you can imagine, recruiting players from a tough, working-class community to don tennis whites was going to be a challenge. Baseball was the game of choice for Hamtramck boys. Tennis was derided as a "sissy" sport, particularly one coached by a woman. Hoxie was a great salesperson and convinced several boys that tennis was to be their ticket to college. Few Hamtramck High School graduates attended college, and Hoxie's primary objective during the early stages of her coaching career was to develop her players' tennis skills in order for them to obtain college scholarships. Later, Hoxie's goal was to produce nationally prominent players. She assembled three players to be the core of her new team, convincing them that they were "going to be winners because we are going to practice longer and harder and better than any other team." Hoxie had an intuitive feel for the deliberate-practice model. She pressured her team to win, often stating, "No losers play for Hoxie." From the sheer force of her personality, her team believed they were invincible.

The Hamtramck High School tennis team played its first interscholastic match in the spring of 1934 against Detroit's Eastern High School and lost badly. Hoxie and her team were shocked at this initial loss. They recovered quickly and worked harder at their games to win three matches during that season. The following season, the team made it to the league semifinals. In 1936, they made it to the finals and then secured their first championship trophy in 1937.

Hoxie began developing "feeder" programs for her high school team, starting a tennis program at the junior high school and promoting handball tournaments for elementary school students. Fred Kovaleski was Hoxie's first star. Fred came to Hoxie's attention by winning the Pulaski Elementary School handball championship at age eleven. Hoxie provided Kovaleski with his first tennis racket and took him to "The Wall" for practice.

"The Wall" was to become the trademark of the Hoxie trainees, a 60-foot expanse of concrete, almost 20 feet high with a 3-foot line to mark the height of a net. Another line was drawn approximately 4 feet above the net-mark line. Kovaleski spent hours hitting balls between the two lines of "The Wall." During the summer months, Kovaleski practiced for twelve hours per day. Hoxie had him practice hard in the summer so that he and other students wouldn't be adversely affected by the heat during a match.

Hoxie was committed to making her high school team a national powerhouse. She told her boys, "If you can beat them in tennis, you can beat them in everything." By "them," she was referring to the elite players from around the country who were competing for national honors. Hoxie continued, "We're ready for them. They've not practiced twelve months a year the way *you* have. You're my Polacks and you're hungry to win. There's no way anyone's going to beat you." In *Jean Hoxie: The Robin Hood of Tennis*, Jean Pitrone wrote, "They listened. They believed. And most of all, they continued to practice . . . relentlessly."

During the winter months, Hoxie had her team practice in the Copernicus Junior High gymnasium which had no heat during the weekends. Since most of Hamtramck's competitors came from wealthy communities, Hoxie knew that year-round practice gave her players a huge advantage when the tennis season started. Hoxie was aware that, for the children of the wealthy, "there was the distraction of an endless succession of lessons – dancing lessons, fencing, skating, skiing, French lessons, riding lessons." Meanwhile, her players were hitting thousands of balls against the gymnasium walls in the cold. The children from the "advantaged" families were at a distinct *disadvantage* when the tennis season began.

In 1939, Hoxie took her charges to the annual indoor championships held in New York City during late December. She procured funding from her fellow teachers for the trip and even got a local automobile dealership to provide her with four new tires for her car. The Hoxies used their personal funds to pay for the rest of the expenses. Jean and her "Hoxie kids," as they were beginning to be referred, piled into her Dodge automobile for the trip to New York.

The tournament was held at the 7th Light Guard Armory; most of the players were from the New York metropolitan area. When the Hoxie kids arrived from this small, ethnic Midwest community, they received considerable attention from tournament officials, fellow competitors, and, significantly, the press. How could it be otherwise? Here were these players with difficult-to-pronounce Slavic names taking on the elite of the New York tennis scene. Hoxie was a master at public relations and instructed her players to speak only Polish. The New York press loved their story and highlighted the Hamtramck players in several newspaper articles.

Frank Kovaleski made it to the semifinals of the singles and to the finals of the doubles. Another Hoxie kid, Ed Roszak, made it to the finals of his age division. The Hoxie kids were beginning to make their mark on the national stage, and they returned to Hamtramck intoxicated by their success and the subsequent media attention.

The Hamtramck tennis program received increasing attention from Detroit's tennis elite. Several members of the Ford family, among others, contacted Hoxie for private lessons. More importantly, they provided Hoxie with financial support for her growing tennis program.

The fifteen-year-old Kovaleski made it to the quarterfinals of the men's division of the Detroit City Open Tournament and, in 1942, ended the year with a number nine national ranking in his age division. He was named to the Junior Davis Cup squad that year along with several elite players from California and Florida. He earned a tennis scholarship to the College of William & Mary. In 1947, he won the National Public Parks singles and doubles championships. He played at Wimbledon and Forest Hills, traveled the world as a tennis player, and eventually secured employment as an executive with the Nabisco Corporation. Kovaleski attributed his success on and off the court to Hoxie.

Hoxie promoted Kovaleski as a symbol for Hamtramck tennis excellence. Aspiring Hamtramck players wanted "to be like Fred." When outdoor practice for the high school team began in March, many of the players believed they could be the next Kovaleski. Regardless of the weather, Hoxie demanded that her team wore shorts although she did allow them to wear pullover sweaters. If any of her players complained of the cold, she yelled, "This is not a country club!"

The Hoxie kids loved beating the hell out of the privileged Grosse Point team. If any of Hoxie's team were to lose to a Grosse Point player, they were banished to "The Wall" for an extended period of solitary confinement until Hoxie believed they were ready to return to team play.

"Killer" Koliba

Hoxie knew that her starting-them-young philosophy would produce champions. Her first "little Hoxie kid" was Johnny Koliba, whom Hoxie nicknamed "Killer." Hoxie was aware of the "tremendous public relations value in shiny-faced, primary-grade children, dressed in tennis whites and wielding tennis rackets." Hoxie played up "Killer" to the media because not only was he a good tennis player, he was also really cute. Killer entered his first out-of-town tournament at age nine, where he played and lost to the teenager Jerry Evert, who later became the uncle of Chris Evert. The press tagged Johnny Koliba as "the youngest player in the world." The immigrant Koliba family, who knew nothing about tennis, was mystified why the newspapers were publishing photos of their "little Johnny."

Always looking for a public relations stunt, Hoxie arranged for the nine-year-old "Killer" to play an exhibition match against women's champion Alice Marble at Detroit's Olympia Stadium before ten thousand spectators. Marble's coach, Eleanor Tennant, told the press that "Killer" had "the makings of a champion."

By the time he was twelve, "Killer" had to produce, and it was no longer sufficient to just look cute on the tennis court. When he lost in a tournament at Kalamazoo, Hoxie directed an older player to take him to the Greyhound bus station where he was sent back to Hamtramck…alone. The other Hoxie kids got the message – a loss would mean banishment, shame, and humiliation. A more sensitive person might have withered under Hoxie's pressure and demands. Koliba responded by working harder on his game and became one of Hoxie's stars on the high school team.

TENNIS FOR GIRLS

In 1943, Hoxie began her tennis program for girls. The girls did not escape Hoxie's wrath either. One time, Hoxie directed two players to sweep the puddles off the courts following a rain storm. The two made a rather half-hearted attempt to dry the courts. Hoxie yelled, "Come on, come on you two! You're not the Pope's daughters! You've got to *work*, girls. You've got to work if you want to amount to something in this world."

June Stack was one of Hoxie's promising star players. After she lost a match in a ten-and-under tournament in Chicago, Hoxie gave Stack the send-her-home-alone-on-the-bus treatment. At the next tournament in which Stack participated, Hoxie informed her just prior to the start of the match, "I want this over in eight minutes." Talk about pressure. Stack responded to Hoxie's dictatorial style by becoming the youngest girl to win the Michigan Interscholastic Championships in 1948 at age twelve.

Hoxie began conducting tennis clinics at various colleges around the country, including several elite women's schools including Smith, Vassar, and Radcliffe. Beginning in 1947, Hoxie conducted tennis clinics internationally, traveling to England, Brazil, Norway, the Netherlands, Scotland, France, Egypt, and Russia. She visited with and charmed all types of foreign dignitaries; Jean Hoxie became an international tennis celebrity.

In January 1951, Hoxie was in Jamaica setting up tennis programs. Several months later, Hollis Dann of the USLTA arranged to have Althea Gibson go to Hamtramck to be coached by Hoxie. Gibson remembered being directed by Hoxie to hit at "The Wall." With reference to "The Wall," Hoxie often asserted, "The first 10,000 shots are the hardest."

THE FIRST TENNIS CAMP

For years, Hoxie envisioned developing a summer tennis training center. The Hoxie Tennis House, which she proclaimed to be "The Original Tennis

Camp," opened during the summer of 1954; several campers stayed there at a rate of $75 per week. By 1957, forty students enrolled at the camp; two of the campers were granddaughters of John Foster Dulles, who served as Secretary of State in the Eisenhower administration. Camp enrollment increased to 186 students by 1961. One camper, Stanley Pasarell, was later named to the U.S. Junior Davis Tennis Cup squad. Julie Heldman attended the camp for six consecutive summers and attained a number five world ranking during her tennis career.

Former Hoxie kids returned to assist Hoxie with her camp and with the new group of Hamtramck trainees. Hoxie exhorted them to "help the program that produced *you*." Thus, as with the case of the Australian players of the 1950s and 1960s, the new Hamtramck trainees were apprenticed by the more experienced players.

"Peaches"

At age fifty-seven, Hoxie wanted to eclipse all of her previous accomplishments by producing an extraordinary player, a "phenom" who would dominate the national and international tennis scenes. She directed her assistant, Richard Sunday, who was a former Hoxie kid, to search for a "thoroughbred." Unknown to them at the time, their thoroughbred lived fewer than a hundred yards away from "The Wall" at Veteran's Memorial Park.

John and Eugenia Bartkowicz immigrated to the United States in 1948. John was Polish and Eugenia Russian. Jane Marie was born on April 16, 1949. The family moved to the south end of Hamtramck, Michigan, in 1954, and purchased a home located within sight of "The Wall." By age six, Jane became intrigued by all of the activity at "The Wall," noticing all these kids dressed in tennis whites hitting balls against it for hours at a time with a rather stocky, blonde woman shouting instructions to them and stating, "Do you know how long Heifetz (violinist Jascha Heifitz) practices each day? Six or seven hours every day – that's how long!"

One day, the seven-year-old Jane found a broken tennis racket in the bushes and wandered out to one of the courts at Veteran's Memorial Park. As one of the park's instructors, Richard Sunday provided her with some basic instruction and a used but unbroken tennis racket and directed her to "The Wall" to hit as many forehands as she could. Sunday observed her hitting style and later addressed her as "Peaches." When Jane asked him why he was calling her Peaches, he responded, "You're such a cute peach; I'm going to call you Peaches." Since all of the Hoxie kids had nicknames, Jane Marie Bartkowicz became known as "Peaches."

Peaches observed that the most accurate of "The Wall" hitters proceeded to the tennis courts for match play. So, little Peaches returned to "The Wall" every day to practice – and she did so day after day for several hours. Eventually, someone alerted Coach Hoxie regarding this little girl who was becoming quite proficient at hitting against "The Wall." Hoxie observed her for a few minutes and realized that she was looking at a future champion. Hoxie devised a rein-forcement system in which trainees who started hitting against "The Wall" could earn a piece of licorice for hitting twenty-five consecutive shots without missing. Peaches amassed a ton of licorice.

Bartkowicz set two records on another wall that no other Hoxie kid even came close to achieving. During her lunch break at Pulaski Elementary School, Peaches took her tennis racket to the "boiler" room of the school. It was a rather small room with exposed pipes and several windows but in one area there was sufficient wall space against which to hit tennis balls. Peaches began hitting and reached 1775 balls without a miss by the time her lunch break was over. She could and would have gone longer, but she had to return to class. Bartkowicz later set a wall-volley record of 980 con-secutive shots. As any tennis player knows, these two wall records are truly phenomenal.

Peaches's practice sessions were intense, including three to five hours after school, depending on the weather, and from six to eight hours per day on the weekends. During the summer months, she spent all day at the courts. Peaches Bartkowicz was a prime, and early, example of the deliberate-prac-tice model. Her practice regimen resulted in approximately 1800 to 2000 hours of deliberate practice per year. There were essentially no focused tennis training programs for girls in the 1950s; few even played competitive tennis. Peaches had to be the only girl, possibly in the world, who engaged in this type of deliberate training.

Bartkowicz did not consider herself to have a lot of natural talent, stating that she loved the game and wanted to excel. She denied that anyone pushed her with respect to her austere training regimen. She improved her game by playing against older and more skilled opponents, including select players from the boys' high school team or returning Hamtramck collegiate players during the summer months.

At age eight, Peaches won a tennis trophy at some local public parks event. She was excited as she went home to show her trophy to her parents, but they weren't sure how to respond since they basically didn't even know what tennis was or how she won the trophy. With John and Eugenia's consent, Hoxie purchased tennis clothing for Peaches and provided baby-sitting services for her younger sister, Christine, so Peaches could continue with her daily practice sessions. Christine later took up the game and was nicknamed (ready for this) "Plums" by Coach Hoxie.

Bartkowicz's rise in the junior tennis ranks was meteoric. At age ten, she won a 13-and-under doubles tournament in Ottawa, Canada. In 1960, she entered her first national tournament in both the 11- and 13-under divisions in Chattanooga, Tennessee. Initially, the tournament committee was not going to let her play in two divisions. One of the officials eventually concluded, "She won't win it anyway so why not let her play." Bartkowicz put on a dazzling display of tennis, winning the 11-and-under division easily, including a 6-0, 6-0 thrashing of Connie Capozzi in fourteen minutes. She then surprised the tournament committee by winning the 13-and-under division defeating the number one seed, Vicki Holmes, 5-7, 6-2, 6-0. And she won both of these events serving underhanded. Her standard serve was not well-developed, so she used the pronounced sliced, underhand serve that Michael Chang made famous in his match against Ivan Lendl in the 1989 French Open. I'm sure her opponents did not know how to handle this low trajectory, strongly-sliced serve. And once the ball was in play, Bartkowicz wore her opponents down with her consistency.

Bartkowicz was the premier Hamtramck player. As such, she was beginning to experience the same stress and pressure to win that earlier Hoxie kids had endured. One of Hoxie's favorite threats was "Win or you don't eat!"

Although presumably none of the players ever experienced food deprivation, they were acutely aware of the possibility of being sent home alone on a bus following a tournament loss and being banished from the group for an extended time period. Hoxie often reminded her players, "I'm a champion developer. I don't like second raters. I don't teach that." An early Hoxie kid, Tony Lamarato, noted, "Everybody was afraid of Jean Hoxie." Bartkowicz was no exception, describing Hoxie as a "tough cookie."

Bartkowicz responded to Hoxie's demands by winning the 13-and-under national title again in 1961. By the end of her junior tennis career, she had won twelve national singles titles. She won the 18-and-under title three times. She *never* lost a match during her junior tennis career. To appreciate the enormity of this accomplishment, let's contrast this with Chris Evert's junior tennis record. Chris, whom many consider to be one of the greatest female players in history, won three national singles titles as a junior and lost a number of individual matches. No wonder Peaches Bartkowicz was Chris Evert's and Tracy Austin's tennis idol.

Peaches was not the only national title holder in the Bartkowicz family. Plums was the number one ranked player in the 12-and-under division in 1966 having defeated "Chrissie" Evert 6-3, 6-8, 6-4 in the finals of the USLTA Girls' Championships at Lake Bluff, Illinois.

When Peaches was not on the road competing for national titles, she trained at Hamtramck with the high school boys' team. After the boys' varsity matches, she would often play the opposing team's number one player in a type of exhibition match and never lost. On one occasion, the women's team from Michigan State came to Hamtramck and Peaches, age fourteen, took on the Spartans' top player. Bartkowicz reflected, "The high school guys were pretty cool about playing me, but the Michigan State player wasn't too thrilled when this local kid beat her."

By June 1964, Peaches was ready for international competition. At age fifteen, she entered the Wimbledon Junior Championships, which is an 18-and-under event. With the media present, Jean Hoxie detailed the reasons Bartkowicz would win the Wimbledon Junior title stating, "*She's tough . . . the greatest strategist in the game today . . . relentless . . . she fights the game and never makes mistakes . . . she's already won 105 championships.*"

Despite Hoxie's prediction, Bartkowicz almost didn't make it past the first round. Her opponent, a Russian, towered over the five feet six Peaches. They split the first two sets. Peaches was down a break in the third set when Arthur Ashe, during the changeover, shouted, "Come on, Peaches!" She was amazed that Ashe even knew who she was. Bartkowicz bore down, broke the Russian's serve to even the score and then took the third set and the match. Several weeks later, Wimbledon officials determined that her first-round Russian opponent was actually twenty-one years old. Peaches reported that she never saw the Russian player again in any international competition.

With her trademark two-fisted backhand and penetrating forehand, Bartkowicz demolished her next several opponents to make the final round against Mexico's Elena Subirats. Dispatching Subirats 6-3, 6-1, Peaches Bartkowicz of Hamtramck, Michigan, became the youngest player to win the Wimbledon Junior title.

Bartkowicz felt the pressure to win every match she played. Following her return from Wimbledon, Peaches entered a women's tournament at River Forest, Illinois. When she lost in the semifinals, she felt that she had disappointed Coach Hoxie. Years later, Bartkowicz admitted being terrified of Hoxie.

Bartkowicz had a solid, but not stellar, professional tennis career. When she started competing on the women's tour, Peaches realized she had some significant limitations in her game, primarily attributable to Hoxie's coaching style. Bartkowicz never developed a net game that would have been important, particularly during that era when three of the four major championships were played on grass. Another limiting factor was Coach Hoxie. Her dictatorial, demanding coaching style had a deleterious impact on the developing Peaches. And despite all her coaching successes, Hoxie had significant limitations in her understanding of the game. By the time Bartkowicz was fourteen years old, she would have benefited from and probably flourished with another coach.

Regardless, Bartkowicz engineered wins against some of the dominant players of the era including Margaret Court, Virginia Wade, Rosie Casals, Evonne Goolagong, Francoise Durr, Ann Hayden Jones, and Chris Evert. There were only two elite players she never defeated: Billie Jean King and

Nancy Richey. Bartkowicz won fourteen professional titles and attained a world ranking of eight in 1969. She reached the quarterfinals of the U.S. Open in 1968 and 1969. She was also one of the original nine members of the Virginia Slims tour that commenced in 1970.

Jerry Hoxie once addressed the achievements of the Hoxie kids by reflecting, "Everyone thinks we have some sort of elaborate set up to coach all these kids. All we've got are several outdoor courts here at the park, 'The Wall' ..., and this crazy woman."

Note that the "crazy woman," Jean Hoxie, integrated many of the elements for developing a successful tennis community – deliberate practice, a competitive environment, and an emphasis on sustained effort - all within the framework of an apprenticeship program. With significant contributions from her husband, Jean Hoxie built a successful tennis community in an ethnic, working-class neighborhood with no tennis tradition. If a major tennis training center can be established in Hamtramck, Michigan, it can be established almost anywhere.

IN MEMORIAM
WILLIAM A. HARRIS
JANUARY 14, 1947 - MARCH 8, 2002

"Bill Tilden was reincarnated as Bill Harris."

Several years ago, I conducted an informal survey of select tennis players in the Tallahassee community, the majority of whom were over fifty years old with an age range from twenty-five to seventy-seven. The survey concerned Florida junior tennis and involved only two questions. The first question was "Who was the greatest junior girls' player of all time?" The second question was a corresponding one about the boys. I asked participants to focus only on the players' junior tennis careers. With only one exception, the twenty-five-year-old, all survey participants agreed that Chris Evert was Florida's greatest girls' junior player. The twenty-five-year-old respondent mentioned Jennifer Capriati.

The question about Florida's greatest junior boy's player resulted in looks of puzzlement and consternation. Each of the survey participants pondered the question before responding. They noted the difficulty of the question given the apparent lack of a clear choice across several decades of Florida tennis. After a significant delay, each produced an answer. With the exception of Jim Courier, whom fifteen of the respondents rated as the greatest boys' junior player, there was minimal consistency across the answers. Other players mentioned were Brian Gottfried, Larry Gottfried, Eddie Dibbs, Frank Froehling, Vince Spadea, Larry Turville, Armistead Neely, and Cameron Corse. Finally, the twenty-five-year-old respondent thought Roscoe Tanner was a good candidate for the boys. Interestingly, Roscoe *was* a resident of the Florida Department of Corrections from January 31, 2006 to February 1, 2007, having been convicted of grand theft and depositing a check with intent to defraud. During his junior tennis playing days, he actually hailed from Lookout Mountain, Tennessee.

My idea for this informal survey came from a formal study initially published in *Florida Tennis Magazine* in 1992. The authors of that study, Phil Secada and Jim Martz, considered a number of variables in their decision-making process including the number of years that a player was ranked among the top ten in the state and the nation, number of years with a state ranking of number one, and the number of national titles.

And who were considered to be the elite of all the great Florida junior tennis players in history? Consistent with the results of the informal Tallahassee survey, Chris Evert was the top player among all the great female junior players – and with good reason. Chris garnered national titles in 1968, 1970, and 1971. She was ranked number one among Florida players in her age division from 1968 through 1971.

And Florida's number one male junior player in history is a name that most tennis players and readers of this book will not be familiar – Bill Harris. Consider just a few of his junior tennis accomplishments: Harris burst onto the Florida tennis scene at age ten when he was ranked number seven in the 13-and-under division. The following year he was ranked number three. From 1959 through 1965, Harris was ranked number one in his age division. In 1960, at age thirteen, Harris was also ranked number three in the 15-and-under division. In 1962, he was ranked number three in the men's division. And in 1963, Harris was ranked number one in both 16- and 18-and-under divisions. He won three national titles – in 1960, 1961, and 1963. He was the number one seed at the National Boys' Championships in 1960, 1961, 1962, 1963, and 1965. He was seeded number two behind Butch Seewagen in 1964. Harris won more national titles than he lost matches. From my review of the extant literature on Harris, I could determine that he lost only nine matches from 1959 through 1965. He won thirteen national singles titles.

Harris's contemporaries hold him with a special reverence reserved for the truly extraordinary. Stan Smith, former number one player in the world, noted that Bill "was sort of a god among the players of our era." Charles Darley described him as a "tennis genius." Jaime Pressley, Bill's hitting partner for three years in high school, described Bill as a "demigod." One of Bill's closest friends, Frank Tutvin, stated that he was "the best junior tennis player in the world." My favorite quote was from Butch Seewagen, who noted, "Bill Tilden was reincarnated as Bill Harris."

I remain astounded that few tennis players remember Bill Harris. Of all the great tennis players developed in the state of Florida, Harris was unequivocally the best. His junior record eclipses even that of Chris Evert's.

All of the issues previously discussed in this book – innate talent, the rage to master, deliberate practice, environmental design, and the multiplier effect – require examination to provide even a partial account for the accomplishments of this remarkable young man. If Frankie Parker was the tennis "boy wonder" of the 1930s, Bill Harris was definitely the boy wonder of the 1960s.

CHARLES HARRIS

"What was silent in the father speaks in the son; and often I found the son the unveiled secret of the father."

~ Friedrich Nietzsche

Bill wasn't the only tennis player in the Harris family. His older siblings, Robert and Betty, were also accomplished players. Secada and Martz ranked Robert Harris 91st among the top 100 junior Florida boys from 1960 to 1992. And Betty once played Billie Jean Moffitt in the juniors, losing 6-3, 6-3.

The tennis patriarch was the father, Charles Harris. He was an extraordinary tennis player in his own right. In 1937, Charles was ranked number seven in the United States, winning state championships in Florida, New Jersey, Colorado, and Utah. He was the Florida State champion for three consecutive years from 1935 to 1937 and was the West Palm Beach city champion eight times. His most impressive tennis accomplishment came in 1939 when he won the French Championships in doubles with partner Don McNeil.

Charles Harris competed against many of the tennis greats of the 1930s: J. Donald Budge, Bobby Riggs, Frankie Parker, Bitsy Grant, Joe Hunt, Gene Mako, Frank Kovacs, Gottfried Von Cramm, and his doubles partner, Don McNeil. He defeated Frankie Parker 6-3, 3-6, 6-3, 4-6, 6-4 in the semifinals of the 1936 Kentucky State tournament. Charles took a set from the great Don Budge in a semifinal match in the 1937 Miami-Biltmore tournament, losing 2-6, 6-2, 6-2, 6-1. The one player who seemed to have Charles's "number" was Bobby Riggs. Charles lost all of his seven encounters with Riggs but extended him to five sets in the finals of the 1938 Palm Beach Invitation. Charles once played the great Australian, Frank Sedgman, in the first round of the 1949 U.S. Championships at Forest Hills, losing 5-7, 6-4, 6-3, 6-2.

Charles played tennis in the classic style of the 1930s. His daughter, Betty, noted that her dad had the "most beautiful backhand." He was extremely steady, wearing opponents down from the baseline. Gardnar Mulloy (who won four U.S. men's doubles titles with partner Billy Talbert, won the Wimbledon doubles title in 1957 with Budge Patty, and lost in the final of the U.S. Singles Championships in 1952 to Frank Sedgman) noted that Charles was "very tough on clay – he beat my ass all the time. We called Charlie the 'Big Cat' because he pounced on every ball. Never missed."

From 1938-39, Charles represented the United States in a series of exhibition matches played in various international sites including Sweden, Norway, Finland, Germany, the Netherlands, Egypt, and Japan. He also played an exhibition match in the princely state of Baroda, which was incorporated into the union of India in 1949. Charles and his teammates had several adventures during their international travels. They went on a hunting trip with Sir Sayajirao Gaekwad III, Maharaja of Baroda. And they had the dubious honor of either seeing or meeting Adolf Hitler in Pre-World War II Germany.

BILL HARRIS – TENNIS LEGEND

Bill Harris started playing tennis at age seven or eight under the tutelage of his father. During the weekends, Charles drove his children to the public courts of Lantana, Florida, for several hours of practice. Unlike a Mike Agassi or Richard Williams, Charles did not specifically design a tennis-production machine. But he did provide his children with the essentials of tennis, molding their games after the tennis greats of the 1930s. His forte was groundstrokes, and it was no accident that several of his children became human backboards.

The Harrises were a hard-working, middle-class family who lived in West Palm Beach. Charles and his wife provided their children with a well-balanced and physically active life. The family owned the J.C. Harris Company, a clothing store established in 1913 by Bill's grandfather. The store specialized in formal and casual attire. It was the oldest retail store in West Palm Beach and recently closed after one hundred years of continuous operation.

During the summer months, on his way to work at the store, Charles would take his children to the Howard Park public courts. They played tennis for many hours until their mom picked them up at 5 p.m. Although several of his siblings were accomplished players, Bill really took to the game. Having a rather obsessive, perfectionistic streak, Bill once asserted that he would not leave the courts until he had hit the ball 500 times without missing. He spent hours hitting tennis balls against the family garage door. His target was a basketball-sized circle drawn on the door. He considered it losing if he did not hit the circle dead center. Bill apparently never did formal groundstroke drills. He didn't run or do weight training. He just played tennis all day long. In a very real sense, when it came to tennis, Bill had the "rage to master."

In 1958, at age eleven, Bill won his first major junior tournament, defeating Hugh Curry 6-2, 6-4 at the Florida State Hard-Court Championships. And that was just the beginning. He won the first of three national titles in 1960 when he was thirteen years old.

But it was a quarterfinal match of the 1961 Boys 15-and-under National Championships at Kalamazoo where his legendary status emerged. Harris was the number one seed, and he was scheduled to play the sixth-seeded Cliff Richey of San Angelo, Texas. This was Richey's first time at the tournament, which he referred to as "the Wimbledon of junior tennis." Richey had worked hard to be the best among the juniors, and he recognized this match with Harris was pivotal to reaching his goal. Richey was a tough, gritty clay-court player; he was ready for Harris. Richey dominated the match by winning the first set 6-1 and then raced out to a 5-1 lead in the second set.

Richey recalled that when he was up 5-1 in the second, he overhead several spectators in the stands say, "Let's move on; this match is over." Not quite. Bill Harris had this remarkable capacity to focus and pressure his opponent when on the verge of defeat.

Frank Tutvin informed me that the strongest part of Harris's game was "when he decided not to miss a ball." After the match, Bill told his brother that when he was down 5-1 in the second set, he was determined not to miss another shot. Harris engineered a furious comeback. He rallied from this staggering deficit to defeat Richey 1-6, 8-6, 6-2. Robert Harris reported that it took Richey at least a year to recover from that match.

Richey reflected on the match. He described Harris as a "wily" sort of player and a "cool customer." Harris never seemed rattled by Richey's big lead. Richey noted that this 1961 match was similar to other matches he had in his career that when it came down to "crunch time," he had no big weapon to finish off his opponent. Richey acknowledged that he was "hurt and stung" by the loss, but it didn't affect him long. His dad, who had been watching the match, was supportive of his son, encouraging him to learn from the loss. And learn he did. Richey won the Kalamazoo tournament for the next two years including a thrilling 5-7, 6-3, 9-7 win over Butch Seewagen in the semifinals of the 18-and-under championships in 1963.

Charles Darley, one of Bill's fellow competitors and one of only several Americans to defeat Harris during a seven-year period, was courtside to watch the match against Richey. He described the comeback as "absolutely amazing." He also mentioned that Harris said something "very quirky" after the match. Someone asked Bill what he was thinking about when he was down match point against Richey. Bill replied that he had heard a train go by just prior to match point and thought it would be fun to place a penny on the track.

This comment requires some explanation. Two things captured the attention of the tennis players during their off-court time during the championships. One was to aggravate the local teenage boys, known as "the townies." And the townies attempted to harass and intimidate the tennis players, perceived as snotty, rich kids who were receiving a lot of attention from the local girls of Kalamazoo. Darley noted that the townies drove by and gave "the finger" and yelled obscenities at the players. The tennis players responded in kind. The other form of entertainment for the players was to flatten pennies on the local railroad track. The phenomenon of kids placing pennies on railroad tracks has occurred as long as there have been trains and kids with pennies. A penny is placed on a railroad track and, when the train runs over the penny, it is transformed into a flattened, fifty-cent sized souvenir. I have to admit, I did this penny flattening maneuver several times as a thirteen-year-old. Nevertheless, this is not the wisest thing to do. Sometimes, when the train runs over a penny, it may shoot it out as a potential deadly projectile. There have also been several instances in which the person placing the penny on the track has been flattened, along with the penny, by the train.

Darley's "shocking" defeat of Bill Harris came several days after Bill's victory at the 1961 national championships. Bill was seeded first at the Jaycee's International Tennis Tournament held in East Lansing, Michigan, a hard-court event. Bill was almost invincible on clay, but he was somewhat vulnerable on a hard-court surface. This vulnerability was only relative, however. Bill had great groundstrokes and was incredibly steady, but a good serve-volley player and one who routinely attacked the net against Harris's serve had a chance, albeit a small one, of defeating him.

This was Darley's strategy when he played Harris in the quarterfinals. He reported that it was an incredibly hot day, somewhere around 95 degrees. Darley attacked the net at every conceivable opportunity. He won the first set 7-5, but Harris took command of the second set, winning it 6-1. It was beginning to look dim for Darley. After all, he was unseeded and facing the best fourteen-year-old player in the world. Darley had nothing to lose and resumed his attack strategy. He took Bill's second serve and chipped and charged the net. He tried to pressure Harris whenever the opportunity presented itself. He informed me that, in classic tennis player fashion, he even remembered one particular point that involved hitting a winning crosscourt forehand. He then hesitated and said, "You know, it's strange but I think Bill was coming to the net when I hit that shot." This match occurred over fifty years ago, but Charles talked about it as though it happened yesterday.

The third set was a thriller, with Darley winning it 12-10. He reported that his whole body cramped up after the match, and he felt horrible for the next twenty-four hours. I suppose one could describe this as a Pyrrhic victory. Darley stated that Harris's shots were deep and well-placed and that he rarely missed. Harris covered the court well, and his open-stance forehand was particularly tough. Harris did not express much emotion on the court but made some comments following one of his rare misses. Charles described Bill as being rather introverted.

Charles Darley, from Rochester, Minnesota, played collegiate tennis for the University of California – Berkeley. Following his graduation, he played the circuit from 1966-68. But his greatest victory had to be that win over Bill Harris on August 10, 1961. And with all respect to David Wheaton, it was probably the greatest win for any tennis player from Minnesota.

King Lambert and the Flying Insect

I had the opportunity to watch Harris play tennis in late December 1962. Bill had just won the Orange Bowl 16-and-under Championships, defeating Francisco "Pancho" Guzman of Ecuador in the finals 6-1, 7-5. Several days after his Orange Bowl victory, he was asked to play an exhibition match against King Lambert at the Silver Thatch Inn of Pompano Beach. My family and I were staying at the Inn that December.

I was recruited to be a linesperson for the match. The tennis director at the Inn, Wayne Sabin, figured it would be a good experience for me. This was to be my first and last experience as a linesperson. I think my reaction to Harris arriving at the court was like seeing some tennis god stepping down from Mount Olympus with a Jack Kramer racket to spend several hours with the rest of us tennis mortals. I was a rather introverted thirteen-year-old, and, being keenly sensitive to the tennis "pecking order," I don't believe I said a word to him.

Lambert was probably in his midtwenties and worked as a Dunlop representative. He was an excellent player and highly ranked in the Florida men's division. You had to figure he would be the favorite because of his significant physical developmental advantage. After all, Harris was only a kid.

I was assigned to observe one of the singles sidelines. I found the task a little difficult because I wanted to watch the match. Harris had these classic groundstrokes - an open stance forehand and an almost entirely flat backhand. Bill's older sister, Betty, stated that his groundstrokes were like Chris Evert's. I think it may be more appropriate to say that Evert's groundstrokes were like Bill's. His shots had great depth and penetration. His anticipation and foot speed were tremendous. He took the first set against Lambert 6-2. Lambert, taking a page from the Charles Darley playbook, attacked the net whenever possible. Harris passed him many times, but Lambert managed to win the second set 6-4.

The third set was hard-fought with the match tied at 5-5. With Harris serving, Lambert had a break point. They probably exchanged twenty shots during the breaker. Lambert took a forehand and drove it deep to Harris's backhand and approached the net. Just as this was happening, I was startled by a rather large, strange-looking flying insect that landed on the armrest of the chair upon which I was sitting. Just for a split second, I diverted my attention from the singles sideline to the insect. At that moment, Harris, who was on the opposite side of the net from where I was sitting, passed Lambert with a down-the-line backhand that was close to the line. Unfortunately, I did not have a good look at the shot because I was distracted by the insect. All of a sudden, I could sense thirty pairs of eyes bearing down on me to make the call. I started to panic and thought, "Why me and why on such a critical point?" I didn't have the presence of mind, being a rather goofy thirteen-year-old, to say I didn't see the call and have the point replayed. So, I managed to screw up some false courage, pointed my right hand out to the side, and yelled, "Out!" So, with my screwed-up false courage, I probably screwed up the call. Lambert jogged toward me and said, "You sure about that call, kid?" I meekly replied, "Yes." He said, "Thanks, I needed a break." Bill was gracious about the call – he didn't say a word. I can only imagine what John McEnroe would have done. Well, Lambert held serve to take the next game and the match. I didn't linger around the court after the exhibition, retreating as quickly as possible to our hotel room and thinking, "I'm glad this was only an exhibition match."

1963: THE PHENOMENAL YEAR

Harris turned sixteen in 1963 and probably had the greatest year of any male junior tennis player in history. He was the first seed in every tournament he played. He played multiple tournaments in Florida and routinely competed in both the 16- *and* 18-under divisions. At times, he played six matches a day, between singles and doubles. All the players were gunning for him. And you can only imagine how the guys in the 18-and-under division must have felt. Here's this sixteen-year-old kid dominating players who were several years older. By this time, Harris was supremely confident when playing tennis. When he stepped onto the court for a match, Harris knew that he would win. Armistead Neely, one of Bill's contemporaries and later the number one tennis player for the University of Florida, noted that a mystique began to evolve around Harris. Neely added that Harris owned the game others were trying to play. There were times when Harris played an entire tournament left-handed and won. No one even noticed that he was right-handed.

During that era, there were four national tournaments in which the elite junior players competed:

1. St. Louis, Missouri – a hard-court event
2. Louisville, Kentucky – a clay-court event
3. Springfield, Ohio (known as "the Westerns") – a clay-court event
4. Kalamazoo, Michigan for the national championship – this was a clay-court event until 1964 when the tournament changed to a hard-court format.

In 1963, Harris won the first three events leading up to the national championships at Kalamazoo. Easily defeating Bernard Watson 6-0, 6-2 in his first match, Harris was the juggernaut of the Kalamazoo tournament. He then destroyed Richard Cohen of Merion Station, Pennsylvania, in the third round 6-1, 6-1. Harris had his first "test" of the tournament facing Stanley Pasarell. As noted earlier, Pasarell was one of the Hoxie Tennis House campers. Pasarell gave it his all but fell to Harris 6-2, 6-4. Harris dominated the seventh seed, Robert Goeltz of Bethesda, Maryland, 6-1, 6-1 in the quarterfinals. Harris easily defeated his friend and doubles partner, Robert Speicher in the semis 6-0, 6-2.

The surprise of the Kalamazoo tournament was unheralded Chuck Brainard from, of all places, Hamtramck, Michigan. He was another Hoxie kid who began training at age seven. Like other Hoxie trainees, Brainard was a backcourt specialist, a "human wall." By the 1960s, Hoxie's primary objective expanded from an emphasis on obtaining tennis scholarships for her players to securing national titles. She enjoyed nothing more than to have her players defeat the privileged "elites."

Brainard had the toughest draw of the tournament, facing many of the "elites" as he progressed to the final round. His first two matches were straightforward, readily dispatching his opponents. In the third round, he faced the accomplished Dan Bleckinger, defeating him 6-1, 6-3. He then faced his first "elite," the third-seeded Bob Lutz from Los Angeles; Brainard prevailed 6-4, 6-3.

In the quarterfinals, Brainard's opponent was the tenth seed, Zan Guerry. Guerry had a remarkable junior tennis career, winning thirteen national singles or doubles titles plus a win at the Orange Bowl in 1964. Between his junior and professional careers, Guerry had wins against Eddie Dibbs, Mike Estep, Frank Froehling, John McEnroe, Victor Pecci, Dick Stockton, and Guillermo Vilas.

Guerry described his loss to Brainard at the 1963 national championships as the toughest of his life. Guerry noted that he could have defeated Brainard on 99 out of 100 occasions, obviously not showing him much respect as a tennis player. Given his self-proclaimed superiority, it's amusing that Guerry only won four games against Brainard, losing 6-3, 6-1.

Brainard played the second seed, the great Armistead Neely from Tampa in the semifinals. This was the match of the tournament. Neely won the first set, 7-5; Brainard won the second set, 6-4; and the third set was a struggle with both boys refusing to yield. It was Neely's attacking style versus Brainard's steady backcourt game. Neely approached the net whenever possible and put away many volleys; Brainard countered by firing multiple deadly passing shots. Neely had two match points in the third set but couldn't convert. Brainard, who had spent hours perfecting his groundstrokes against "The Wall" at Hamtramck, prevailed 9-7 in the third set.

Brainard's semifinal win set up an interesting final-round encounter. Coach Hoxie and her husband had worked on Brainard's game for twelve months a year for the last nine years. He hit tennis balls for hours against "The Wall" and played many matches under Hoxie's watchful eye; and he had just defeated some of the best junior players in the nation to reach the final round.

Even though Harris was not from a particularly privileged background with his parents inculcating a strong "immigrant" work ethic, Hoxie most likely perceived him as the ultimate "elite" player, viewing this match-up as a contest between the tough blue-collar "Hoxie kid" from Hamtramck and the advantaged prodigy from West Palm Beach. I'm sure Coach Hoxie sensed this may have been her moment. But she and Chuck Brainard never saw anything like Bill Harris on a tennis court. Despite Brainard's superb preparation and great backcourt game, he was facing the best junior clay-court player on the planet. Having prevailed in the final, destroying Brainard 6-1, 6-0 in thirty-eight minutes, Harris secured his third national championship in four years.

When Bill returned to school in late August, the high school athletic director attempted to recruit him to play other sports, acknowledging his great athletic skills. Wanting to concentrate on tennis, Harris declined. And how could he have done otherwise? In addition to being the best sixteen-year-old tennis player in the world, his high school was named Forest Hill(s) and its athletic director and football coach had the name of one of tennis's most infamous players, Bobby Riggs.

By the end of 1963, Harris was the nation's top-ranked player in the 16-and-under division. In Florida, he was ranked number one in the 16-and-under as well as the 18-and-under divisions. He also was the state men's champion. What a year!

From the information I had available to me, it appears that Harris only lost two matches in 1963. He lost the state high school championships in the final round to his long-time friend, Frank Tutvin. Bill was a sophomore and Frank a senior. The other loss occurred at the 1963 Orange Bowl Championships. Harris bypassed the 16-and-under division to play at the 18-and-under level; this was something unheard of during that era. Remember, this is one of the premier junior tournaments in the world where Harris competed against the elites of international junior tennis. He made it to the final round, where he lost to the great Brazilian, Tomas Koch. In the 16-and-under division, Chuck Brainard defeated Bill's hitting partner Jamie Pressley, 6-2, 6-4. Had Bill played in the 16-and-under division that year, he most likely would have won his second Orange Bowl title given how easily he had dispatched Brainard several months earlier at Kalamazoo.

Shrouded in a Mysterious Blazer

There was a rather mysterious quality to Bill Harris. He had a certain aura about him – complex, distant, enigmatic. The individuals with whom I spoke about Harris mentioned that he seemed to step out from a grander era of tennis, reminiscent of the times of Bill Tilden, J. Donald Budge, and Gottfried Von Cramm. And like those tennis legends, Harris was an impeccable dresser. His trademark was his famous blue blazer. He probably started wearing the blazer to matches during his mid-teens. He showed up to matches with the blazer, often times wearing it during the warm-up. He removed it just prior to the start of the match and put it back on after dismissing an opponent. Over time, the sight of Harris removing the blazer represented an impending defeat for whomever he was facing. Neely stated the blazer had a fear-inducing quality equivalent to the effect of the serape worn by Clint Eastwood. One can almost imagine Harris approaching the tennis court from the distance through a haze, walking onto the court, approaching his opponent, and, in that distinctive, rasping Clint Eastwood voice, saying, "You've got to ask yourself one question: Do I feel lucky?" Harris would then remove the blazer, and his opponent would be reduced to tennis mush.

Some of Harris's persona seems attributable to the tennis instruction received from his dad. Charles trained Bill in the style of the early to mid-twentieth century – classic, steady groundstrokes. No wonder many considered him to be the reincarnation of Bill Tilden. But there was more to Harris's game and his personal "aura" than just being a throwback to some other era. Elements of his game can be seen as a prototype for players such as Jim Courier, Jimmy Connors, and Andre Agassi. Harris was an aggressive counterpuncher with a great return of serve. He knew how to develop a point better than anyone. Harris exhausted his opponents by moving them from corner to corner. Since he rarely missed his groundstrokes, attempts to outsteady him were bound to fail. If opponents were to approach the net, Harris routinely ripped passing shots by them. He played the net well when necessary. He had an effective overhead. His only one possible "weakness" was the serve. It wasn't overpowering but it was consistent, deep, and well-placed. Harris was certainly one of the greatest junior players in history. I had the opportunity to ask Jaime Pressley, given all that he now knows about the game, would he have played Harris differently. He replied, "It would be impossible," meaning there was no way for him to defeat Harris.

With few exceptions, Harris did not socialize with other players. Even in grade school, there was a different quality about him. His twin sister, Mary, shared that Bill was a loner throughout his school years. Neely described Bill as dominant, rather "foreign," and quiet but supremely confident. Harris did not run with the pack. He played his matches and went home. Neely stated they never practiced together or exchanged pleasantries.

Like Tilden several decades before him, Harris had a reputation for baiting players. There were times when he intentionally lost the first set and the first several games of the second set. Word spread at the tournament site and people would congregate around his court. Some would say, "The great Bill

Harris is about to lose." Harris would smile, begin to focus, and win the next twelve games. This had to have a devastating effect on all his potential opponents.

In his article, *The Search for Bill Harris*, Eliot Berry detailed one match, the finals of the Florida juniors that was played in 95-degree heat. Harris wore his blue blazer throughout the warm-up and continued wearing it during the first set. He lost the set 6-0 but didn't remove the blazer until he was down 4-0 in the second set. He casually strode over to the sidelines, removed the blazer and only then started to play. He won the next six games to take the second set 6-4. He won the third set 6-1. Berry speculated that "heart," "talent," and supreme confidence may not have provided an adequate explanation for why Harris wore his blazer in 95-degree heat. And Berry asked, "Why had Harris not emerged from the amateur ranks to blaze a trail across the pro circuit?"

Harris had a talent for devising games of skill. One of Harris's childhood friends, Bob Speicher, said that Bill enjoyed performing various skilled tasks with his eyes closed such as walking on top of a fence. During a tournament at Louisville, Kentucky, club officials threw a party for the players. The tennis club was located by a river, and Bill noticed a rather slippery-looking, moss-covered rope that ran from the bank of the river to a barge. Harris was dressed in a nice pair of slacks and his blue blazer. He stated that he could walk the length of the rope to the barge and back to the river bank without falling. Several of his fellow players bet against him, wanting to see the great Bill Harris fall headlong into the river. Well, Harris managed to traverse the length of the rope to the barge and back without any problem, much to the chagrin of his "peers."

There was a game of skill popular in this country during the 1950s and 1960s: the Labyrinth was a wooden box with a suspended maze on top that rotated on two axes, each controlled by a wooden knob. The maze contained sixty holes, and the object of the game was to navigate a small steel marble to the end of the maze without it falling into any hole. The game required a considerable amount of physical dexterity, and it took me several weeks of concentrated play to master it. Mary, Bill's twin sister, shared with me that Bill could do it with his feet.

1964 was another stellar year for Harris. He won almost every tournament he entered. Neely stated that in early 1964, Florida players began hearing about a "mystery" player from Pasadena, California, by the name of Stan Smith. Smith was a basketball player who switched to tennis and was having great success in the California juniors. He was physically large with a big serve-volley game. Smith committed to playing in several of the four major junior tournaments outlined above. When Harris was informed about Smith's decision to play in these tournaments, his response was, "Hmm, we'll see." Harris was usually rather dismissive of California players.

So, Smith traveled east to play at the Westerns in Springfield, Ohio, a clay-court event. Harris met Smith in the quarterfinals and defeated him 6-1, 6-1. Welcome to "Florida" clay-court tennis, Stan. Smith said that match was a wake-up call for him. Smith did defeat Harris in the finals of the 18-and-under National Championships at Kalamazoo later that summer. As noted earlier, in 1964 the Kalamazoo tournament changed to a hard-court format. Had it remained a clay-court event, it is almost inconceivable that Smith could have defeated Harris.

Smith recounted a story that occurred at the 1964 championships in which a girl approached Harris with a scrapbook of all his wins and asked Bill to sign it. Obtaining all of Harris's news clippings must have been quite a feat. She probably had to do some serious library work to assemble her scrapbook. Neely reported that no one, with the possible exception of Bjorn Borg, attained such legendary status during one's junior tennis career.

Later that year, both Smith and Harris represented the United States in the Sunshine Cup. Smith stated, "Since it was on clay and Bill was nearly unbeatable on this surface, he would win his match, I would lose mine, then we would win the doubles."

Smith, of course, had a stellar professional tennis career. He was the world's number one ranked player in 1972. He won the Wimbledon singles title that year and also was victorious at the U.S. Open in 1971. Together with partner Bob Lutz, they won multiple doubles titles, including the Australian Open in 1970 and four U.S. Open titles (1968, 1974, 1978, and 1980). Harris had a winning record against both Smith and Lutz in the juniors.

WHAT ACCOUNTS FOR BILL HARRIS'S GREATNESS?

When I asked several of his family members this question, they all replied, "He was born with it." They may be advocates of Sir Francis Galton's innate talent hypothesis. And this would be understandable. Several of his siblings were exposed to similar environmental conditions and yet Bill's tennis skills were vastly superior to those of his older, tennis-playing siblings, Robert and Betty. At age fourteen, Bill was routinely defeating the seventeen-year-old Robert.

Putting innate talent aside for a moment, let's examine some factors that may provide a plausible account for his incredible tennis skills. Bill had the advantages his siblings shared: (1) tennis instruction from a world-class tennis-playing father, (2) they lived in South Florida, the epicenter of competitive junior tennis, and (3) the Harris family had the means to support state, regional, and national tournament play.

There were several factors that were advantageous to Bill alone. The first was a significant innate, biological advantage involving his physical stature. Harris was physically quite mature at an early age. Butch Seewagen joked that Bill was probably shaving at age thirteen. He also noted that playing Harris in the juniors "was like a boy competing against a man."

Another factor was that Harris's birth month was January. This can have a huge advantage in the early development of an athlete. There can be a significant developmental advantage for someone born in the early months of the year competing against a "same-aged" peer born in, say, October to December. Furthermore, Harris had the advantage of being significantly more mature than even peers born a year or two earlier. For example, when Harris competed in the 13-and-under national championships in Chattanooga, Tennessee, tournament officials demanded a copy of his birth certificate because they couldn't believe he was only twelve-and-a-half years old.

During his early tennis years, Harris played all the time. His practice sessions, like Borg's, did not involve formal tennis drills. Borg apparently could keep a ball in play for at least thirty minutes during a practice session. Harris could do the same, if not longer. Those two didn't have to drill; their rallies were more than sufficient practice. So, between Harris's competitive play and practice sessions, he most likely logged in more than 10,000 hours of deliberate practice.

Harris was the recipient of the multiplier effect. As a function of his early tennis successes, because of the above-noted factors, Bill was exposed to an increasingly higher level of competitive play than almost any of his peers. He was competing, and winning, in multiple age divisions starting at an early age. By doing so, he was competing against highly skilled players; this only made his game more effective. He had the opportunity to play as a member of the Junior Davis Cup for several years. Not unexpectedly, Harris was undefeated in Junior Davis Cup play.

And yet, as many have noted, there was something different about Harris. There were qualities that set him apart from his fellow competitors. Perhaps Ellen Winner's conceptualization of giftedness applies to him. Recall Winner's three defining characteristics: (1) gifted children are precocious, (2) they march to their own drummer – they learn in a qualitatively different way and faster than their accomplished peers, and (3) they have the *rage to master* – they are intrinsically motivated to excel. All of these factors appear to apply to Harris's tennis development.

TRINITY BOUND

Harris's last year in the juniors was 1965, having turned eighteen years old in January. He won the majority of tournaments in which he competed that year. He ended the year as the number one ranked player in Florida and number two nationally. He lost the opportunity to be the top-ranked national player that year having been dismissed by the hard-hitting, serve-volley player, Steve Avoyer, from San Diego during the semifinals in the 18-and-under National Championships at Kalamazoo. Bob Lutz defeated Avoyer in the finals. Had this event been played on clay, Harris would have defeated both of them.

Following his graduation from high school in the spring of 1965, Harris was highly recruited by the top tennis universities in the nation. The major tennis powers during that era included USC, UCLA, University of Miami,

Rice University, and Trinity University of San Antonio. Trinity had a great tennis tradition. Clarence Mabry, Trinity's coach, recruited many accomplished players including Frank Froehling, III, Chuck McKinley, and later Dick Stockton and Brian Gottfried. Prior to recruiting Harris, the Trinity University tennis team was 75-0 in intercollegiate tennis competition during the previous several seasons. Mabry wanted that streak to continue.

Mabry offered Harris a full scholarship to attend Trinity. There were several advantages for Bill to accept this offer. First, Trinity was one of the few universities that allowed freshman to play on the varsity team. Second, consistent with the majority of university tennis teams, their matches were played on hard courts. Bill was already one of the greatest clay-court players in the world. By attending Trinity and playing collegiate tennis, he could develop the one area where he was somewhat vulnerable and become a more effective player. The conditions were ideal to provide Harris with a tennis environment to continue to develop his remarkable skills. And note something important here – by enrolling in college in 1965, Bill would have been scheduled to graduate in 1969, the first full year of Open-era tennis. He would have been poised to unleash his unstoppable skills on the pro circuit upon graduating from college.

There was one issue to resolve before Bill accepted Coach Mabry's offer of a full tennis scholarship. It involved his twin sister, Mary, who was having some difficulty in getting admitted to the college of her choice. She and Bill had attended school together for many years and wanted to continue this arrangement through college. Bill informed the university that he would only play tennis for them if Mary was also accepted to the school. Bill and Mary enrolled at Trinity in September 1965.

Harris assumed the number one position on the tennis team as a freshman. Coach Mabry described Harris as a "complete tennis player," with the best tennis fundamentals the former had ever seen. This was high praise given that Mabry had coached the great Chuck McKinley.

McKinley was a terror on the courts in the early to mid-1960s. He won the Wimbledon title in 1963, defeating Fred Stolle 9-7, 6-1, 6-4; McKinley did not lose a set throughout the tournament. McKinley also reached the Wimbledon final in 1961, losing to Rod Laver. Other highlights of McKinley's tennis career included wins at the U.S. Clay Court Championships in 1963 and 1964 and at the U.S. Indoor Championships in 1962 and 1964. He teamed with Dennis Ralston to wrest the Davis Cup from Australia in 1963, defeating a young John Newcombe in the deciding match 10-12, 6-2, 9-7, 6-2. McKinley was built like a fire plug. He was five feet eight and weighed 160 pounds. Like Boris Becker years later, McKinley threw himself into his shots with reckless abandon. As great as McKinley was, Harris was better.

During the 1966 tennis season, Harris led the Trinity team to multiple victories which, Mabry noted, was *very* unusual for a freshman. On the court, he continued to manifest supreme confidence. Of increasing concern was Bill's off-court behavior; he was becoming increasingly erratic and unpredictable. He took solitary walks for hours at a time and often missed practice sessions. His teammates had to locate and bring him to the courts to play his scheduled matches. There was one incident in which a fellow student teased Bill that if he ever lost a match, they were going to send him to fight in Vietnam. Bill became upset about this and disappeared for several days. Following his return, Coach Mabry assembled a team meeting at the court bleachers. Suddenly, Bill jumped off the back of the bleachers and disappeared again.

The most important tennis event for the Trinity players was the Rice Invitational played in March. Bill won the event with his stellar play and led Trinity to the overall team title. Later that night Bill's behavior reached a crisis point. He telephoned his mother, but she was unable to understand a word he was saying. His verbalizations were rapid, digressive, and highly idiosyncratic. Listening to his barrage of incomprehensible verbalizations, she became quite alarmed. She immediately telephoned Coach Mabry and asked him to assist her in getting Bill back to West Palm Beach.

Upon Bill's return home in March 1966, he was evaluated by a psychiatrist and initially diagnosed with schizophrenia, which is one of the major mental disorders with symptoms including auditory hallucinations (i.e., hearing voices), delusions (e.g., ideas of persecution), disorganized speech, and disorganized motor behavior. Individuals with schizophrenia also may exhibit pronounced deficits in emotional expressiveness (e.g., blunted affect) and self-initiated activities. Bill's diagnosis was only tentative. There was the possibility that Bill could be manifesting one of the more "benign" of the psychotic disorders that resolve within a relatively brief period of time. There was some hope that Bill could return to his previous high level of functioning.

Bill responded well to his initial psychiatric treatment and returned to Trinity in May 1966. His older brother, Robert, left college in South Carolina and joined Bill at Trinity. Bill's symptom picture did not remain stable. He confided to his brother that he was depressed and was hearing voices and seeing things. To what degree Bill was adherent with his prescribed psychotropic medication was somewhat unclear. Bill did not like the side effects associated with his prescribed antipsychotic medication and was periodically non-adherent.

Since leaving the university in March, Harris had not touched a racket in two months. Coach Mabry wanted to withhold him from competitive tennis upon his return to Trinity. But Trinity was scheduled to play the powerful University of Miami in May. Miami finished the year second to UCLA in the NCAA standings. The number one player for Miami was the Chilean Jaime Fillol. He was a member of the Chilean Davis Cup team and later competed on the professional tour, reaching a world ranking of fourteen in 1974.

Despite Bill's psychiatric status, he convinced Mabry to put him in the lineup at number one singles. The night prior to the match, Bill became agitated and threw some chairs. He managed to compose himself the next day. But when he walked on to the tennis court, he was in his own private domain – he owned it. One can only guess at his subjective state. He may have been experiencing auditory hallucinations and feelings of paranoia, but his tennis skills were so well-entrenched and finely tuned that he was still able to display expert-level performance. He defeated Fillol in singles and also won his doubles match, leading Trinity to a 5-1 victory. Few, at the time, could appreciate the enormity of Bill's victories. Harris had recently experienced a major psychotic break only two months earlier and was still experiencing active psychotic symptoms, and yet he was able to defeat one of the top collegiate tennis players in the country. I can't conceive of any other tennis player being able to do this.

Harris returned to West Palm Beach that summer to continue his psychiatric treatment. He was stable enough to compete in several tournaments, reaching the final round of the prestigious Tri-State Championships in Cincinnati. He returned to Trinity in Fall 1966. On October 10, Harris played Chuck McKinley in an exhibition match as part of what was billed as "Chuck McKinley Day." Following the match, McKinley was scheduled to conduct a tennis clinic for aspiring San Antonio junior players. The match started off well for Harris. McKinley won the first game but then Harris took the next three, running McKinley from corner to corner. Harris was in control and took the first set 6-4. McKinley won the next two sets 6-1, 6-2. One of Bill's classmates speculated that Harris may have allowed McKinley to win the match. There was a distinct possibility that Harris did not want to upstage his opponent during Chuck's special day.

Harris's psychiatric issues precluded his return to school for the spring semester. There was an article published in the school newspaper that addressed Bill's departure from Trinity. It read: "Trinity University Tennis Coach, Clarence Mabry, announced that Trinity tennis star, Bill Harris, has been forced to withdraw from classes because of an illness. Mabry said Harris is suffering from a nervous condition and it is doubtful that he will be able to return to Trinity this spring. Harris has returned to his home in West Palm Beach, Florida. Mabry said that Harris plans to return to Trinity as soon as he is physically able." Sadly, this was not to be.

CINCINNATI - 1968

During the initial years of his psychiatric illness, Bill attained several significant periods of symptom remission. It was during these times that he returned to competitive tennis. There continued to be hope among the Harris family that Bill might achieve a complete remission of his psychiatric symptoms. Encouragingly, he won a tournament in Lake Worth, Florida in 1967, defeating Jaime Pressley 6-3, 6-1.

Harris's most impressive win came at the 1968 Tri-State Tennis Tournament in Cincinnati. Tennis in Cincinnati has a rather rich and storied history. Cincinnatians proudly proclaim that their annual tournament is "*the oldest tournament in the United States still played in its original city.*" The oldest American tournament is, of course, the U.S. National Championships, initially played at the Newport Casino in Newport, Rhode Island, in 1881. The tournament continued to be played in Rhode Island until 1915, when it moved to the West Side Tennis Club in Forest Hills, New York.

Some prominent Cincinnatians, who were vacationing in Newport, Rhode Island, in 1874, saw the sport played at the Newport Casino. One of their group, Stewart Shillito, brought tennis back to Cincinnati. Upon returning home, Shillito built a tennis court at his father's residence. The sport grew in popularity, and a group of players launched the Cincinnati Tennis Club in 1880.

The first tournament in Cincinnati was known as the Cincinnati Open. It was played at the Avondale Athletic Club from 1899 to 1902, when its location was changed to the Cincinnati Tennis Club. The "open" designation meant that the tournament was open to anyone, not just residents of Cincinnati. The 1899 inaugural event, played on brick dust, was won by Nat Emerson (I wonder if they called him "Emmo") over Dudley Sutphin 8-6, 6-1, 10-8. The women's champion was Myrtle McAteer, who dispatched Juliette Atkinson in the final round 6-4, 6-2.

The name of the tournament was changed in 1901 to the Tri-State Tennis Tournament and remained so until 1969, when it was known as the Western Tennis Championships. It is presently known as the Western and Southern Open, one of the ATP World Tour Masters events.

The history of the Cincinnati tournament is a who's who of tennis greats. Previous champions in the men's division include Bill Tilden, Bitsy Grant, Bobby Riggs, Pancho Segura, Cliff Richey, Ken Rosewall, Jimmy Connors, John McEnroe, Ivan Lendl, Pete Sampras, Andre Agassi, Roger Federer, and Rafael Nadal. Those victorious in the women's division include Alice Marble, Pauline Betz, Peaches Bartkowicz, Margaret Court, Evonne Goolagong, and Serena Williams.

Charles Harris played Bobby Riggs in the 1936 final, losing 6-1, 6-3, 6-1. Charles also lost to Riggs in the 1938 semifinal round 6-0, 6-1, 6-4. I suspect Riggs disrupted Charles's game with drop shots, lobs, and strategic "junk." And, of some minor historical interest, the last player to win the Cincinnati tournament with a wood racket was John McEnroe in 1981.

There was a thirty-one year hiatus for the women in the Cincinnati tournament, before it once again became a stop on the WTA tour in 2004. In 2011, the tournament became a joint event for both men and women professional players.

When Harris won the event in 1968, the tournament was played on a red clay-court surface, ideally suited for his game. He hadn't played much tennis that year but did compete in a few regional tournaments prior to the Cincinnati event.

Although 1968 saw the advent of Open-era tennis, the Cincinnati tournament remained an amateur event until the following year. Harris was the fourth seed behind Joaquin Loyo-Mayo, Jaime Fillol, and Peter Van Lingen. Fearing that the stress of the tournament could trigger a psychiatric relapse, Bill's parents were quite concerned about his decision to play. But Harris had a remarkable tournament. He won his first two rounds with ease and then played Larry Turville, defeating him 3-6, 6-2, 6-1. He dismissed John Sheaffer in the next round, 6-1, 6-1.

Harris defeated Steve Faulk in the round of 16 and faced Premjit Lall in the quarterfinals. Lall was a solid player. In 1958, Lall reached the finals of the Wimbledon Junior Championships. He played on the Indian Davis Cup team from 1959-73. His best performance in a Grand Slam was in 1962, when he reached the round of 16 in the Australian Championships, losing to John Newcombe 6-3, 6-4, 10-8. In typical Bill Harris fashion, he lost the first set but won the next two, defeating Lall 5-7, 7-5, 7-5. He defeated the Australian, Alan Stone, in the semis 4-6, 9-7, 6-0.

In the finals, Harris played Tom Gorman. This apparently was an entertaining match for the fans, with both Bill and Tom engaging in some on-court "banter." Eliot Berry detailed one point in the third set that involved in excess of an 80-shot exchange. Unexpectedly, Harris ended the point by catching the ball and joking with Gorman, "That's real good, Tom. Now that's the way you should be playing me!" This sounds like the appeal of "Brer Rabbit" in the Uncle Remus story to be thrown into the briar patch. The one way you did *not* want to play Harris was by attempting to outsteady him. If Gorman could play an 80-ball exchange, Harris could double that. Bill won the match 3-6, 6-2, 6-2. This was an especially remarkable accomplishment. Harris was into his third year of a major psychiatric disorder and was manifesting signs of his illness during the tournament.

An article in the Cincinnati Post & Times Star the next day reported, "Harris returned to tennis after a two-year layoff and appears capable of returning to the promise that he showed as a junior." This was not to be. Tragically, Bill was embarking on a psychiatric journey that adversely impacted his life for the next thirty-four years.

The 1968 U.S. Open was particularly exciting because it was the first United States championship of the Open era. The amateurs and professionals could compete together for the first time. There was an expectation that one of the professionals, such as Laver or Rosewall, would win the event. But Arthur Ashe, who was playing as an amateur and had this uncanny ability to seize the moment, won the event by defeating Tom Okker in the final round 14-12, 5-7, 6-3, 3-6, 6-3.

One little known but historically interesting feature of the inaugural U.S. Open was that the two "boy wonders" of tennis - Frank Parker from the 1930s and Bill Harris from the 1960s - played their last major tournament at the Open. Parker had won the event, when it was known as the U.S. Nationals, in 1944 and 1945. He wanted to play one event in the Open era. So, at the spry age of fifty-two, Parker entered the event and played Arthur Ashe in the second round, losing with the respectable score of 6-3, 6-2, 6-2.

Harris drew Paul Gerken in the first round. I recently spoke with Gerken about the match, and he stated that they played on one of the side grass courts at the West Side Tennis Club. He was aware of Harris's reputation as a "tennis machine." Gerken, a recent high school graduate, relied heavily on serving and volleying. He served and volleyed and, on Harris's service games, Gerken chipped and charged the net. Gerken won the match 6-2, 3-6, 6-3, 6-0. One surprising fact about Gerken's tennis career is that he had a winning record against Borg, defeating him during two of their three encounters.

Harris's psychiatric disorder was having a destructive impact on his life and game. Bill continued to play tournament tennis on a sporadic basis for the next several years, but his skill level declined precipitously. His peers noted that he could still play well, but he wasn't the "old Bill Harris." A number of them shared that had Bill not had his psychiatric issues, he would have dominated the European clay-court circuit. And I can only believe he would have had great success at the French Open, possibly winning it multiple times. His brother, Robert, was more succinct about Bill's prospects, stating, "He would have been the number one player in the world."

Perhaps this was the "unveiled secret" of the father.

THE NEXT THIRTY-FOUR YEARS

"His eyes stare out at his aging mother
as if unsure of who she is
and why she is taking care of him."

~ Pete LeForge

Bill's schizophrenia took a progressively deteriorating course, one that had a profound impact not only on himself but also on his family. Unless one is a family member of a severely mentally-ill individual or a mental-health worker specializing with this clinical population, it is difficult to convey the challenges that arise on a daily basis when caring for the mentally ill. It can be quite stressful.

I found out about Bill's psychiatric issues when I started jotting down some ideas for this book. Throughout the years, I occasionally wondered what had happened to him. Harris was such a dominant junior player that I couldn't understand how he just disappeared from the tennis scene. I encountered a brief Wikipedia piece about him several years ago, and I found myself staring at the computer monitor in disbelief. I probably had a stunned expression on my face while thinking, "Is *that* what happened to him?" Strangely, I had a rather profound emotional response to the news. And I didn't think this would be possible. I worked for three decades as a clinical psychologist specializing in the treatment of the severely mentally ill within the context of a state psychiatric hospital. With respect to the major mental illnesses, I have pretty much seen it all. Although I have empathy for those so affected, my emotional reactions became rather muted over time. The news about Bill Harris affected me deeply.

Compared to many individuals with a severe and persistent mental illness, Bill was one of the lucky ones. His mom and dad were able to care for him at home. They attempted to keep him as independent as possible, setting him up in a small cottage in the backyard of the main house. The family provided him with a cloistered, protective environment.

One of the sad things about Bill's psychiatric journey is that he retained sufficient insight for a time to see himself deteriorating. In response to this, he acted out against his own and his family's tennis legacy. On one occasion, he destroyed all newspaper accounts of his tennis triumphs. He gave away his tennis trophies to strangers. He threw all of his father's tennis trophies into a lake. He even cut himself out of the family's photo album.

Bill's adherence with his medication regimen was sporadic. He required several crisis stabilization unit (CSU) admissions throughout the years whenever his psychiatric condition worsened.

The early signs of Bill's disorder were, in retrospect, most likely present during adolescence. His discomfort around others and detachment from his peers were widely interpreted at the time to be part of his "aura"; these might have been signs of his emergent psychiatric disorder. Unknown to others outside the family, after Bill played at the National Boys' Championships in Kalamazoo, he withdrew and did not play tennis for several months until two weeks prior to the Orange Bowl tournament. The fact that he did so well at the Orange Bowl is a testament to his incredible tennis skills.

Where are you, Amy Giletz?

Whenever Bill was feeling well, he took his racket and went to the courts to "hit a few." He had a friend, Jim Bochte, who was the head pro at the

Palm Beach Tennis Club. One day, Bill went to the club and asked Jim if he could use the club's backboard and if there was an established record for the number of consecutive hits on that particular board. Jim told him that some girl, Amy Giletz, set the record by hitting 967 in a row. Bill was always up for a challenge. For those of you who have ever used a backboard, 967 consecutive hits is a hell of a lot of balls. I once hit 200 and wasn't able to maintain sufficient concentration to continue. Bill proceeded to the backboard and began hitting balls. He kept hitting and hitting. After approximately forty-five minutes, Jim walked to the backboard to see how Bill was progressing. He was standing there smiling and informed Jim that he had stopped at 966 because he didn't want to break Amy's record. Could Bill have surpassed Peaches Bartkowicz's wall record of 1,775? I wouldn't have bet against him.

With the progression of his psychiatric illness, Bill's interest in tennis gradually subsided although he occasionally rallied with his good friend, Frank Tutvin. Frank reported that Bill retained his "stylish" groundstrokes. In her article for the Palm Beach Post, Vicki Michaelis eloquently stated, *"Bill let go of tennis only as one releases a love, with painstaking slowness, following every strand of hope to its frayed end."* Bill and his dad continued to follow the major tournaments on television. One can only imagine Bill's response to seeing players he dominated in the juniors having successful professional careers. After his dad died, Bill had nothing further to do with the sport.

BILL'S FINAL DAYS

In early March 2002, Bill required a psychiatric admission due to an exacerbation of his illness. The family reported that Bill had some type of adverse reaction to psychotropic medication. He was subsequently transferred to another facility because of an emergent medical crisis. Tragically, he died on March 8, 2002.

In addition to being a world-class tennis player, Bill was an artist and poet. He accomplished more in his first eighteen years than most do in a lifetime. Whenever some player is inducted into the International Tennis Hall of Fame or during discussions of who was the greatest tennis player in history,

I often think of Bill Harris, marvel at his accomplishments, and wonder at what might have been.

You Will Not Be Forgotten

American men's tennis is, at this time, in a rather challenged state. Since the days of Sampras, Agassi, Chang, and Courier, American tennis, at least for the men, has fallen considerably. Check the men's ATP Points Standings as of September 12, 2016. The highest ranked American player is Steve Johnson, who is currently ranked number 23, followed by Jack Sock and John Isner. While all three are accomplished players, none of them, in my opinion, has the versatility or focus to make it to the top of the men's game.

France and Spain lead the top 20 rankings with four and three players respectively. Other countries represented include Serbia, Switzerland, the Czech Republic, Austria, Croatia, and Belgium. What is the common element for the players in these countries? They all learned the game on a clay-court surface. As several bloggers have noted, the USTA has either missed or ignored the point that the game has changed and that some of the best players in the world developed their game on a slow, red-clay surface. This is where one can learn to develop or "work" a point. The surface demands versatility, steadiness, and sustained concentration.

And who was possibly the greatest junior clay-court player in history? Bill Harris. He could work a point better than anyone. He was incredibly steady with great anticipation. His passing shots were deadly, with a devastating accuracy. He was a great counter-puncher. He had a magnificent return of serve. His game, with some modifications to include topspin ground-strokes, would have flourished in the current environment.

CHAPTER 9

THE CHALLENGE

"How many of those life units do *you* want to devote to tennis?"

How often has this happened to you? You just finished a match and think, "I *know* I can play better than that." And there are good reasons for you to believe this. After all, there have been times when you have played really well and effectively. The problem may be that you just don't sustain it over time. You may even double your practice efforts but find yourself slipping back into old patterns that limit your game.

PERSONAL COMMITMENT

Are you ready to break out of this self-limiting pattern? Are you willing to take an honest appraisal of your game, with all its strengths and weaknesses, and commit to a program of tennis excellence? If your answer is yes, then here is the challenge for you: by combining the elements in this book – deliberate practice, growth mindset, values clarification, mindfulness, competitive environment, micro-periodization, fartlek training, imaginal rehearsal, iPlans, and recuperative naps – I will guarantee that you will become a more effective tennis player, perhaps even a great one.

There is one significant caveat. Tennis excellence will take hard work and lots of it. There is no secret formula to a deliberate-tennis regimen. You have to put in the time and effort, and you have to maintain it for an extended period. But if you do, the rewards will be considerable.

As previously noted, the best time to implement a deliberate-practice regimen is in childhood. This appears to be the only time in which to accumulate sufficient practice hours to become an expert-level performer. If you happen to be the parent of a child who has taken to the game, you have the opportunity to design or expose your child to an innovative tennis environment to possibly produce an international-level player, the Peaches Bartkowicz or Bill Harris of the 21st century. But deliberate practice is not limited for those who happen to be exposed to the right environmental conditions at an early age. Anyone, regardless of their circumstances, can benefit from a program of deliberate practice.

Granted, not everyone will become an international-level performer. But does that really matter? What we are talking about here is maximizing your tennis potential given your current circumstances. You need to articulate your tennis values and determine how much time you are able to devote to a tennis-development program. Depending on your particular circumstances, this may be considerable with the possibility of putting in one to three hours per day. Others, with multiple responsibilities involving work and family, will have less time to practice or play tennis. This all comes down to those life units discussed earlier. The critical question is this: How many of those life units do *you* want to devote to tennis? Once you provide an answer, you are ready to go. The present moment is the perfect time to put this deliberate-tennis model to the empirical test.

And don't think that just because you may be middle-aged or older that this type of program will be ineffective. Deliberate tennis is not only for the young. Data from the sports psychology literature suggest that performers *do* reach their highest skill level in their mid to late 20s. It is the rare athlete who can maintain top form beyond the fourth decade. The aging process reduces cognitive, perceptual, and psychomotor performances as measured by standard psychological tests. Individuals in their seventies require about 1.6 to 2 times as long to process these tasks as someone in their twenties. Interestingly, individuals with a history of expert-level performance show the same age-related declines on standard measures of cognitive functioning and processing speed as do individuals who do not have this expert performance history. Nevertheless, the older experts show fewer age-related declines on specific skill-related tasks. There are data suggesting – and this is a critical point for those tennis players middle age or older – that maintaining skills requires as much effort as acquiring them. I doubt that there are many middle-aged or senior tennis players who would be willing to commit to a deliberate-practice regimen. For those of you who do, you will have a marked competitive edge over your same-aged peers.

TWO CRITICAL ISSUES

There appear to be two primary issues to consider when designing a deliberate-tennis regimen: *the establishment of a competitive environment and high volume repetition programmed toward incremental improvement.* In order to improve your skills, you need to engage players who are somewhat above your current level. A tennis ladder established through a site like the Global Tennis Network provides a steady stream of competition. A player's position on the ladder is determined empirically. By playing individuals who are one to several positions ahead of you, you have the opportunity to incrementally improve your skills. Once you are able to defeat a higher-level opponent, challenge players on a higher rung. USTA leagues and tournaments are other competitive venues for skill development.

I, like Mike Agassi, believe in math. High volume repetition, particularly under the direction of a skilled coach, can effect major skill improvements. You are only going to improve by hitting thousands of balls. And if you can hit thousands more than the competition, particularly in a way that facilitates continued skill development, you may become a dominant player.

Finding reliable practice partners can be problematic. Depending on your financial circumstances, you may want to consider purchasing a tennis-ball machine. In the spring of 2014, I purchased the Lobster Elite Two portable machine. With a tennis-ball machine, it is always ready for action. The Elite Two is battery-operated so you don't need a tennis court near an electrical outlet. A completely charged battery provides four to eight hours of ball machine use, more than sufficient for a given practice session. The hopper has a 150-ball capacity. You can set the ball speed from 20 to 80 mph, and the machine has a feed rate from two to twelve seconds.

The Elite Two is a versatile machine. It allows you to work on almost any shot imaginable – forehands, backhands, approach shots, lobs, volleys, drop shots, and overheads. The machine will produce a shot with topspin, slice, or without spin. You can hit multiple variations of shots from the middle of the court to behind the baseline. The only shot it cannot produce is a serve. Although you may not have Mike Agassi's mechanical skills to modify the machine to produce a tennis-serving "dragon," you can periodically talk one of your tennis friends into practicing serves and returns.

The Elite Two has several additional features including a random left to right horizontal sweep function and the capacity to oscillate shots vertically. By setting both the horizontal and vertical functions, the machine will essentially simulate match conditions by creating shots that cover the entire court – right, left, deep, and short. This provides quite a workout.

One of the great things about tennis is that it yields objective results. You either win or lose, and there are multiple tournaments or leagues in which to test your skills. And even if you are not particularly successful during competitive play, you remain physically active, perhaps travel some, and have the opportunity to meet people and "talk tennis." What could be better than that?

EPILOGUE

"[B]eing a psychologist does have its advantages."

A llow me to step out of the here-and-now for a minute and speculate about my past. If I had been exposed to and applied the concepts presented in this book when I first started learning the game, would I have been a more effective tennis player? I believe the answer would be unequivocally yes. Examining my tennis history from a deliberate-practice perspective, I probably accumulated from 500 to 1000 hours of deliberate practice during my lifetime. No wonder I only got as good as I did. Speculating about one's past can be fun, but it is not particularly productive. All we have to work with is the present moment.

In conjunction with writing this book, I began a program of deliberate tennis in early March 2014. I reached that magic age of sixty-five in 2014, signed up for Medicare, dragged myself out to the tennis court and began practicing. I was now eligible to play in the 65-and-over division, and I wanted to take full advantage of being the "youngest" in this particular age group. I incorporated every element discussed in this book to see if I could create a "geezer" tennis machine.

There are obviously many challenges in implementing such a program. At my current age, there is always the possibility of injury, serious illness, or death. Nevertheless, to quote Admiral Farragut, "Damn the torpedoes, full speed ahead!" So, there I was, hitting thousands of balls with my Elite Two portable tennis-ball machine, running M-drills and fartleks, playing guys twenty to forty years younger than I from our local Global Tennis Network ladder, and practicing mindfulness skills at the tennis court. It was all rather absurd. The best parts were the recuperative naps in the afternoon and a glass of red wine in the evening.

In early May 2014, I was ready to test my skills at the 10th Annual Rosemary Beach Open tennis tournament in Rosemary Beach, Florida. For ranking purposes in Florida, this tournament is classified as "designated," meaning that one could accrue 200 ranking points by winning the tournament. The types of tournaments from which a state ranking is derived include: Category I National Championships, Super Category II tournaments, Category II tournaments, State Closed events, designated, and local tournaments. Final rankings are based on the number of points earned during a calendar year with the higher-level tournaments having more ranking points.

Approximately one week before the tournament, I managed to defeat one of my tennis friends who, at the time, was ranked in the top 50 in the nation in the 65-and-over division. He is the consummate senior tennis player and deliberate-practice advocate. He had defeated me in our previous six encounters so this 7-6, 6-3 win was a special one for me and provided at least some validation for my deliberate-training regimen. The next day I defeated one of the better guys from the tennis ladder.

I scheduled several practice sessions and one match for the five days before the tournament began. But then, in true "Sunshine State" fashion, it started to rain. And it rained and rained. In fact, it rained almost continuously for the five days prior to my first round match at Rosemary Beach. There were times during the week when it only drizzled, so I gathered my racket and a hopper of used tennis balls and proceeded to the courts for service practice. I must have looked rather ridiculous, this sixty-five-year-old guy with rain-soaked tennis clothes, standing out there practicing serves. Water flew off the balls as I worked through my various serves – flat, slice, kick, and the lefty bread-and-butter serve, the can opener to the ad court. I also took a used ball and hit some against a local backboard, stepping around gingerly and trying not to fall. Try hitting 1,775 consecutive hits under those conditions, Peaches. (She could probably do it.)

The weather started to clear by the time of my first match. There were eight players in the 65-and-over division. For my first round match, I was scheduled to play a former high school tennis coach from Alabama who is also a certified United States Professional Tennis Association (USPTA) instructor. He appeared to be in superb shape. During the warm-up, he manifested solid groundstrokes and moved about the court with ease. I thought, "This is going to be a battle." Despite his classic 1960s style groundstrokes, including a slightly topspin forehand and slice backhand, he was a little inconsistent. I prevailed in this first round match 6-1, 6-0 and played well.

In the semifinals, I played the number one seed. I had encountered him before, approximately five years earlier, in another tournament and lost 6-1, 6-2. This guy is a good tennis player. From what I recalled from our previous match, he appeared to be a basher type so my initial iPlan was to hit some low-paced junk down the middle of the court to see if this would disrupt his play.

One of the challenges about *automatic thoughts* is that they occur quickly and often contain negative predictions. During the warm-up, I caught myself thinking, "This guy could kill me," given our previous match in which he actually did run right through me. I've always preferred the metaphor of thoughts as leaves falling into a swiftly moving stream. Fortunately, I was aware enough to detect this automatic thought, quickly assigned it to a leaf and, in my imagination, watched it float downstream and out of sight. These types of negative thoughts occurred several times during the match, and I managed to successfully distance from them with this leaf-in-the-stream metaphor. The other thing I always do is *diaphragmatic breathing* while saying to myself "relax" as I exhale during the time period between points. By doing this, I was able to attain a state of *attentive relaxation* before playing the next point. Finally, for my serve, I used *imaginal rehearsal,* imagining a perfectly executed serve just prior to actually hitting it.

I won the toss and, following the advice in Brad Gilbert's best-selling book *Winning Ugly,* elected to receive serve. I was certain that my opponent did not have the opportunity to practice much during the past six days given the extent of the rain, so I thought I could jump out to an early lead with a break of serve. Well, it didn't exactly happen that way. He hit four great first serves and held serve at love. He then broke my serve at love to take a 2-0 lead. I found out later that my opponent had spent the entire previous week playing doubles in a tournament in sunny central Florida. At this point in the match, it would have been easy to think, "Here we go again," but I made a conscious effort to be more mindfully aware of the task at hand. My opponent was actually less of a basher than I had remembered, so I changed tactics. I went on the attack, got to the net, and put away multiple volleys. He appeared unnerved by my attacking game and started to over hit. I won the first set 6-3.

My opponent's game then caught fire. His groundstrokes became deep and consistent, and he was passing me at the net and lobbing well. He forced me to change my game plan, so I camped out on the baseline to see if I could outsteady him. This had some initial success, but then he unleashed some of the greatest drop shots I had ever seen. He executed them perfectly, some hit from just inside the baseline. Despite my good court coverage as a result of my fartlek training, I couldn't quite run them down. He won the second set 6-1.

During the first game of the third set, my opponent hit another well-executed drop shot; I was determined to run it down. As I was racing toward the ball, I experienced a tearing or wrenching sensation in my right groin area. Well, I didn't reach the shot but, despite the groin injury, I was still able to maneuver around the court reasonably well. My opponent took that first game and, during the changeover, I said to him, "Man, your drop shots are incredible. You are hitting them perfectly." After that, he wasn't able to execute another one for the rest of the match. Perhaps I got him thinking about them; being a psychologist does have its advantages. He did break me in the second game of the third set, however, to take a 2-0 lead. My prospects for winning the match appeared rather dim at that point.

As a result of my reduced mobility attributable to the apparent groin pull, I elected to stay in the backcourt and hit numerous high-arcing, "quasi" moonballs. And then something rather interesting happened: my opponent, who up to that point was nailing his groundstrokes, started missing. He fell into the "pusher's trap," becoming frustrated with the monotony of my moonball strategy. Because he no longer could execute his drop shots, he started aiming for the lines to shorten the points, and the majority of his shots were landing either just long or wide. I evened the match at 2-2 and then took the third set 6-3.

This match highlights the importance of being flexible with respect to strategic plans. I had initially started with the basher iPlan. When that did not appear necessary, I shifted to an attack-the-net strategy. Then, following my injury, I shifted again to becoming a pusher. Effectiveness is the key to deliberate tennis. On that particular day, I was the more effective player.

I played the second seed in the finals, who was a fellow southpaw. We both acknowledged the fact that we hated playing lefties and laughed that being a southpaw tennis player was our one big advantage in this world. I had stretched and iced my injured groin area the previous evening and was moving around sufficiently well to play the match. My opponent, who had a great inside-out forehand, didn't have enough variety in his game to stay with me. I won the match 7-5, 6-3.

I actually won my first 65-and-over tennis tournament! This was undoubtedly the result of my deliberate-tennis training regimen. If I had approached the tournament with my typical preparation, I would not have won the semifinal match.

I received a rather heavy, glass beer mug as the first place trophy. And, to my surprise, this tournament provided prize money to the winner and runner-up of each division. So, in addition to the trophy I received a check for $60. Not too bad for a sixty-five-year-old, over-the-hill tennis hack. The $60 check covered the cost of the entry fee and gas money to and from the tournament. Of course, that doesn't factor in the impact of taxes. Perhaps I should move to Monte Carlo to shield my "career earnings" from the tax man.

As I was driving home to Tallahassee that afternoon, I was feeling rather pleased with my performance and began setting my sights on some national tournaments. I was ready to resume my deliberate-tennis practice the next day. When I woke up the following morning, however, I could barely walk. The groin pull appeared to be a severe one. I took several weeks off from training, but my condition was not improving to any significant degree.

After several weeks, I consulted with an orthopedist who diagnosed me with osteoarthritis, pelvic region and thigh. Bob Herschel's words were coming back to haunt me: mobility *is* the key to playing at this age.

The orthopedist recommended a treatment regimen that initially involved a cortisone shot plus some physical rehabilitation. The cortisone shot provided some temporary relief, enough for me to resume my tennis activities. But once I started playing competitive matches, I would re-aggravate my arthritic condition. Another cortisone shot provided similar relief but it didn't last.

The orthopedist then recommended an experimental procedure known as platelet rich plasma (PRP). This procedure involves extracting some blood and then placing it in a centrifuge that separates the blood into two layers. The platelet-rich blood is then injected into the injured area and is believed to "mimic" an injury and subsequently stimulates the body's healing system. In addition, there are chemicals and growth factors contained in the blood sample that may promote healthy tissue development.

I have curtailed all my tennis activities while undergoing the PRP procedure. This is a slow process that takes from four to six weeks before any initial improvement is evident. If the PRP procedure does not produce sufficient improvement for me to return to competitive tennis, then the next step may involve a hip replacement.

If it turns out that the Rosemary Beach tournament is my last, what a way to go out. I won the tournament and a check and, on the basis of this one tournament, was ranked number 20 on the 2014 Florida tentative rankings for the 65-and-over division. And this was all because of the deliberate-tennis regimen I had designed for the two months prior to the tournament. The problem, of course, is that this tennis regimen may have accelerated my arthritic condition. Ah, to be sixty again.

I consider it a great honor to have been able to play this game for the past fifty-five years. I have made many friends through tennis and have, with the exception of some arthritis, remained physically active and healthy. I learned many of life's most important lessons on the tennis court – how to deal with victories and defeats, how to be a member of a team, the importance of sustained effort, and how to cope with adversity and self-doubt. In the end, what matters most is the process. Engage and enjoy the journey.

CHAPTER 1. THE GARDEN AND DREAMS OF TENNIS GLORY

1 *Gonzales "was annoyed by cameramen":* Alison Danzig, "Gonzales loses at Garden,7-5, 7-5; Falters after Comeback in both sets. Laver ousts Gimeno 6-0, 6-1," *The New York Times*, March 26, 1966.

2 *He destroyed Gimeno in thirty-three minutes:* Ibid., March 26, 1966.

3 *Laver was the complete tennis player:* Eugene L. Scott, *Ivan Lendl's Power Tennis* (New York: Simon & Schuster, 1983), 3.

3 *Laver's left forearm:* Dave Anderson, "The Greatest? Don't Forget Laver's Lost Years," *The New York Times*, August 30, 2009.

4 *Jack Kramer promoted the $25,000 tournament:* Jack Kramer with Frank Deford, *The Game: My 40 Years in Tennis* (New York: G.P. Putnam's Sons, 1979), 261.

4 *Traditionally there are two answers to this important question:* Geoffrey Colvin, *Talent is Overrated: What Really Separates World-Class Performers from Everybody Else* (New York: Penguin Books, 2008), 4-5.

5 *One established finding:* K. Anders Ericsson, Ralf Th. Krampe, and Clemens Tesch- Romer, "The Role of Deliberate Practice in the Acquisition of Expert Performance," *Psychological Review* 100 (1993), 363-406.

5 *Carol Dweck, Ph.D., and her students:* Carol S. Dweck, *Self-Theories: Their Role in Motivation, Personality, and Development* (Philadelphia: Taylor & Francis, 2000).

6 *Looking back, it seems as though I frittered:* The Man From U.N.C.L.E. (Arena Productions, MGM Television

1964-68) and *The Soupy Sales Show* (WNEW, New York, 1964-66).

12 ***Peter towered over the young Mac:*** John McEnroe with James Kaplan, *You Cannot be Serious* (New York: G.P. Putnam's Sons, 2002), 28.

13 ***Ed looked like the character:*** Ernest Hemingway, *The Old Man and the Sea* (South Africa: Indigenous Works, 1983).

14 ***"I'm through":*** Alison Danzig and Peter Schwed, *The Fireside Book of Tennis* (New York: Simon & Schuster, 1972), 267.

15 ***Drobny was one of the giants of the game:*** Jaroslav Drobny, *International Tennis Hall of Fame*, www.tennisfame.com.

18 ***For the uninitiated, NTRP stands for:*** www.usta.com.

20 ***When I turned forty:*** Bob Anderson, *Stretching: 20th Anniversary, Revised Edition* (Bolinas, CA: Shelter Publications, 2000), 188-189.

21 ***What in the world is a fartlek??:*** Jenny Hadfield, "What's the Difference Between Fartlek, Tempo, and Interval Runs," *runnersworld.com*, November 21, 2012.

22 ***This drill is helpful for enhanced mobility and footwork:*** Arthur Ashe with Alexander McNab, *On Tennis: Strokes, Strategy, Traditions, Players, Psychology, and Wisdom* (New York: Alfred A. Knopf, 1995), 109-110.

23 ***The Australian Davis Cup teams:*** George Vecsey, "Sports of the Times; One Man Dynasty," *The New York Times*, January 1, 1986.

CHAPTER 2. SIR FRANCIS GALTON AND THE INNATE TALENT HYPOTHESIS

26 ***His I.Q. was estimated to be 200:*** Duane P. Schultz and Sydney Ellen Schultz, *A History of Modern Psychology: Fourth Edition* (New York: Harcourt Brace Jovanovich, 1987), 115.

27 ***He was particularly influenced by Darwin's:*** Charles Darwin, *The Origin of Species By Means of Natural Selection or the Preservation of Favored Races in the Struggle for Life* (New York: The Modern Library, 1993), 24-64.

27 ***He began investigating:*** Francis Galton, *Hereditary Genius: An Inquiry into its Laws and Consequences* (New York: D. Appleton and Company, 1900), ix.

27 ***In his book, Hereditary Genius:*** Ibid., 1.

27 ***"It is in the most unqualified manner":*** Ibid., 14.

27 ***These individuals were "urged by an inherent stimulus" to excel:*** Ibid., 38.

28 ***Galton acknowledged the need:*** Ibid., 15.

29 ***"The same kind of experience awaits him":*** Ibid., 16.

29 ***As Geoff Colvin, author of:*** Geoffrey Colvin, *Talent is Overrated: What Really Separates World-Class Performers from Everybody Else* (New York: Penguin Books, 2008), 62.

29 ***She noted that there are two "diametrically opposed" myths:*** Ellen Winner, *Gifted Children: Myths and Realities* (New York: Basic Books, 1996), 8-9.

30 ***Although Winner suggested that giftedness is neither:*** Ibid., 153.

30 ***Winner raised an interesting issue:*** Ibid., 180.

31 ***For instance, an individual's visual acuity:*** David Epstein, *Sports Gene: Inside the Science of Extraordinary Athletic Performance* (New York: Penguin Group, 2013), 39.

31   ***Recent research indicates that twenty-one gene variants:*** Ibid., 82.

31   ***Even with this apparent "simple" trait:*** Ross Tucker and Malcolm Collins, "What Makes Champions: A Review of the Relative Contribution of Genes and Training to Sporting Success," *British Journal of Sports Medicine* 46 (2012), 555-561.

31   ***A ridiculous assertion:*** Billy Mitchell, "Billy Mitchell Interview on MTV," www.youtube.com.

CHAPTER 3. CAN ORDINARY PEOPLE DO EXTRA-ORDINARY THINGS?

33   ***The authors investigated the oft-noted limited capacity:*** K. Anders Ericsson, William G. Chase, and Steve Faloon, "Acquisition of a Memory Skill," *Science* 208 (1980), 1181-1182.

34   ***The authors concluded, "With an appropriate mnemonic system":*** Ibid., 1182.

35   ***We turn now to another stringed instrument:*** K. Anders Ericsson, Ralph Th. Krampe, and Clemens Tesch-Romer, "The Role of Deliberate Practice in the Acquisition of Expert Performance," *Psychological Review* 100 (1993), 363-406.

38   ***The earliest reference to this ten-year issue:*** William Lowe Bryan and Noble Harter, "Studies on the Telegraphic Language. The Acquisition of a Hierarchy of Habits," *The Psychological Review* 6(4) (1899), 345-375.

38   ***"Our evidence is that it requires":*** Ibid., 358.

38   ***Simon and Chase (1973), in a landmark study:*** Herbert A. Simon and William G. Chase, "Skill in Chess," *American Scientist* 61 (1973), 402.

39   ***This rule was articulated by:*** Malcolm Gladwell, *Outliers: The Story of Success* (New York: Little, Brown, and Company, 2008), 39-40.

39   ***Ericsson does not use the term:*** K. Anders Ericsson, "Training History, Deliberate Practice and Elite Sports Performance: An Analysis in Response to Tucker and

Collins Review – What Makes Champions?" *British Journal of Sports Medicine* 47 (2013), 533-535.

40 ***For the vast majority of us, skill development follows a similar path:*** K. Anders Ericsson, "The Influence of Experience and Deliberate Practice on the Development of Superior Expert Performance." In K. Anders Ericsson, Neil Charness, Robert R. Hoffman, and Paul J. Feltovich, *The Cambridge Handbook of Expertise and Expert Performance* (New York: Cambridge University Press, 2006), 684-685.

41 ***Ericsson defined deliberate practice as:*** Ericsson, "Training History, Deliberate Practice and Elite Sports Performance: An Analysis in Response to Tucker and Collins Review – What Makes Champions," 534.

41 ***There are several important, interrelated components:*** Geoffrey Colvin, *Talent is Overrated: What Really Separates World-Class Performers from Everybody Else* (New York: Penguin Books, 2008), 66-72.

43 ***Allen Fox, the celebrated:*** Allen Fox, *Tennis: Winning the Mental Match* (Kearney, NE: Morris Publishing, 2010), 135.

45 ***Geoff Colvin concluded:*** Colvin, *Talent is Overrated*, 206.

CHAPTER 4. GAME, MINDSET, MATCH

46 ***One area that has profound implications:*** Carol S. Dweck, *Self-Theories: Their Role in Motivation, Personality, and Development* (Philadelphia: Taylor & Francis, 2000), 5-13.

46 ***Belief systems or "mindsets" give meaning:*** Carol S. Dweck, *Mindset: The New Psychology of Success* (New York: Random House, 2006), 6-7.

47 ***Dweck, through years of deliberate:*** Carol S. Dweck and Ellen L. Leggett, "A Social-Cognitive Approach to Motivation and Personality," *Psychological Review* 95(2) (1988), 256-273.

48 ***Allow me to illustrate:*** Carol I. Diener and Carol S. Dweck, "An Analysis of Learned Helplessness: Continuous Changes in Performance, Strategy, and Achievement Cognitions

Following Failure," *Journal of Personality and Social Psychology* 36(5) (May, 1978), 451-462.

49 **In the next study, Elliott and Dweck (1988):** Elaine S. Elliott and Carol S. Dweck, "Goals: An Approach to Motivation and Achievement," *Journal of Personality and Social Psychology* 54(1) (1988), 5-12.

53 **In McEnroe's autobiography:** John McEnroe with James Kaplan, *You Cannot Be Serious* (New York: G.P. Putman's Sons, 2002), 44.

53 **Arthur Ashe described McEnroe:** Arthur Ashe with Alexander McNab, *On Tennis: Strokes, Strategy, Traditions, Players, Psychology, and Wisdom* (New York: Alfred A. Knopf, 1995), *85.*

53 **He started playing tennis at the Douglaston Club:** McEnroe, *You Cannot Be Serious*, 22.

53 **There was more to Seewagen:** Butch Seewagen, personal communication.

54 **As a developing junior player:** McEnroe, *You Cannot be Serious, 22.*

54 **Palafox had the young McEnroe:** Ibid., 26.

54 **Despite the impressions of many:** Ibid., 24.

55 **"It was as if one day John woke up":** Joel Drucker, "Summer of '77: Forest Hills and Two Emerging Stars," *ESPN.com*, August 24, 2007.

55 **"The kid is difficult to play":** Ibid., 2.

55 **Over the course of McEnroe's legendary:** McEnroe, *You Cannot Be Serious, 13-14.*

55 **He stated, "I'll confess it":** Ibid., 14-15.

56 **Following a particularly energetic match:** Richard Evans, *McEnroe: A Rage for Perfection* (New York: Simon & Schuster, 1982), 41.

56 **That same year, George Lott:** McEnroe, *You Cannot Be Serious*, 32.

56   *McEnroe reflected:* Ibid., 31.

56   *"He'd just stand there":* Ibid., 31

57   *These messages essentially communicate:* Dweck, *Mindset, 173.*

57   *He had to fight the thought, "I'm a loser":* McEnroe, *You Cannot Be Serious,* 120.

57   *McEnroe described his loss:* Ibid., 175.

57   *He stated that match:* Ibid., 174.

58   *At one point, he walked over to the headset:* Ibid., 177.

58   *Despite having a stellar year in 1984:* Ibid., 177.

58   *McEnroe compared Gilbert:* Ibid., 220.

59   *McEnroe's response was:* Ibid., 219-220.

59   *He initiated a serious training regimen:* Ibid., 224.

60   *Arthur Ashe commented:* Eugene Scott, *Ivan Lendl's Power Tennis* (New York: Simon & Schuster, 1983), 29.

60   *One of her favorite expressions:* Tony Schwartz, "Obsession – Ivan Lendl's Lonely Quest for Perfection," *New York Magazine,* June 26, 1989, 36.

60   *Lendl defeated his mother:* Ibid., 37.

60   *Sometime in 1979:* Ibid., 37.

61   *Fibak suggested overhauling Lendl's game:* Ibid., 37.

61   *The first step involved Lendl developing:* Ibid., 38.

61   *The next step in Lendl's tennis makeover:* Ibid., 39.

61   *Lendl consulted with:* Robert Haas, *Eat to Win: The Sports Nutrition Bible* (New York: New American Library, 1985).

62   *He stated, "[T]he faraway goal is not the real objective":* Scott, *Ivan Lendl's Power Tennis,* 27.

62   *Knowing how committed Lendl was:* Schwartz, "Obsession," 40.

63   *She had Lendl practice a mental exercise:* B. Alexis Castori, *Exercise Your Mind: 36 Mental Workouts for Peak Performance* (New York: Barnes & Noble, 1992), 16-18.

63   *Lendl practiced another exercise:* Ibid., 75-77.

64   *Castori also helped Lendl:* Schwartz, "Obsession," 40.

64   *Malcolm Gladwell argued that our culture:* Bridget Murray, "Why We Don't Pick Good Quarterbacks," *American Psychological Association Monitor* 33(10) (November, 2002), 22.

65   *In true growth-mindset fashion:* Dweck, *Self-Theories*, 155.

66   *"It is important to praise":* Melissa L. Kamins and Carol S. Dweck, "Person Versus Process Praise and Criticism: Implications for Contingent Self-Worth and Coping," *Developmental Psychology* 35(3) (1999), 846.

67   *In one study, Kamins and Dweck (1999):* Ibid., 835-847.

68   *Dweck concluded, "[I]f you learn from person praise":* Dweck, *Self-Theories,* 114.

68   *Josh Waitzkin, the eight-time:* Fred Waitzkin, *Searching for Bobby Fischer: The Father of a Prodigy Observes the World of Chess* (New York: Random House, 1988).

68   *He stated, "The most gifted kids in chess":* Flora Carlin, "The Grandmaster Experiment," *Psychology Today,* 38(4) (2005), 82.

68   *Would these results hold with older children?:* Claudia M. Mueller and Carol S. Dweck, "Praise for Intelligence Can Undermine Children's Motivation and Performance," *Journal of Personality and Social Psychology* 75(1) (1998), 835-847.

CHAPTER 5. IT'S THE ENVIRONMENT, STUPID

72   *He was born on a farm near:* Duane P. Schultz and Sydney Ellen Schultz, *A History of Modern Psychology: Fourth Edition* (New York: Hartcourt Brace Jovanovich, 1987), 195.

72   *Watson's teachers described him as:* Ibid., 195.

72   *At his mother's insistence:* Ibid., 195.

72   *In 1908, Watson accepted:* Ibid., 197.

72   *Following Baldwin's dismissal:* Ibid., 197.

73 *In the former text, published in 1914, Watson declared:* John B. Watson, *Behavior: An Introduction to Comparative Psychology* (New York: Henry Holt & Company, 1914), 1.

73 *Watson asserted: "I should like to go one step":* John B. Watson, *Behaviorism* (New York: Norton, 1925), 104.

73 *In the next sentence to the above cited passage:* Ibid., 104.

74 *Watson and Rayner reported:* John B. Watson and Rosalie Rayner, "Conditioned Emotional Reactions," *Journal of Experimental Psychology* 3(1) (1920), 5.

74 *A group of researchers in 2009:* Hall P. Beck, Sharman Levinson, and Gary Irons, "Finding Little Albert: A Journey to John B. Watson's Infant Laboratory," *American Psychologist* 64(7) (2009), 613.

75 *A media frenzy ensued:* James Stimpert, "Hopkins History: John Broadus Watson: The Father of Behavioral Psychology," *The Gazette Online: The Newspaper of the Johns Hopkins University*, January 22, 2001.

75 *As a result of his affair with:* Schultz and Schultz, *A History of Modern Psychology*, 199.

75 *Upon entering the business world:* Kerry W. Buckley, "The Selling of a Psychologist: John Broadus Watson and the Application of Behavioral Techniques to Advertising," *Journal of the History of Behavioral Sciences* 18(1982), 211.

75 *Watson had a major impact:* Ibid., 212.

75 *Later, the director of research for General Motors:* Ibid., 215.

76 *There was a rejection of mind-body dualism:* Fred S. Keller, *The Definition of Psychology: Second Edition* (New York: Appleton-Century-Crofts, 1973), 139.

77 *This work, perhaps more than any other:* Charles Darwin, *The Origin of Species By Means of Natural Selection or The Preservation of Favored Races in the Struggle for Life* (New York: The Modern Library, 1993).

77 ***Darwin argued that:*** Charles Darwin, *The Descent of Man* (Amherst, New York: Prometheus Books, 1998), 67.

77 ***This position constituted a radical break:*** Schultz and Schultz, *A History of Modern Psychology*, 123.

77 ***The work of E.L. Thorndike (1898):*** Edward L. Thorndike, "Animal Intelligence: An Experimental Study of the Associative Processes in Animals," *The Psychological Review* 2(4) (1898), 8-31.

78 ***Thorndike reported that by:*** Edward L. Thorndike, *Educational Psychology, Volume II: The Psychology of Learning* (New York: Columbia University, 1913), 9.

78 ***Thorndike called this stamping in process:*** Geraldine Joncich, *The Sane Positivist: A Biography of Edward L. Thorndike* (Middletown, Connecticut: Wesleyan University Press, 1968), 266.

78 ***This has also been called:*** Ibid., 350.

78 ***Thorndike made an important discovery:*** A. Charles Catania, "The Nature of Learning." In John A. Nevin and George S. Reynolds (Eds.), *The Study of Behavior: Learning, Motivation, Emotion, and Instinct* (Glenview, Illinois: Scott, Foresman, & Company, 1973), 39.

78 ***A productive research program:*** Ibid., 39.

79 ***As with Thorndike's experiment:*** Ibid., 52.

80 ***Skinner reported:*** B.F. Skinner, *Science and Human Behavior* (New York: Macmillan, 1953), 64-65.

80 ***When the consequences result:*** Ibid., 73.

81 ***Skinner drew an analogy:*** Ibid., 91.

81 ***The operation responsible for:*** Catania, "The Nature of Learning," 52.

82 ***There is an important property:*** Ibid., 52.

82 ***Brad Gilbert, in his wonderful book:*** Brad Gilbert and Steve Jamison, *Winning Ugly: Mental Warfare in Tennis – Lessons From a Master* (New York: Simon & Schuster, 1993), 152.

83 *One of their more entertaining projects:* B. F. Skinner, "Two "Synthetic Social Relations"," *Journal of the Experimental Analysis of Behavior* 5(4) (1962), 531-532.

85 *Were you aware:* Ryan Murphy, "10 Most Superstitious Athletes," *Mensfitness.com* 2014.

85 *Similarly, Jason Terry:* Ibid., 5.

85 *Tennis players are not immune:* Ibid., 4.

86 *Andre Agassi had a version:* Andre Agassi, *Open: An Autobiography* (New York: Alfred A. Knopf, 2009), 291-292.

86 *And then there's Goran Ivanisevic:* Friday 10 to 1, "Player Superstitions," *Tennis.com.au,* July 13, 2012.

86 *Jack Sock requires:* Will Brodie, "Superstitions and Idiosyncrasies of Tennis Players," *The Age Online,* January 12, 2014.

86 *Rafael Nadal has a preoccupation:* Stuart Miller, "If It Works, Tennis Players Stick With It, Whatever It Is," *International New York Times,* August 31, 2013.

87 *The King of Quirk title:* Mariana Borg, *Love Match: My Life With Bjorn* (London: Sidgwick & Jackson, 1981), 16.

87 *How is it that these otherwise:* B.F. Skinner, "'Superstition' in the Pigeon," *The Journal of Experimental Psychology* 38 (1948), 168-172.

88 *Skinner reported a:* Ibid., 168.

89 *There is even one credible establishment:* www.loshorcones. org.

89 *This community is based on:* B.F. Skinner, *Walden Two* (Englewood Cliffs, New Jersey: Prentice-Hall, 1948).

90 *Laszlo Polgar had an educational vision of sorts:* Cathy Forbes, *The Polgar Sisters: Training or Genius?* (London: B. T. Batsford, 1992), 13-14.

90 *In 1965, Laszlo met:* Ibid., 13.

91 *When Susan was four years old:* Flora Carlin, "The Grandmaster Experiment," *Psychology Today,* 38(4) (2005), 77-78.

91 *Garry Kasparov, former world chess champion:* Ibid., 82.

91   *Nigel Short, chess prodigy:* George Pyne, "Judit Polgar is New Queen of the Chess World," *The Gainesville Sun*, December 11, 1993.

91   *Laszlo and Klara quit their jobs:* Serena Allott, "Queen Takes All," *Telegraph*, January 16, 2002.

91   *After about six months of intensive training:* Carlin, "The Grandmaster Experiment," 78.

92   *Laszlo would not allow them:* Forbes, *The Polgar Sisters*, 24.

92   *Laszlo was obsessive and driven:* Allott, "Queen Takes All."

92   *Susan followed up her win:* Ibid.

93   *At sixteen, Susan took the New York:* Carlin, "The Grandmaster Experiment," 76.

93   *Susan became the first woman:* Ibid., 83.

93   *Susan once famously stated:* Forbes, *The Polgar Sisters*, 23.

93   *As the girls were emerging:* Carlin, "The Grandmaster Experiment," 83.

93   *There is agreement among the Polgar family:* Ibid., 81.

94   *In 1988, a British chess correspondent:* Allot, "Queen Takes All."

94   *Another journalist described Judith:* Ibid.

94   *As the youngest in the family:* Carlin, "The Grandmaster Experiment," 82.

94   *One typically attains:* Robert D. McFadden, "Youngest Grandmaster Ever is 15, Ferocious (and Female)," *The New York Times*, February 4, 1992.

94   *In 2005, at age twenty-nine:* Carlin, "The Grandmaster Experiment," 76.

95   *Garry Kasparov once said:* Forbes, *The Polgar Sisters*, 30.

95   *One final note on the Polgar project:* Carlin, "The Grandmaster Experiment," 84.

95   *During their off-duty time:* Mike Agassi with Dominic Cobello and Kate Shoup Welsh, *The Agassi Story* (Toronto: ECW Press, 2004), 19-20.

95   *Emmanuel described his initial reaction:* Ibid., 20-21.

96   *He had no one to practice against:* Ibid., 25.

96   *Emmanuel was quick, agile, and athletic:* Ibid., 26

96   *One day at age sixteen:* Ibid., 26-27.

97   *Taking Emmanuel under his wing:* Ibid., 29.

97   *Following several months of intense training:* Ibid., 29.

97   *These games were significant:* Ibid., 29.

97   *So, how did Emmanuel do:* Ibid., 35.

98   *As Emmanuel was surveying Centre Court stadium:* Ibid., 37.

98   *Emmanuel participated in the 1952:* Ibid., 40.

98   *For a man with great ambitions:* Ibid., 43-48.

98   *In Chicago, Emmanuel adopted "Mike" as:* Ibid., 48.

98   *Mike got involved in the Chicago:* Ibid., 51-55.

99   *After his boxing career ended:* Ibid., 66.

99   *In a weird way:* Ibid., 69.

99   *Mike secured a job at:* Ibid., 72.

100   *Mike Agassi was a tennis visionary:* Ibid., 77.

100   *Andre, in his book:* A. Agassi, *Open*, 28.

100   *Mike had his first three children:* M. Agassi, *The Agassi Story*, 77.

100   *For every stroke:* Ibid., 78-79

101   *Andre described his father as:* A. Agassi, *Open*, 35-36.

101   *Mike acknowledged that he ruined:* M. Agassi, *The Agassi Story*, 79.

101   *By age thirteen:* Ibid., 94-95.

102   *Mike started referring to him as a:* A. Agassi, *Open*, 57.

102   *Mike took a more balanced approach:* M. Agassi, *The Agassi Story*, 80.

102   *He wrote, "By the time Andre":* Ibid., 81-82.

103   *Even Andre believes some:* A. Agassi, *Open*, 28.

103   **Mike instructed Andre to attack:** Ibid., 42.

103   **Andre referred to the ball machine:** Ibid., 27-31.

104   **He stated in his autobiography:** Ibid., 27

104   **Andre reported, "Though I hate tennis":** Ibid., 29.

105   **Mike was aware that:** M. Agassi, *The Agassi Story*, 105.

105   **Segura offered to coach Andre:** Ibid., 102.

105   **Around this time:** Ibid., 104.

106   **Despite Andre's objections:** A. Agassi, *Open*, 71.

106   **His father noted, "After a decade":** M. Agassi, *The Agassi Story*, 115-116.

106   **Andre's rise in the men's:** Ibid., 118.

107   **Andre realized that Mike was choked up:** A. Agassi, *Open*, 165.

108   **Andre continued to have:** M. Agassi, *The Agassi Story*, 135.

109   **Laszlo initially wanted:** Forbes, *The Polgar Sisters*, 15.

109   **Emmanuel's father was a skilled:** M. Agassi, *The Agassi Story*, 12, 18.

109   **Several Cornell University researchers:** Stephen J. Ceci, Susan M. Barnett, and Tomoe Kanaya, "Developing Childhood Proclivities into Adult Competencies: The Overlooked Multiplier Effect." In R.J. Sternberg and E.L. Grigorenko (Eds.), *The Psychology of Abilities, Competencies, and Expertise* (New York: Cambridge University Press, 2003), 70-92.

110   **Geoff Colvin reported:** Geoffrey Colvin, *The Talent Myth: What Really Separates World-Class Performers from Everybody Else* (New York: Penguin Books, 2008), 200.

111   **The match came down to a "sudden death,":** A. Agassi, *Open*, 38.

111   **Andre's response was telling:** Ibid., 38.

111   **As Andre strolled:** Ibid., 97.

CHAPTER 6. THE MENTAL GAME

112 **Peter Bodo, in The Courts of Babylon:** Peter Bodo, *The Courts of Babylon: Tales of Greed and Glory in the Harsh New World of Professional Tennis* (New York: Scribner, 1995), 390.

112 **She reported to Bodo:** Ibid., 386-387.

114 **Albert Ellis, of Rational Emotive Therapy fame:** Albert Ellis, *Reason and Emotion in Psychotherapy* (New York: Citadel Press, 1962), 18.

114 **Aaron Beck, known primarily:** Aaron T. Beck, *Cognitive Therapy and the Emotional Disorders* (New York: International Universities Press, 1976), 237.

114 **Characteristics of Automatic Thoughts:** Matthew McKay, Martha Davis, and Patrick Fanning, *Thoughts and Feelings: Fourth Edition* (Oakland, California: New Harbinger Publications, 2011), 18-21.

117 **Ten Types of Problematic Thinking:** Matthew McKay, Martha Davis, and Patrick Fanning, *Thoughts and Feelings: The Art of Cognitive Stress Intervention* (Oakland, California: New Harbinger Publications, 1981), 19-25.

118 **A great example of dichotomous thinking:** John McEnroe with James Kaplan, *You Cannot be Serious* (New York: G.P. Putnam's Sons, 2002), 215.

121 **Do you recall that chapter:** Mark Twain, *The Adventures of Tom Sawyer* (Philadelphia: Running Press, 1987), 83-86.

122 **More important, what would you like to have:** Steven C. Hayes with Spencer Smith, *Get Out of Your Mind and Into Your Life: The New Acceptance & Commitment Therapy* (Oakland, California: New Harbinger Publications, 2005), 170.

123 **As formulated here, goals are used:** Kelly G. Wilson and Troy Dufrene, *Things Might Go Terribly, Horribly Wrong: A Guide to Life Liberated From Anxiety* (Oakland, California: New Harbinger Publications, 2010), 108.

123 ***For instance, having attained:*** Franz Lidz, "Suddenly, A Door – Mats," *Sports Illustrated Vault*, May 15, 1989.

125 ***There is a psychiatric condition:*** American Psychiatric Association, *Diagnostic and Statistical Manual of Mental Disorders: Fifth Edition (DSM-5)* (Washington, DC: American Psychiatric Publishing, 2013), 202-208.

126 ***Data from psychological studies:*** Hayes, *Get Out of Your Mind and Into Your Life*, 24.

126 ***The problem is that our thoughts:*** Wilson and Dufrene, *Things Might Go Terribly, Horribly Wrong*, 59.

126 ***There is an important distinction between:*** McKay, Davis, and Fanning, *Thoughts and Feelings: Fourth Edition*, 127.

126 ***Defusion is "the process":*** Wilson and Dufrene, *Things Might Go Terribly, Horribly Wrong*, 87.

127 ***Several types of specific imagery:*** McKay, Davis, and Fanning, *Thoughts and Feelings: Fourth Edition*, 130-131.

128 ***What would reality be like:*** Thomas D. Borkovec, "Life in the Future Versus Life in the Present," *Clinical Psychology: Science and Practice* 9 (2002), 76-80.

128 ***Borkovec noted, "So seeking":*** Ibid., 79-80.

129 ***The molecular biologist:*** Jon Kabat-Zinn, "Mindfulness-Based Interventions in Context: Past, Present, and Future," *Clinical Psychology: Science and Practice* 10 (2003), 144-156.

131 ***The most common involves observing:*** Jon Kabat-Zinn, *Full Catastrophe Living: Using Wisdom of Your Body and Mind to Face Stress, Pain, and Illness: Fifteenth Anniversary Edition* (New York: Delta Trade Paperbacks, 2009), 22-23.

132 ***This exercise, an adaptation from:*** Marsha M. Linehan, *Day 1: Observing Just This Moment* (Seattle: Behavioral Tech, LLC, 2005), Track 2.

133 ***Mindful eating is a totally different:*** Kabat-Zinn, *Full Catastrophe Living*, 27-29.

134 ***Practicing mindfulness is:*** Ibid., 29.

134 *Through this process of systematically:* Ibid., 65.

134 *This issue with your thinking:* Ibid., 67-69.

135 *Kabat-Zinn referred to this as:* Ibid., 70.

135 *A critical element to mindfulness involves:* McKay, Davis, and Fanning, *Thoughts and Feelings: Fourth Edition*, 120, 129.

137 *The great Arthur Ashe believed:* Arthur Ashe with Alexander McNab, *On Tennis: Strokes, Strategy, Traditions, Players, Psychology, and Wisdom* (New York: Alfred A. Knopf, 1995), 31.

138 *Gilbert persuasively argues:* Brad Gilbert and Steve Jamison, *Winning Ugly: Mental Warfare in Tennis – Lessons From a Master* (New York: Simon & Schuster, 1993), 113-114.

138 *Allow me to retell this short story:* Leo Tolstoy, "The Emperor's Three Questions." In Thich Nhat Hanh, *The Miracle of Mindfulness: An Introduction to the Practice of Mindfulness* (Boston: Beacon Press, 1975), 69-75.

143 *He was the first Russian novelist:* Leo Tolstoy, *Anna Karenina: A Novel in Eight Parts* (New York: Penguin Books, 2002), 62.

143 *The description of tennis played:* Vladimir E. Alexandrov, "Tolstoy and Tennis." In Lazar Fleishman, et al. (Eds.), *Word, Music, History: A Festschrift for Caryl Emerson* (Stanford, California: Stanford Slavic Studies, 2005, Part 1), pp. 340-54.

143 *Upon the first strike of the ball:* Elif Batuman, *The Possessed: Adventures with Russian Books and the People Who Read Them* (New York: Farrar, Straus, and Giroux, 2010), 121.

143 *According to entries in his wife's diary:* Alexandrov, "Tolstoy and Tennis," pp. 340-54.

144 *Allen Fox stated:* Allen Fox, *Think to Win: The Strategic Dimension of Tennis* (New York: Harper Collins, 1993), 14.

144 *Here is the good news:* Jeff Greenwald, *The Best Tennis of Your Life: 50 Mental Strategies for Fearless Performance* (Cincinnati: Betterway Books, 2007), 126.

146 *But the concept is a good one:* Jim Loehr and Tony Schwartz, *The Power of Full Engagement: Managing Energy, Not Time, Is the Key to High Performance and Personal Renewal* (New York: The Free Press, 2003), 28.

147 *Despite spending hundreds of hours:* Ibid., 32-33.

148 *This type of breathing can be mastered:* Douglas A. Bernstein, Thomas D. Borkovec, and Holly Hazlett-Stevens, *New Directions in Progressive Relaxation Training: A Guidebook for Helping Professionals* (Westport, CT: Praeger Publishers, 2000), 163-164.

149 *The diaphragm is a rather large piece:* Kabat-Zinn, *Full Catastrophe Living*, 54.

150 *The development of the progressive relaxation:* Bernstein, Borkovec, and Hazlett- Stevens, *New Directions in Progressive Relaxation Training*, 5-6.

150 *As with any skill:* Ibid., 27.

151 *The primary goal of progressive muscle relaxation:* Ibid., 27-28.

151 *Progressive relaxation begins with:* Ibid., 35-36.

151 *The basic procedure for the tense-relax cycle:* Ibid., 36-38.

152 *As the trainee becomes proficient:* Ibid., 51-56.

152 *The therapist then proceeds:* Ibid., 56-57.

152 *Once the trainee achieves:* Ibid., 57-58.

152 *The next stage:* Ibid., 58-59.

152 *With differential relaxation:* Ibid., 63-66.

153 *Conditioned relaxation is particularly important:* Ibid., 66-67.

153 *This school was a perfect fit:* Walter Isaacson, *Einstein: His Life and Universe* (New York: Simon & Schuster, 2007), 67.

153 *While at this school:* Ibid., 3.

154 *To borrow a phrase from:* Thomas D. Borkovec and

Brian Sharpless, "Generalized Anxiety Disorder: Bringing Cognitive-Behavioral Therapy into the Valued Present." In Steven C. Hayes, Victoria M. Follette, and Marsha M. Linehan (Eds.), *Mindfulness and Acceptance: Expanding the Cognitive-Behavioral Tradition* (New York: The Guilford Press, 2004), 225.

154 *Here is a wonderful story:* Andrew Fogg, "Mental Golf Practice to Improve Your Swing and Your Golf Performance," *The Golf Hypnotist*, May 11, 2009.

154 *Jack Nicklaus, widely recognized:* Steve Bull, *The Game Plan: Your Guide to Mental Toughness at Work* (Chichester, West Sussex: Capstone Publishing Limited, 2006), 63.

155 *Imaginal rehearsal involves the use:* Shane M. Murphy, "Imagery Interventions in Sport," *Medicine and Science in Sports and Exercise*, 26 (1994), 489.

156 *There are two dimensions of imaginal rehearsal:* Shane Murphy, "Imagery: Inner Theater Becomes Reality." In Shane Murphy (Ed.), The Sport Psych Handbook: A Complete Guide to Today's Best Mental Training Techniques (Champaign, IL: Human Kinetics Publishers, 2005), 131.

161 *Selectively speed up play:* Ashe, *On Tennis*, 41.

161 *Bring the pusher to net:* Gilbert and Jamison, *Winning Ugly*, 87.

162 *Relax and take a good swing:* Ibid., 97-99.

162 *If you are able to execute this:* Ibid., 101.

162 *Some contend that it is legitimate:* Ibid., 99-100.

163 *Ivan Lendl was a proponent:* Eugene Scott, *Ivan Lendl's Power Tennis* (New York: Simon & Schuster, 1983), 26

165 *With the assistance of Donald Dell and Dennis Ralston:* Ashe, *On Tennis*, 41.

167 *This is the Mike Agassi:* Andre Agassi, *Open: An Autobiography* (New York: Alfred A. Knopf, 2009), 41.

167 *There was a classic match:* "As They Saw It," astheysawit.com.

167 *The twenty-three-year-old Parker:* "Davis Cup – Tie Details – 1939 – USA v Australia," daviscup.com.

168 *He was born:* Cynthia Beardsley, *Frank Parker: Champion in the Golden Age of Tennis* (Chicago: Havilah Press, 2002), 2-7.

168 *Under Beasley's tutelage:* Ibid., 16.

168 *He won his first national singles title:* Ibid., 12.

168 *The press referred to him as:* Alison Danzig and Peter Schwed, *The Fireside Book of Tennis* (New York: Simon & Schuster, 1972), 42.

169 *In his autobiography, Jack Kramer opined:* Jack Kramer with Frank Deford, *The Game: My 40 Years in Tennis* (New York: G.P. Putnam's Sons, 1979), 175.

169 *The "Brom" challenged Parker's:* Danzig and Schwed, *The Fireside Book of Tennis*, 42-43.

CHAPTER 7. THE TENNIS COMMUNITY

181 *Jack Kramer reported:* Jack Kramer with Frank DeFord, *The Game: My 40 Years in Tennis* (New York: G.P. Putnam's Sons, 1979), 231.

182 *Gonzales, whom some consider:* Lew Hoad – Tennis, *Sport Australia Hall of Fame*, www.sahof.org.au.

182 *Peter Bodo commented:* Peter Bodo, *The Courts of Babylon: Tales of Greed and Glory in the Harsh New World of Professional Tennis* (New York: Scribner, 1995), 32.

182 *John Newcombe articulated:* Rich Hillway, "Historical Perspective: Q&A with the Aussies," Coloradotennis.com.

183 *Thus, the Australian national team:* Daniel Coyle, *The Talent Code: Greatness isn't Born, It's Grown. Here's How* (New York: Bantam Books, 2009), 64-66.

183 *And then there was Harry Hopman:* Harry Gordon, "Hopman, Henry Christian (Harry) (1906-1985), *Australian Dictionary of Biography* 17 (2007), 549-551.

184 *Ken Rosewall stated:* Kramer, *The Game*, 225.

184   *One of the lesser known Australian:* Hillway, "Historical Perspective."

188   *In his autobiography:* John McEnroe with James Kaplan, *You Cannot be Serious* (New York: G.P. Putnam's Sons, 2002), 56.

188   *Ivan Lendl made an important:* Eugene Scott, *Ivan Lendl's Power Tennis* (New York: Simon & Schuster, 1983), 23.

188   *Jack Kramer understood this competitive dynamic:* Kramer, *The Game*, 28.

189   *He also noted:* Ibid., 31.

189   *Kramer argued for a:* Ibid., 28.

191   *Peter Bodo characterized these individuals:* Bodo, *The Courts of Babylon*, 84-85.

192   *From the 1940s to the 1960s:* Jean Maddern Pitrone, *Jean Hoxie: The Robin Hood of Tennis* (Hamtramck, Michigan, 1985), 45.

192   *Hamtramck was a tough, working-class:* Ibid., 8.

192   *In 1930, there was no tennis tradition:* Ibid., 20.

192   *Public county records:* Ibid., 1.

192   *An event took place:* Ibid., 12.

193   *Jean Hoxie worked hard on her game:* Ibid., 17.

193   *She approached the Hamtramck:* Ibid., 18.

193   *As you can imagine:* Ibid., 20.

193   *Hoxie was a great salesperson:* Ibid., 20.

193   *She assembled three players:* Ibid., 21.

193   *The Hamtramck High School tennis team:* Ibid., 21.

193   *The following season:* Ibid., 22.

193   *Hoxie began developing "feeder" programs:* Ibid., 22.

194   *Fred Kovaleski was Hoxie's first star:* Ibid., 23.

194   *She told her boys:* Ibid., 25.

194   *During the winter months:* Ibid., 41.

194   *In 1939, Hoxie took her charges:* Ibid., 28-30.

195   *Several members of the Ford family:* Ibid., 30.

195   *The fifteen-year-old Kovaleski:* Ibid., 24-25, 34.

196   *Regardless of the weather:* Ibid., 41.

196   *The Hoxie kids loved beating the hell:* Ibid., 41.

196   *Her first "little Hoxie kid" was:* Ibid., 47-48.

196   *Always looking for a public relations stunt:* Ibid., 48.

196   *By the time he was twelve:* Ibid., 48-49.

197   *The girls did not escape:* Ibid., 81.

197   *June Stack was one of Hoxie's:* Ibid., 49.

197   *Hoxie began conducting tennis clinics:* Ibid., 46.

197   *Beginning in 1947:* Ibid., 67.

197   *In January 1951:* Ibid., 70-71.

197   *For years, Hoxie envisioned:* Ibid., 85.

198   *Hoxie exhorted them:* Ibid., 76.

198   *She directed her assistant:* Ibid., 74.

198   *John and Eugenia Bartkowicz:* Jane Marie Bartkowicz, personal communication.

198   *By age six, Jane became intrigued:* Pitrone, *Jean Hoxie*, 95.

198   *One day, the seven-year-old Jane found a broken tennis racket:* Bartkowicz, personal communication.

199   *Peaches observed that the:* Pitrone, *Jean Hoxie*, 96.

199   *Bartkowicz set two records:* Bartkowicz, personal communication.

199   *Peaches's practice sessions:* Ibid.

200   *Bartkowicz did not consider herself:* Ibid.

200   *At age eight:* Pitrone, *Jean Hoxie,* 96-97.

200   *Bartkowicz's rise in the junior tennis ranks:* B.B. Branton, "Zan Guerry, "Peaches" and Tennis Titles," *The Chattanoogan.com,* July 22, 2010.

200 *One of Hoxie's favorite threats was:* Pitrone, *Jean Hoxie*, 97.

201 *An early Hoxie kid:* Ibid., 18.

201 *Bartkowicz responded to Hoxie's demands:* Ibid., vii.

201 *When Peaches was not on the road:* Branton, "Zan Guerry, "Peaches" and Tennis Titles."

201 *With the media present:* Pitrone, *Jean Hoxie*, 103-104.

202 *Despite Hoxie's prediction:* Bartkowicz, personal communication.

202 *Bartkowicz felt the pressure:* Pitrone *Jean Hoxie*, 104-105.

202 *When she started competing:* Ibid., 114.

202 *Regardless, Bartkowicz engineered:* Buck Jerzy, "From "The Wall" to "The Hall," *Polish-American Sports Hall of Fame – Induction Banquet*, June 24, 2010.

202 *There were only two elite players:* Bartkowicz, personal communication.

203 *Bartkowicz won fourteen professional titles:* Branton, "Zan Guerry, "Peaches" and Tennis Titles."

203 *Jerry Hoxie once addressed:* Pitrone, *Jean Hoxie*, 99.

CHAPTER 8. IN MEMORIAM: WILLIAM A. HARRIS

205 *My idea for this informal survey:* Phil Secada and Jim Martz, "Florida's all-time great juniors," *Florida Tennis Magazine*, (1992), 1-2.

205 *Stan Smith, former number one:* Vicki Michaelis, "How Mental Illness Felled a Tennis Great," *The Palm Beach Post*, November 19, 1994.

206 *Charles Darley described him:* Charles Darley, personal communication.

206 *Jaime Pressley, Bill's hitting partner:* Jaime Pressley, personal communication.

206 **One of Bill's closest friends:** Frank Tutvin, personal communication.

206 **My favorite quote:** Butch Seewagen, personal communication.

206 **"What was silent in the father":** Friedrich Nietzsche, *Thus Spoke Zarathustra: A Book For All and None* (W. Kaufmann, Trans.). (New York: The Viking Press, 1966), 100.

206 **The tennis patriarch was the father:** Charles Harris – Tennis, *The Palm Beach County Sports Hall of Fame.*

207 **Charles Harris competed against:** Charles R. Harris, tennisarchives.com

207 **Gardnar Mulloy (who won four:** "Youth has been Served in the Palm Beaches," *Palm Beach Illustrated.*

207 **From 1938-39:** Mary Harris Dewald, personal communication.

207 **Bill Harris started playing tennis:** Michaelis, "How Mental Illness Felled a Tennis Great."

208 **During the summer months:** Ibid.

208 **In 1958, at age eleven:** Robert Harris, personal communication.

208 **But it was a quarterfinal match:** Associated Press, "Bill Harris Pulls Off Big Rally," *The Miami News,* August 5, 1961.

208 **This was Richey's first time:** Cliff Richey, personal communication.

209 **Richey recalled that when he was up:** Ibid.

209 **Frank Tutvin informed me:** Tutvin, personal communication.

209 **Richey reflected on the match:** Richey, personal communication.

209 **Charles Darley, one of Bill's:** Darley, personal communication.

210 *Darley's "shocking" defeat:* "Gilbart in Jaycee Semifinals with Three Other Floridians," *St. Petersburg Times*, August 11, 1961.

210 *This was Darley's strategy:* Darley, personal communication.

213 *By this time, Harris was supremely:* Michealis, "How Mental Illness Felled a Tennis Great."

213 *During that era, there were four:* Armistead Neely, personal communication.

214 *Easily defeating Bernard Watson:* National Boys' Singles Championship, 1963 Draw Sheets.

214 *Guerry had a remarkable:* B.B. Branton, "Zan Guerry, "Peaches" and Tennis Titles," *The Chattanoogan.com, July 22, 2010.*

215 *Neely had two match points:* Neely, personal communication.

215 *When Bill returned to school:* Michaelis, "How Mental Illness Felled a Tennis Great."

216 *From the information I had:* Phil Secada, "Bill Harris, Florida's Greatest Junior Player, Passes On," *Florida Tennis*, May 2002.

216 *Neely stated the blazer:* Neely, personal communication.

217 *Elements of his game can be seen:* Eliot Berry, "The Search for Bill Harris," *Tropic Magazine,*" August 7, 1994.

217 *I had the opportunity:* Pressley, personal communication.

217 *His twin sister, Mary:* Dewald, personal communication.

217 *Neely described Bill as:* Neely, personal communication.

217 *Like Tilden several decades before:* Michaelis, "How Mental Illness Felled a Tennis Great."

218 *Harris wore his blue blazer throughout:* Berry, "The Search for Bill Harris."

218 *Harris had a talent for devising:* Michaelis, "How Mental Illness Felled a Tennis Great."

218 *There was a game of skill:* Dewald, personal communication.

219 *Smith committed to playing:* Neely, personal communication.

219 *Smith said that match was a wake-up call:* Secada, "Bill Harris, Florida's Greatest Junior Player, Passes On."

219 *Smith recounted a story:* Michaelis, "How Mental Illness Felled a Tennis Great."

219 *Neely reported that no one:* Neely, personal communication.

219 *Later that year:* Secada, "Bill Harris, Florida's Greatest Junior Player, Passes On."

220 *Butch Seewagen joked:* Seewagen, personal communication.

220 *Another factor was that Harris's birth month:* Malcolm Gladwell, *Outliers: The Story of Success* (New York: Little, Brown, & Company, 2008), 20-26.

220 *For example, when Harris competed in the 13-and-under:* Betty Harris Modell, personal communication.

220 *Borg apparently could keep a ball in play:* Eugene L. Scott, *Bjorn Borg: My Life and Game* (New York: Simon & Schuster, 1980), 84.

221 *Harris was the recipient of the:* Stephen J. Ceci, Susan M. Barnett, and Tomoe Kanaya, "Developing Childhood Proclivities into Adult Competencies: The Overlooked Multiplier Effect." In R.J. Sternberg and E.L. Grigorenko (Eds.), *The Psychology of Abilities, Competencies, and Expertise* (New York: Cambridge University Press, 2003), 70-92.

221 *Recall Winner's three defining characteristics:* Ellen Winner, *Gifted Children: Myths and Realities* (New York: Basic Books, 1996), 3-4.

222   *Prior to recruiting Harris:* Michaelis, "How Mental Illness Felled a Tennis Great."

222   *Mabry offered Harris a full scholarship:* Secada, "Bill Harris, Florida's Greatest Junior Player, Passes On."

222   *There was one issue to resolve:* Dewald, personal communication.

222   *Coach Mabry described Harris as:* Berry, "The Search for Bill Harris."

223   *During the 1966 tennis season:* Michealis, "How Mental Illness Felled a Tennis Great."

223   *There was one incident in which:* Berry, "The Search for Bill Harris."

223   *The most important tennis event:* Ibid.

223   *Upon Bill's return home in March 1966:* American Psychiatric Association, *Diagnostic and Statistical Manual of Mental Disorders: Fifth Edition* (DSM-5) (Washington, DC: American Psychiatric Publishing, 2013), 87-88.

224   *Bill's symptom picture did not remain stable:* Berry, "The Search for Bill Harris."

224   *To what degree Bill was adherent:* Modell, personal communication.

224   *Since leaving the university in March:* Berry, "The Search for Bill Harris."

225   *On October 10, Harris played:* Mark Hortsmeyer, "McKinley Exhibits Davis Cup Form," *The Trinitonian*, October 14, 1966.

225   *There was an article published:* "Tiger Net Team Loses Top Man," *The Trinitonian*, February 3, 1967.

225 *Cincinnatians proudly proclaim:* Phillip S. Smith, *From Club Court to Center Court: The Evolution of Professional Tennis in Cincinnati* (2013 Edition), 5.

226 *Some prominent Cincinnatians:* Ibid., 5.

226 *The first tournament in Cincinnati:* Ibid., 5, 68.

226 *The name of the tournament was changed:* Ibid., 10, 31, 39.

226 *The history of the Cincinnati tournament:* Ibid., 56-65.

226 *Those victorious in the women's:* Ibid., 56-67.

226 *Charles Harris played Bobby Riggs:* Ibid., 271-272.

227 *Although 1968 saw the advent:* Ibid., 167.

227 *Fearing that the stress:* Harris, personal communication.

227 *But Harris had a remarkable tournament:* Smith, *From Club Court to Center Court,* 261-262.

227 *Eliot Berry detailed one point:* Berry, "The Search for Bill Harris."

228 *An article in the Cincinnati:* Ibid.

228 *The 1968 U.S. Open:* atpworldtour.com, 1968 draws, 1-4.

228 *I recently spoke with Gerken about the match:* Paul Gerken, personal communication.

229 *His peers noted that:* Pressley, personal communication.

229 *His brother, Robert, was more:* Harris, personal communication.

229 *"His eyes stare out at his aging mother":* Pete LeForge, *Ways to Reshape the Heart* (Grand Ridge, Florida: Black Bay Books, 2009), 68.

229 *I found out about Bill's:* Bill Harris (Wikipedia, the free encyclopedia).

230 *Compared to many individuals:* Modell, personal communication.

230 *Whenever Bill was feeling well:* Berry, "The Search for Bill Harris."

231 *Frank reported that Bill retained:* Tutvin, personal communication.

231 *Vicki Michaelis eloquently stated:* Michaelis, "How Mental Illness Felled a Tennis Great."

231 *In early March 2002:* Modell, personal communication.

232 *As several bloggers have noted:* Greg Couch, "From Spoiled to Rotten, the Story of American Men's Tennis," aolnews. com, August 9, 2010.

CHAPTER 9. THE CHALLENGE

234 *Data from the sports psychology literature:* K. Anders Ericsson, "The Influence of Experience and Deliberate Practice on the Development of Superior Expert Performance." In K. Anders Ericsson, Neil Charness, Robert R. Hoffman, and Paul J. Feltovich, *The Cambridge Handbook of Expertise and Expert Performance* (New York: Cambridge University Press, 2006), 688-689.

234 *Individuals in their seventies:* Ralf Th. Krampe and Neil Charness, "Aging and Expertise" In K. Anders Ericsson, Neil Charness, Robert R. Hoffman, and Paul J. Feltovich, *The Cambridge Handbook of Expertise and Expert Performance* (New York: Cambridge University Press, 2006), 730.

235 *There are data suggesting:* Ibid., 726.

235 *In the spring of 2014:* lobstersports.com, 1-2.

AUTHOR INFORMATION

Bill Himadi, Ph.D., is a freelance writer, avid tennis player, and clinical psychologist with expertise in the cognitive-behavioral treatment of anxiety disorders and schizophrenia. Dr. Himadi lives with his wife and their daughter in Tallahassee, Florida. He can be reached via email at wghimadi@yahoo.com.

INDEX

D

Lambert, King, 211-13
Laver, Rod, 2-4, 54, 56-57, 118, 129, 164, 181, 184, 222, 228
Law of Effect, 78
LeForge, Pete, 229
Lendl, Ivan, 57-65, 101, 106, 135, 146, 163, 175, 182, 188-89, 200, 226
Lendl, Olga, 60
Linehan, Marsha, 132
Little Albert, 73-74, 104
Lloyd, John, 87
Lobster, Elite Two, 235-36
Loehr, Jim, 147-48
Lombardi, Vince, 103
Los Angeles Tennis Club, 188-89
Los Horcones, 89
Lott, George, 56
Loyo-Mayo, Joaquin, 227
Lucas, Warren, 175
Lutz, Bob, 214, 219, 221

M

m-drill, 22, 136-37
Mabry, Clarence, 222-25
Macy's, 75
Madison Square Garden, 1-4, 6, 58, 98-99
Madoff, Bernie, 174
Mako, Gene, 188, 207
Marble, Alice, 196, 226
Marciano, Rocky, 3
Marengo, Tyler, 145
Martz, Jim, 205
Masso, Eduardo, 107
Matisons, Michael, 145
Mayer, Sandy, 55